INSIGHT *City* GUIDES

Created and Directed by Hans Höfer
Edited and Updated by Grace Coston
Photography by Ping Amranand

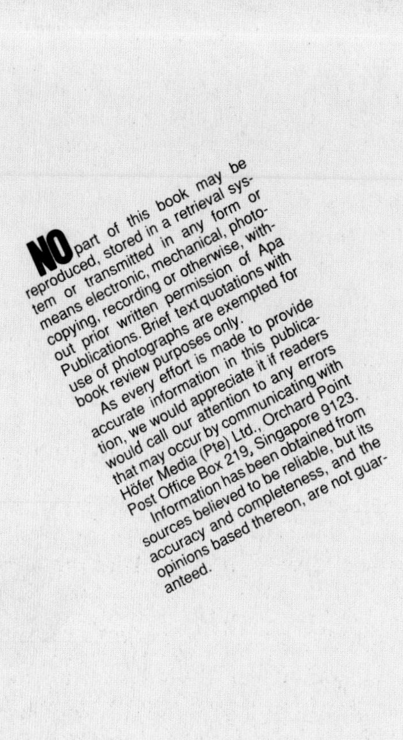

Second Edition

Printed in Singapore by Höfer Press Pte. Ltd

About This Book

Who does not love Paris, The City of Light (*la Ville Lumière*)? For centuries Paris played a pivotal role in the civilization of mankind. And today it is still one of the most important centers for educational, intellectual, cultural and artistic pursuits.

Who has not heard of Paris? The city is known all over the world for its cuisine, wine, *haute couture*, painting, theaters and museums, which makes it all the more difficult to write and publish a guide book about a place as cosmopolitan as Paris. There is no trick involved; the editor must expertly cut through piles of raw footage to save the material which is most important, most valuable and most useful. And at the same time present a new, balanced and refreshing perspective to a well-loved city like Paris.

The *Cityguide* editions are modeled on the highly-successful, award-winning series of *Insight Guides* which covers countries and regions. As with the other series by APA Publications, the *Cityguides* combine fine writing, outstanding photography and objective journalism to produce a unique form of travel literature which gives the serious traveler an insight into the history and culture of his or her destination, and to make every tour a rewarding and meaningful experience.

Publisher **Hans Höfer** remains the driving force behind both series. He first created a guide to Bali in 1970 based on his own experiences there, "not to promote tourism… but to contribute to positive communication between the local people and visitors." Since then, the Apa list of titles has grown to include *Insight Guides* from Alaska to Yugoslavia, and *Cityguides* from Athens to Zurich, and each of them reflects the Bauhaus training of the German-born publisher in the arts of printing, photography and design.

Meanwhile other talents were recruited for this project. *Cityguide: Paris* was put together by the best available writers and photographers under the guidance of project editor **Grace Coston**.

An International Collaboration

Coston, who has not lost any of her enthusiasm for Paris even though she has lived there for nearly a decade, was raised in Virginia and attended college in New England. She wrote several plays which were produced in the United States and France, and has also completed her first novel.

Contacting writers was a fun first step, because Coston could call on the people—French, American, British—whom she met over the years at university, or working in the theater. All the contributors found that working on the Paris project was like standing in front of a bakery shop window trying to choose just a few pastries from the fantastic selection of old favorites and untried delights. There are many distinctive aspects of the city, and many special sites that no traveler should miss. At the same time, Paris is innovation in motion. Culturally, artistically, intellectually, it's a city that never stops and never stops surprising.

The principal photographer for *Cityguide: Paris* was **Ping Amranand** whose work has been published in several other Asian and American publications including *Architectural Digest* and *House and Garden*. Amranand was also the photographer for *Insight Guide: The Bahamas*.

Laurence Orillard's familiarity with the

Coston

Amranand

Orillard

Radkai

McDonald

city makes her the perfect choice for writing the chapters "Heart of Paris", "Intellectual Paris", "Around Town" and "Contemporary Art". Born in the sleepy Norman town of Evreux, she has traveled throughout Europe with her parents and lived her own adventures in Asia, Canada and Ireland. Orillard returned to Paris in 1984, and she is presently working as a writer and language teacher.

Marton Radkai, whose chapter on history is refreshingly lively, sent his text from Munich, where he lives with his German wife and works as a freelance writer. He did his growing up in Paris, London and Geneva, before heading for the United States, where he received degrees in History, German and Communications from universities in Vermont and Massachusetts.

There being as many museums in Paris as there are cheeses in France, an entire chapter was set aside for the subject. **Jane McDonald** had a hard time selecting which museums to highlight, but she loved the research. She did her writing as she was preparing to leave Paris after a five-year stay.

The French Connection

French contributor **Philippe Artru** recently put together the first issue of a new art magazine in Paris. He has published articles on a variety of topics and traveled extensively throughout Canada, the United States, England, Hungary and Israel to research his work. His contribution was translated by **Joanne Forrest**, who also compiled and wrote the Travel Tips. Forrest has lived in Paris since 1978, studying and teaching while pursuing a career in acting. She has performed in several films and numerous plays in the United States and Paris.

Artru and Forrest led the project editor to photographer **Jean-Bernard Sohiez**, who then was working with writer Laurence Orillard on the chapter "Contemporary Art". Coston had wanted this section to be a little jewel in the middle of the book, and Sohiez's photographs of artists and gallery owners in their element sparkle as a rare gem. Orillard's contribution and Sohiez's images blended superbly to open the door to the rich and mysterious world of contemporary art in Paris.

Stephanie Wooley is another transplanted American, but her roots were first planted in the far-away Hawaiian islands. She wrote about the shopping scene in Paris and the activities that are available to visitors. Wooley is the chief translator in the largest law firm in Paris.

Patty Hannock is also a very busy woman. Her acting and directing credits include works in English, French and German, in film and stage, and for television. She currently divides her time between Paris and London.

Susan Andrews is also a performer, with extensive experience in singing and acting. On a personal side, she will only reveal that she "frequents the haunts of Paris By Night".

Cityguide: Paris, like every APA book, is the result of a concerted team effort. The talent and diversity of experience of the contributors are brought together to capture the beauty and the essence of Paris. Each contributor has a special vision of Paris, and in *Cityguide: Paris*, their personal insights are shared with you.

—APA Publications

Artru

Forrest

Andrews

Wooley

Hannock

CONTENTS

HISTORY & PEOPLE

MAPS

PLACES

TRAVEL TIPS

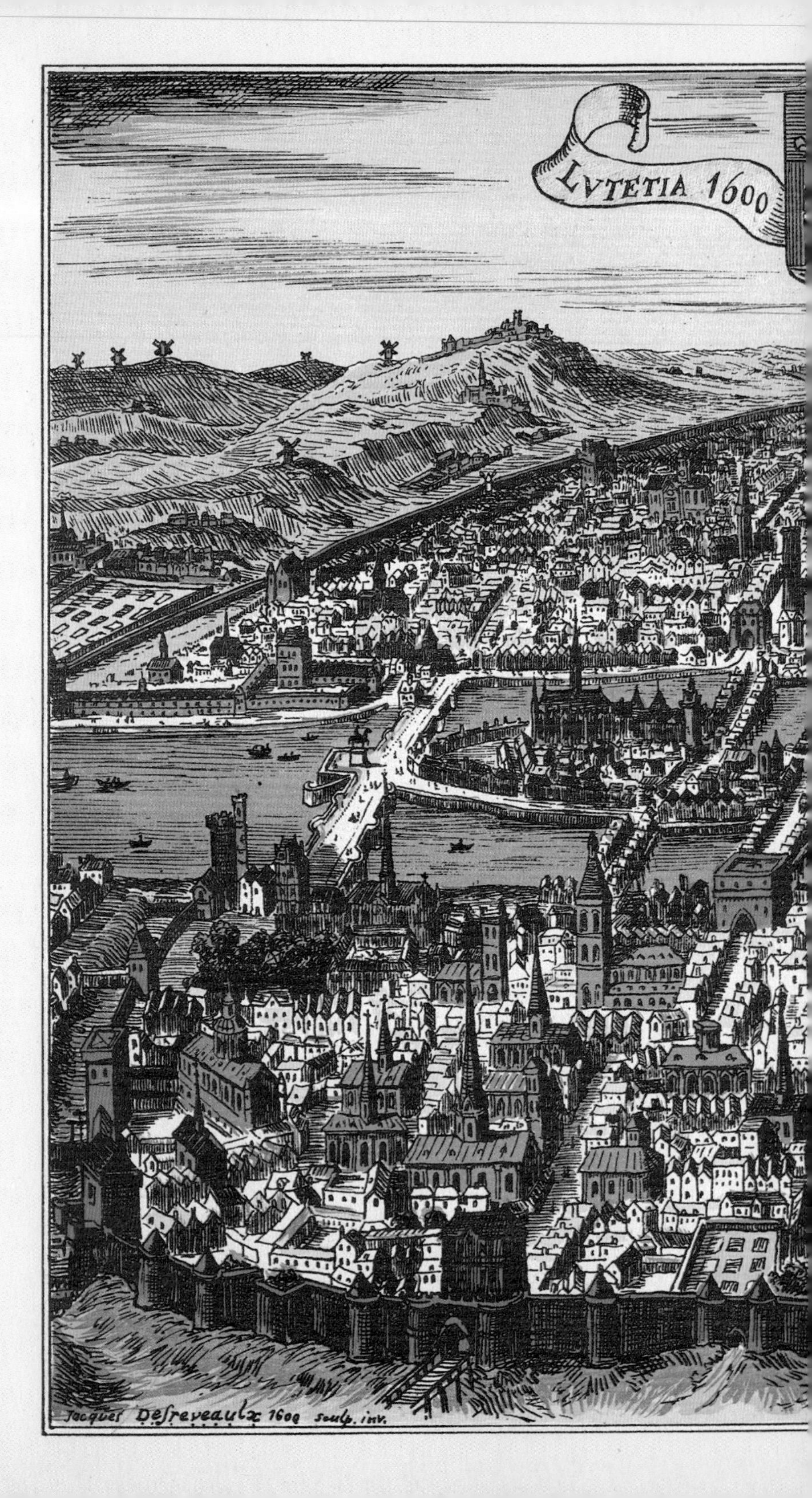
LVTETIA 1600
Jacques Deſreveaulx 1600 sculp. inv.

vulgo PARIS

THE CITY ON THE SEINE

As the 20th century nears its close, Paris has marked two events from its history: the millennial anniversary of the Capetian royal dynasty and the bicentennial of the French Revolution. Together these milestones represent two faces of the city's history and both were celebrated with temporary fanfare as well as longer lasting mementoes including coins, stamps and monuments. Typical of this Cartesian capital, the observances and festivities on both occasions were criticized right and left for being too much or too little, offensive to part of the population, a waste of money, and generally inappropriate.

Nonetheless, Paris turned its face to the past and gathered forces for the next century, newly adorned with an improved Louvre, a modern Opéra, a Great (concrete) Arch joining the classical perspective of the Napoléonic *Arc de Triomphe*. These and other new museums and cultural facilities are the proud results of 200 years of *Liberté, Fraternité et Egalité*, and the public debate they have started promises that the next 200 years—or even one thousand—will be just as lively.

In other ways, too, the city of Paris is a symphony in counterpoint. One of the two Roman ruins remaining in Paris is the ancient arena of *Lutéce*, still in use today as a field for peaceful games of *pétanque*. This popular bowling game adds a taste of what locals call *Paris village* charms to the cosmopolitan city.

Two buildings from the far ends of the spectrum represent Paris; the Gothic Notre Dame cathedral and the Eiffel Tower, which recently celebrated its 100th birthday with a very successful face-lift. Now I.M. Pei's glass pyramid in the stately courtyard of the Louvre and the sleek and shiny *Opéra de la Bastille*, the park and museum complex at La

Preceding pages: "Point Zero" on Notre Dame terrace; the central rose window of Notre Dame; view from the Alexandre III bridge; Bagatelle Rose Gardens; Trocadéro; pinochle in the park; Paris in 1600. Left, a detail from the Arc de Triomphe.

Vilette, the *Grande Arche de la Défense* and other works are part of the aesthetic balance.

In the oldest, central part of the city, the population and traffic have always been dense, and most Parisians adopt a sort of hardened expression when they confront public transportation or rush hour in the streets. Though various projects have been undertaken to improve the situation, including expressways along the *quais* of the Seine river and a giant, new parking area under the Louvre, midtown traffic is unbearable most of the time. Subways and buses get jammed in the morning and evening as people go to and from work. Make your trip smoother by avoiding weekday rush hours.

If the noise and agitation do begin to wear you down, there is ample relief in the multitude of beautiful, green spaces scattered throughout the city. Some, decorated with statuaries and fountains, like the Tuileries or Luxembourg, are ultimate examples of the *jardin à la française*.

Other parks, notably the Buttes-Chaumont in Belleville, are wilder, and recreate natural landscapes. Set in the middle of a small lake, a grassy island rises up sharply, topped with a pink and white Greek-style temple. Here you can catch a breeze and look out over the northeastern Paris neighborhood and see a simpler, but popular side of Paris. Study the faces of the families and lovers who walk in the park to get a closer glimpse into the lives of Parisians who aren't making headlines, just reading them.

Whatever parks you choose to stroll in, and you certainly will be drawn to them as you discover the city, you will find the traces of another Paris—an older one. Many parks originally were the private grounds of royal palaces, or the battle grounds for bloody revolutions. The city's history is etched in its landscapes, written on the stone façades, wrought in the ironwork. Street names recall medieval times or modern generals, bridges are stamped with Napoléon's Imperial "N" or carved with the faces of demons from the dark ages. Traces of early Christian martyrs, Joan of Arc, and resistance fighters bring to mind the people and events that have marked the city over the ages.

The Tuileries Gardens and the Louvre Palace bear much of the history of Paris on their shoulders, but other areas like the famous Montmartre hilltop, the Père-Lachaise Cemetery, and, of course, the numerous monuments ornamenting the city, inevitably recall the past as well.

The traveler will love discovering all of the distinctive *quartiers* that make up Paris. While some will be fascinated by the history of a place, others will enjoy the harmony of public gardens and broad avenues, and still others, the technology and innovation of the Eiffel Tower or the polished, steel sphere at La Villette.

Discover the Paris of the early morning hours, when the smell of fresh baked croissants wafts out of innumerable bakeries, and coffee machines are working up steam in the sleepy cafés. The sidewalks are swept and water rushes along the curbs, shopkeepers crank up steel shutters and open for business, the work-force hits the streets. From the vantage of a comfortable café, watch the city fill up and shed the warm cocoon of morning for the busy mid-day ambience of traffic jams and commerce. To keep out of the fray, head for a spacious, calm museum; but you may prefer to plunge right in and tour the streets instead. Evening in Paris is most sublime. See the lights twinkle on, beckoning you to stroll across the Seine on a magnificent bridge. Enjoy the cool breeze of nightfall while you decide how to spend your evening: in a fine restaurant, at the theater, in a wild club, or a simple midnight excursion to absorb the atmosphere.

Like everything else, the Parisian character is marked by contrast and even contradiction. In turn, rude, mocking, cold and superior or polite, helpful, friendly and open, Parisians are both annoying and charming. Yet no visitor need ever feel too far from home in a city where newspapers, films and books are available in almost every one of the world's languages, restaurants offer hundreds of different *cuisines*, and cultural events celebrate every aspect of civilization. Indeed, it is often said that Paris belongs not to the French, but to the world.

Right, come hither on the Ile St.-Louis.

CLOVIS I.

THE HISTORY OF PARIS

As with many of the world's great cities, the mysterious mists of antiquity hang solemnly over the origins of Paris. In 500 B.C. when the Celts chased each other around Europe, one tribe, the Parisii, settled on the Seine river. They were good farmers and active traders, hence, the name "Parisii," which is said to be derived from a Celt word meaning "boat". A more imaginative interpretation suggests that the tribe's original founder was Paris, the émigré son of King Priam of Troy.

In 53 B.C. a number of Gallic tribes failed to appear at the annual council summoned by the Romans in Ambiani (Amiens). Julius Caesar, sensing rebellion in the air, transferred the council into the midst of the restless tribes, to the Parisii town of Lutetia—nothing more than an agglomeration of huts on an island in the Seine.

Lutetia thrived under the Romans. A wooden bridge connected the island (Cité) to the left bank where a residential neighborhood sprawled, replete with temples, baths, a theater and other hallmarks of Roman civilization. Dominating the right bank, from its hilltop perch, stood a temple to Mercury where, in A.D. 287, Saint Denis, a Christian agitator and the first bishop of Paris, was beheaded. Thereafter, the hill was named *Mons Martyrium*, Montmartre. According to legend, Saint Denis picked up his severed head and walked 6,000 steps before being buried by one of his apostles where the famous basilica now stands.

Lying exposed on a plain, Lutetia fell victim to frequent sackings by marauding barbarian tribes. In A.D. 358, Emperor Constantine sent his son-in-law, Julian, to Gaul to fight the barbarians. The young man promptly fell in love with Lutetia and its inhabitants. When not on the battlefields, he sat in the Palais on the Cité, enjoying Lutetian wine and figs, and putting the town's finances in order. The Lutetians returned the favor in A.D. 360, by proclaiming him emperor.

About a century later, Attila the Hun appeared with his hordes in the Ile-de-France. The Lutetians prepared to flee but were stopped by the 19-year- old Geneviève who assured them that the Huns would not harm the city. Lo and behold! The scourge passed southwest of Lutetia and ran straight into the glaives of a hastily raised army of legionnaires. Sainte-Geneviève became the patron saint of Paris.

The dark ages: Sainte-Geneviève was still alive when Clovis I, king of the Salian Franks and founder of the Merovingian dynasty, invaded much of Gaul, converted to Christianity and swept into Lutetia which he promptly made his capital and renamed Paris. Like Julian he installed himself in the Palais and later had a basilica built where he and Sainte-Geneviève were buried. The so-called church of the Apostles ultimately

Left, early drawing of Clovis I. Right, tomb of Abélard and Héloise.

became the Pantheon; the last resting place for France's "great men," including Rousseau, Mirabeau, Victor Hugo and Jean Jaurés.

Merovingian law of succession was simple: the empire was divided up among the previous ruler's offspring. As a result, family members spent the better part of 250 years squeezing each other out. Paris, instead of being used as an administrative center, served as a favorite battleground for the murderous bickering of Clovis' descendants. Nature also conspired, with floods, fires, epidemics and hurricanes. The brief rule of Dagobert (A.D. 629-639) brought a flicker of relief. He organized an annual trade fair at Lendit, and his minister Saint Eloi struck Parisian coins and organized the municipal finances. The Carolingians who ruled from A.D. 751 on, felt more comfortable nearer to their homelands in the lower Rhine. Paris was put in the charge of a count who created a municipal guard and cared for judicial matters.

The Norman invasions of the mid-9th century brought Paris back into the limelight. After several sackings, in A.D. 885, Count Eudes decided to resist. The first siege of Paris lasted an entire year and almost bore fruit: the Carolingian army arrived to the rescue. But Emperor Charles the Fat, instead of attacking the siege-weary Vikings, paid them tribute and let them sail up the Seine river to pillage Burgundy. Paris and the French felt betrayed.

In defiance of the Emperor, Eudes was crowned King of France. Carolingian unity dissolved. The French crown shifted from one dynasty to the next. The Saracens appeared in the south, Hungarians in the east, and the Vikings ran amok. Millenarian fears ran rife.

By hook, crook, marriage and force, Duke Hugo the Great, a descendant of Eudes, forged a French federation. When the German Kaiser Otto II invaded France in A.D. 978, he met a resolute French army at the gates of Paris. The victory led their general, Hugo Capet, son of Hugo the Great, to become King of France.

The middle ages: Though the early members of the dynasty preferred crusading and hunting to governing, Paris prospered under the Capetians. New fountains brought fresh water to the citizens and the streets were paved. *Sergents de ville* armed with clubs walked a beat and Paris' giant pillory worked overtime.

With its cloisters, churches and cosmopolitan crowds, intellectual activity flourished. Monks, scholars, philosophers, poets and musicians flocked to Paris to learn, to argue, to teach. It was the age of Abélard and Saint Bernard hurling logic at each other in the open air. The University of Paris was founded in 1231 and hardly a Middle Ages' scholar failed to visit its faculties.

Economic life in Paris was in the hands of merchants and craftsmen who wisely organized themselves into guilds. The most powerful one was the water merchants' guild, which covered all river workers and gave its coat-of-arms to the city.

created three governing chambers that met regularly in Paris.

The concessions to the commoners had a long lasting effect on Parisian and French political life. These *bourgeois* (city dwellers) became an independent political force, often corrupt, but equally often striving for democratic reforms.

The first revolution: By the mid-14th century the Capetians had given way to the Valois, and the devastating Hundred Years War began. The French knights seemed powerless before the English footsoldiers. The plague made its first deadly appearance. In 1356, the English captured King John the

Philip August (1180-1223) built Les Halles for the guilds, and improved the Seine docks. The guilds took care of levying taxes, town crying and other municipal duties. In 1190 six guild members, so-called *grands bourgeois,* were chosen to act as the king's officers. The number increased later to 24 and they met in regular sessions to discuss municipal business. Louis IX (1226-1270)

<u>Left</u>, Joan of Arc. <u>Right</u>, coat of arms of the City of Paris. <u>Above</u>, boatmen jousting.

Good at Poitiers. The citizens of Paris, tired of incompetent leadership, rebelled. Their leader, Etienne Marcel, a clothmaker and guild chairman, was the first in a long string of genial, uncorruptibly corrupt demagogs to emerge on Paris' political horizon. A motley crew of poor townspeople and peasants under Jacques Bonhomme, chose the moment to also begin a revolt, later known as the Jacquerie.

For support, Marcel unwisely chose the King of Navarre (Charles the Bad) an English ally. When the Parisians found out about the alliance, they turned on him. On July 31,

1358, Marcel was assassinated by a loyalist. Three days later John the Good's son, Charles, entered the capital.

The new regent, who later became Charles V, first hammered out a truce with the English allowing France some time to put its house in order. Paris was well-treated considering its fickle loyalties: The Parliament still met but its powers were curtailed.

Behind a calm exterior Paris seethed. In 1382, a group of citizens calling themselves the Maillotins rebelled against high taxes, and were brutally repressed. Then in 1407 the Maillotins became enmeshed in the violent struggle for power between the Burgundian John the Fearless and his cousin Louis d'Orléans, brother of the mentally deranged Charles VI. John had Louis murdered, and in 1409 took control of Paris, which backed the Burgundians.

While Louis' son raised a new army, Paris jubilated. Into the fray stepped a butcher, Caboche, demanding fiscal and administrative reforms. All hell broke loose as John's authority slipped into the hands of Caboche and his butchers. The ensuing Reign of Terror gave Charles and his Armagnac army a chance to reenter and "pacify" the city. Seeing France cleft by civil war, the English resumed the hostilities. Siding with the Burgundians, they defeated the Armagnacs at Agincourt in 1415.

In 1419, John the Fearless was murdered, whereupon Henry V of England married Catherine, daughter of mad King Charles, and occupied Paris in December 1420.

English law-and-order were initially welcomed after the anarchic years of John the Fearless and Caboche, but radical application of the gallows soon became tedious to the Parisians. Charles VII, the legitimate king, had some support in the capital, but the bulk of Parisians remained convinced that his vengeance would be merciless. When Joan of Arc besieged Paris in 1429, they put up a stiff resistance.

Six years elapsed before Charles VII recaptured his capital and rolled the English back to the Channel coast. His main task consisted in reconstructing the nation. Elected magistrates upheld public life in Paris and the kings, wary of the sanguine city, moved outside of the city to luxurious castles on the Loire river.

Renaissance and religious troubles: With peace came prosperity, with prosperity came war. By the early 16th century, Louis XII (1498-1515) was rummaging around Italy. François I (1515-1547) began the struggle against Habsburg hegemony in Europe. In 1525, he was captured at Pavia. The Parisians paid his ransom, and he promptly moved into the Louvre. In his wake came hordes of Italian architects, painters, sculptors, goldsmiths, cabinet makers and masons who set about refreshing the city's lugubrious Gothic face.

With the rebirth of the capital under François I's graceful, iron hand, French culture also returned to life. Ronsard, Du Bellay and other members of the *Pléiades* carried French poetry to new heights while Clément Jannequin put the French *chanson* on the map. The tireless printing press increased the range of these creative activities, but it also helped spread the new gospel of Protestantism through Catholic France. François I tolerated the new religion as long as its converts remained orderly. Paris, dominated by the conservative Sorbonne theologists, was outraged. Under the reign of Henry II (1547-1559), the city pushed for measures against the Protestants, creating the *chambre ardente* to try and condemn—usually to burning—religious agitators.

Henry II's heirs, François II, (1559-1560), Charles IX (1560-1574) and Henry III (1574-1589) were not competent enough to control France's religious factions. Nor were they helped by the endless intrigues of their mother, Catherine of Medici.

In August 1572, Paris gave the signal for the Saint Bartholomew massacre. Thousands of Protestants died, including most of their leaders. Of the few to escape was Henry of Bourbon, King of Navarre, cousin of the King of France.

Three Henry's war: King Henry III's concessions to the Protestants infuriated the Catholics led by the popular Henry de Guise and the Paris-based Holy League. In 1584, the Navarre Henry became heir to the throne but he had to fight for the right. In 1589, Henry III had Henry de Guise assassinated.

Paris threw up its barricades, a Council of Sixteen took power and deposed Henry III who willy-nilly joined forces with the Protestant Navarre. His army, however, joined the Catholics. On August 1, a friar, Jacques Clément murdered Henry III and Henry of Navarre became Henry IV.

Civil war dragged on for another five years. Paris was the stage for the Council of Sixteen's gruesome repression of real and perceived plots. In 1593, Philippe II of Spain, who had entered the war on the Catholic side, pressed to usurp the French throne. The Paris parliament, however, solemnly declared that no foreigner would rule.

The glorious epoch: Despite massive deficits incurred by their violent foreign policy, the Bourbons lavished huge sums on Paris, while keeping it on a short political leash. Two deserted islets behind the Cité became the residential Ile St.-Louis. New bridges crossed the Seine. Avenues cut through the dingy labyrinth of streets. Architects received blank checks to build new houses, palaces, schools and restore the old ones. Parks appeared where society could stroll in the shade and exchange ideas, gossip or tender glances.

Under Louis XIV (1643-1715) the spending spree reached its peak. His minister,

Henry IV chose the moment to convert back to Catholism. Paris opened its doors and overnight the war-weary nation fell in line.

Henry IV patched up France spiritually and economically. In 1598, his Edict of Nantes set up guidelines for cohabitation between the two religious groups. His (Protestant) advisor, Sully, reformed the tax system and balanced the budget.

Above, remains of the Roman arena, "Lutèce".

Colbert, sanitized entire sections of the city and set up manufacturing plants to provide the French with luxury items. Louis XIV also had hospices built for the poor, and the Invalides went up to house destitute war-veterans. At night Paris glowed to the light of 6,500 lanterns.

The influx of money and the proximity of the court attracted a huge crowd to the capital. Rich wives and courtesans opened their living rooms to witty conversationalists. Theaters rang with the grandiose verse of Racine and Corneille, the booing of the *cliques* and the applause of the *claques*. The first cafés appeared on the boulevards. Everyone laughed at the writings of Moliére, Boileau, de la Fontaine satirizing the hustling and bustling society.

It was not all peaches and cream. In 1648, Paris revolted, demanding greater representation. The 12 provincial parliaments joined, as did a conspiracy of nobles under Prince Condé. The Fronde, as it was called, eventually collapsed, but Louis XIV, who was a boy at the time, later had his palace, Versailles, built *outside* the city limits.

The road to revolution: Louis XIV's immediate successor in 1715, the regent Duke of Orléans, moved back into the city and left government to his ministers, while he vigorously engaged in amorous pursuits. King Louis XV continued in the same vein, letting his mistress, Madame de Pompadour, have the power to select ministers, generals and other functionaries. Meanwhile, the nation's budget deficits grew and the financial situation worsened.

France lost a drawn out war against England (1756-1763). Tongues wagged. Respect for the King and his court dwindled. Satire turned to dissent. In the *salons* surly philosophers replaced the brisk talkers. French reputation no longer rested on royal glory but on the wisdom of the likes of Voltaire, Rousseau, Diderot and Quesnay.

Paris sat in the restuarant car while the train headed for the precipice. Entertainment grew more extravagant and cafés were filled to the brim while Louis XVI made locks and drew maps. When a bad harvest in 1788 increased the price of bread, the Queen suggested the hungry should eat cake.

In 1789 France's debts reached a critical stage. The King summoned the Estates General, a legislative body made up of the clergy, the aristocracy and the bourgeoisie. For the sake of fairer representation, the latter created the National Assembly. By the

time the King reacted, the absolute monarchy had ended. On July 14, Paris' populace proclaimed a Commune, formed a National Guard, and under the leadership of La Fayette, they stormed the Bastille prison for its weapons.

The revolutionary century: The explosion of 1789 swept the past away. Radicals of one hour became conservatives of the next. Streets changed names, newborn babies were called *Egalité, Liberté,* or *République*. A ballerina representing Liberty sat on the altar of Notre Dame. The First Republic was proclaimed, and in January 1793, King

Louis XVI was was put to his death by decapitation on place de la Concorde.

Paris was the burning center of the Revolution. Its temperamental and bloodthirsty mob was the force behind increasingly radical leaders, from Mirabeau, to Brissot, to Danton, Robespierre and Marat, whose scrofulous constituents regularly filled the Assembly's gallery. Power in France was centralized in the capital, and by 1893, anyone proposing a federal system was dragged off to the guillotine.

Napoléon, later, brought order and respectability to the Revolution. He also reconfirmed Parisian centralism. No French leader until Adolf Thiers in 1871, dared to alter that status. "Paris goes her own way," wrote Victor Hugo in the mid-19th century, "France, irritated, is forced to follow."

Romantic Paris: The glorious Napoléonic empire ended sadly with Paris occupied by three allied armies from 1815 to 1818. Louis XVIII, another Bourbon, headed a constitutional monarchy with emphasis on law-and-order and laissez-faire economics.

The Industrial Revolution might have turned Paris into an opulent and mediocre business center were it not for the torrid apostles of romanticism. Inspired by the anti-establishment spirit of 1789, they waged a struggle against creaky academics and bourgeois respectability in garrets, cafés, journals and the "enemy's" own *salons*. The hirsute Berlioz deafened his audiences, Victor Hugo wrote epically about the poor, and Baudelaire, swabbed in absinthe and hashish, glorified *ennui* in the scintillating city.

The spirit of '89 also survived in the Republican forces who reached for the Parisian mob whenever despotism reared its head. In 1830, Charles X (1824-1830) revoked certain electoral laws. After three days of bloody rioting he abdicated in favor of his cousin, Louis-Philippe, who 18 years later, too, succumbed to another Parisian insurrection. When Louis Napoléon, Napoléon's nephew and president of the Second Republic crowned himself Emperor in 1852, he preemptively arrested over 20,000 suspected political opponents, just to make sure.

Second Empire: The Second Empire (1852-1870) was a gaudy and grandiose period in Paris history. Thousands of kilometers of new train tracks connected it with other European capitals. Twice, in 1855 and 1867, it hosted a world fair. Basked in financial ease, the city abandoned itself to the shimmer of masked balls, Offenbach operettas and gossamer *salon* conversation.

Aided by taxes and eager speculators, the Prefect Haussmann gave Paris a brand new face. He gutted and rebuilt the Cité. New watermains and a sewerage system were installed to service the nearly two million Parisians. Boulevards, avenues and *places* appeared: Champs-Elysées, St.-Michel, St.-Germain, Etoile, to name a few. These served an aesthetic purpose and facilitated troop deployment in the event of trouble.

Unlike the old cobblestones the new asphalt could not be easily transformed into a barricade with ready ammunition. Families disappropriated by the construction were forced to move to eastern Paris. The move only added to that area's already notoriously seditious spirit.

The Commune: On July 15, 1870, Napoléon III went to war with Prussia. Parisians lined the streets to cheer the ill-equipped, ill-led and ill-fated army as they marched east. Two months later, the Second Empire had become the Third Republic, and the Prussians were beseiging Paris. In Bordeaux the government of Adolph Thiers waited for a *levée en masse* in heroic revolutionary style that never materialized. In Paris the National Guard and regulars, mostly from the poor classes, milled around preparing for an heroic *sortie* that failed. To kill time wealthy Parisians carried on with their social life though restaurant offerings became exotic as butchers bought their stock from the zoo at the *Jardin des Plantes*. The poor simply went hungry.

On January 28, 1871, Thiers, without consulting Paris, finally agreed to a ceasefire. A month later the National Assembly ratified a peace treaty. The Prussians

Left, revolutionaries stormed the Bastille prison on July 14, 1789.

triumphantly marched through Paris avoiding, however, the eastern districts, home of the belligerent and vengeful National Guard who felt betrayed by the French government. Sensing trouble, Thiers ordered the National Guard disarmed and moved the government to Versailles. He barely escaped the ensuing explosion of rancor.

On March 28, a Commune was proclaimed at the Hôtel de Ville after a municipal election was boycotted by the bourgeoisie. Civil war erupted.

While the Communards hoisted red flags and argued over political and military strategies, Thiers was busy raising a new army. The *Versaillais* succeeded where the Prussians had failed. From house to house they pushed the Communards back, into the eastern districts of Ménilmontant, Belleville and La Villette until reaching the graves of the Pére-Lachaise cemetery. The Paris bourgeoisie came out to jeer at the columns of bedraggled prisoners. The *Figaro* windily raved against the "moral gangrene" and called for summary justice. Some 25,000 Communards died fighting or were executed in the last weeks of May. With them went the revolutionary spark that had defied tyrants and kindled republics since 1789.

La Belle Epoque: Life returned quickly to normal after the Commune but gunshots crackled even while Paris began clearing away the battle debris. By 1878, the city was ready for a world fair, and in 1879 the government moved back from Versailles.

Paris no longer played a guiding role in French politics. With the insurrectionary working class brutally tamed, it became merely the stage for the squabbles, plots, demonstrations, counter-demonstrations, and oral and written polemics of the Third Republic. Factionalism ran rife. The Republicans split into pro-clerical and anti-clerical factions. In the 1890s, after recovering from the Commune, the left gathered around the socialist, Jean Jaurés. On the right was an array of diehard monarchists and nationalists with a strong vein of anti-Semitism, as revealed by the Dreyfus Affair in the late 1890s. (That *cause célèbre* revolved around the Jewish army captain, Dreyfus, deported on trumped-up spying charges).

Paris, its air crepitating with tension, seemed more than ever ready to accept the perplexing, the controversial and the provocative. The *métro* was dug, the Eiffel Tower built, and the first films were shown. Paris, between 1880 and 1940, housed more painters, sculptors, writers, poets, musicians and other creative citizens per acre than any other metropolis. They chattered in smoky cafés with philosophers, theorists, critics, brawny syndicalists, gazetteers, anarchists and socialites. Almost every literary movement flourished in Paris—realism, impressionism, cubism, surrealism, Dadaism, etc... In the pawnshops of Montmartre, Picassos, Utrillos and Modiglianis hung by clothespegs. Debussy, Zola, Cocteau and his apostles strolled through town. Diaghilev's *Ballets Russes* presented Nijinsky to full houses that periodically broke into riots if Stravinsky was performed.

World War I dampened spirits as the city turned to the slaughter at hand. In September 1914, the German army came within earshot. The military governor Galliéni rushed reinforcements to the counteroffensive on the Marne using every means, including the Paris taxi service.

Life returned after Armistice Day (1918). From the east came Russian émigrés, from the west came American writers preceded by composers who flocked to Nadia Boulanger's classes at the *Conservatoire Americain*. In the 1930s, Paris was a temporary haven to the refugees of fascism.

Between wars: With one and a half million dead, millions of others crippled and the agricultural north destroyed by bombings, France's victory over Germany in 1914 was Pyrrhic. Conservative Republicans and leftwing coalitions, including the 1920-founded Communist Party, alternately juggled unsuccessfully with the economic and social after effects of the war. The far right, meanwhile, made important gains.

Fascist-type organisations appeared in France in the late 19th century. Charles Barras and Léon Daudet, pornographic novelists, founded the *Action Française* in the 1890s. In the 1920s and 30s such groups proliferated fueled by general discontent and the fear of Bolshevism, and spurred by the successes of Mussolini and Hitler. They focused their public relations efforts on Paris which was dreamily swinging to swing music. They paraded in paramilitary garb, vociferated against the internationalists, the socialists, and above all the Jews, and periodically clashed with counterparaders.

On February 6, 1934, a coalition of fascist factions attempted a *coup d'état* in Paris. It failed, but the left was finally goaded into concerted action. In 1836, a front of radicals, socialists and communists headed by the socialist, Blum, won the election. The so-called *Front Populaire* promised to fight fascism and improve the French worker's lot. After major strikes, employers reluctantly agreed to wage hikes, paid vacations and reduced hours.

Above, the Opéra House shortly after its construction in 1888.

Initial euphoria was short-lived. The struggle against fascism split the Front when Blum refused to send help to the Spanish Republicans fighting Franco. He also interrupted the labor reforms because of their negative effect on the economy. In 1937, in a wave of wildcat strikes, the shattered *Front Populaire* sank into the past. "Rather Hitler than Blum," the Conservatives muttered, and their wish came true.

World War II: When war broke out against Nazi Germany in September 1939, France shored up the utterly useless Maginot Line, mobilized an ill-equipped army and waited. In Paris, statues were sandbagged, and the Louvre curators carefully prepared paintings for transport to safety.

On June 14, the Nazis marched into the city. There was no siege, no National Guard, no *levée en masse*, no cabbies hauling howitzers. Instead Pétain, withered hero of Verdun, became the titular head of a puppet régime in Vichy.

Some welcomed the Nazis as racial cleansers, others because they expected the trains to run on time. And there were those who resisted, sacrificing their lives at shooting posts and in bloodstained cellars in Paris' gloomy forts like Mont Valérien, Vincennes, and Issy-les-Moulineaux.

On June 6, 1944, Allied forces landed in Normandy and advanced on Paris. Von Choltitz, the German commanders received orders to blow it up but chose to surrender instead. On August 26, General de Gaulle paraded with his forces down the Champs-Elysées. Crowds rejoiced and collaborators scrambled into hiding or suffered the pains of summary justice. The war still had nine months to rage on but, Paris liberated, light returned to the European continent.

Paris since World War II: With the bane of fascism gone, the poets and artists regained their chairs and habits at the Flore, the Lipp and the Coupole. Political quarreling resumed without the extreme right. Tourists returned in droves. Bebop, Satchmo and Rock 'n' Roll came from across the Atlantic.

The war cast long shadows filled with horrors, the stench of the holocaust and the indelible proof of man's capacity for evil. Postwar thought was dominated by the dark existentialism of Sartre and Camus. In addition, France lost two major colonial wars, the first in Indochina (1946-1954) and the second in Algeria (1954-1962).

May 1968: A bloody wave of bombings swept Paris in the early 1960s, when it became clear that de Gaulle, who came out of retirement to head the Fifth Republic, wanted to pull out of the Algerian quagmire.

De Gaulle's manner in internal matters was patriarchal and authoritarian. His ideas, with few exceptions, were conservative. Time had eroded the legend. A generation had grown up that had not heard the comforting speeches beamed into occupied France by the British Broadcasting Corporation (B.B.C.). It had other ideas and other idols.

The 1968 agitation began uneventfully enough in March with a sit-in by students to demand changes in the antiquated University system. Instead of a civil discussion, the *ancien régime* called in the CRS, France's dreaded riot police, to restore order.

Push led to shove. On the night of May 10, 1968, the police stormed 60 barricades in the Latin Quarter. Unrest spread to the factories and other cities. France was soon paralyzed and Paris left in a state of siege. Gasoline was rationed and cautious housewives hoarded sugar and other essentials. The state-run media shuffled along with ersatz programing, while Parisians got the news from the privateers on France's periphery or, ironically, from the B.B.C. in London.

On May 30, de Gaulle announced new elections, and warned against impending totalitarianism. The Parisian bourgeoisie awoke. An hour later over half-a-million de Gaulle supporters were flowing down the Champs-Elysées. May 1968 was the most important upheaval in the city since the war.

June came. The Gaullists won the election. Parisians headed toward the seashore for a well-deserved vacation.

The 1970s appeared tame, but when the conservative President, Giscard d'Estaing, lost to socialist leader, Mitterand in 1981, a huge crowd emerged to march to the Bastille in celebration.

However, by 1986, the exigent Parisian character revealed itself again, during the legislative elections of that year. Voters on the left were dismayed by what they viewed as Mitterand's turncoat tactics: communist ministers forced out of the government, slowdown of promised social programs (including increased minimum wage, family allowances, and public housing projects). The "Union of the Left" which was responsible for his victory fell apart.

Conservative forces, lead by Paris mayor Jacques Chirac and his Rally for the Republic party, called Gaullist, swept the 1986 elections with a rightist coalition united in the face of the disparate left. The result was the mating of the strangest bedfellows yet, or *cohabitation*, as the French call it. In a short-lived experiment, Socialist Mitterrand occupied the President's chair while the powerful Prime Minister Chirac ruled over a rightist majority in the National Assembly.

As the mayor of Paris, Jacques Chirac is well-suited to the population in his inconsistencies. In his student days, Chirac was a member of the Communist youth movement, and later a gung-ho lieutenant fighting with French anti-independence forces in Algeria. He did a two-year stint as prime minister under Giscard d'Estaing in the early 1970s, before resigning the job that was then handed to his sometime-rival or ally Ramond Barre, leader of another right-wing party. Parisians never seemed bothered by Chirac's stint as Prime Minister, which certainly took time from his mayoral duties. Nor did they particularly rejoice in or resent his replacement when new elections allowed the appointment of a Socialist in his place. As mayor of the capital city, he is still in conflict with the more liberal policies of the national leader.

May 1968 reaffirmed Paris' old rebellious spirit. Be they bilious Conservatives or redhot radicals, Parisians never quite seem satisfied with the status quo, or efforts to change it. They demonstrate at the tip of a hat—against racism or for the rights of gays to broadcast. In 1983, socialist minister Savary tampered with medical studies and private schools, and the streets brimmed with over a million irate marchers. In November 1986, a conservative minister, Devaquet, tried to alter university entrance requirements with the same net result.

The undeniable charm of Paris lies in these exquisite tensions—political, artistic, social or architectural. The old lives together with the new. Beaubourg stands an equal to Notre Dame. Yuppies, punks and Dior share the streets used by beslippered *ménagères* clutching shopping nets bristling with baguettes and smelling faintly of agéd Camembert. Paris, modern and chic, is the heart of western civilization, but in its veins still flows the blood of the rustic, untamed, refractory Gaulois.

Left, the Liberation of Paris, 1944. Above, May 1968 student poster denouncing de Gaulle.

MAJESTIC PROPORTIONS

All roads lead to Paris, the reigning queen of France: highways, railways, airways and even Hertzian waves. Only French rivers escape her magnetic attraction. Situated on longitude 2° 20'13"W (Greenwich meridian) and latitude 48° 50'11"N Paris is in the center of a vast land depression known as the Parisian Basin. But more importantly, Paris is the political, economic, historical, artistic, cultural and tourist hub of France, and *le parisien* is more than a little proud to be part of these "5,000 hectares where," as author Jean Giraudoux puts it, "the most thinking, talking and writing in the world have been accomplished."

Paris actually covers an area close to 10,000 hectares or 40 square miles (100 sq. km), running 7½ miles (12 km) east and west, and 5½ miles (9 km) north and south, an area 40 times greater than the Paris of the 12th century.

On the map, 20 *arrondissements* (administrative districts) spiral out like a snail's shell, a pattern reflecting the city's historical development and successive enlargements. The site of medieval Paris corresponds roughly to the first six *arrondissements*. The Revolution of 1789 added the land included in the next five, while the territory covered by the last nine was obtained in the 19th century by annexing a dozen neighboring villages such as La Villette, Belleville, Auteuil and Montmartre.

Today's city limits are marked by the beltway, *le périphérique*, stretching 22 miles (35 km) around Paris. Constructed in 1973 to reduce traffic jams, the *périphérique* is often congested itself, particularly at rush hours (7 a.m. to 10 a.m. and 5 p.m. to 7:30 p.m.) when an estimated 130,000 cars storm its 35 exits leading to the suburbs.

Umbrellas and raincoats are indispensable to any Parisian visit but thanks to the

Satellite photo of the Ile-de-France region: Paris and urban areas in blue, forests in deep green and tilled fields show in biege and brown.

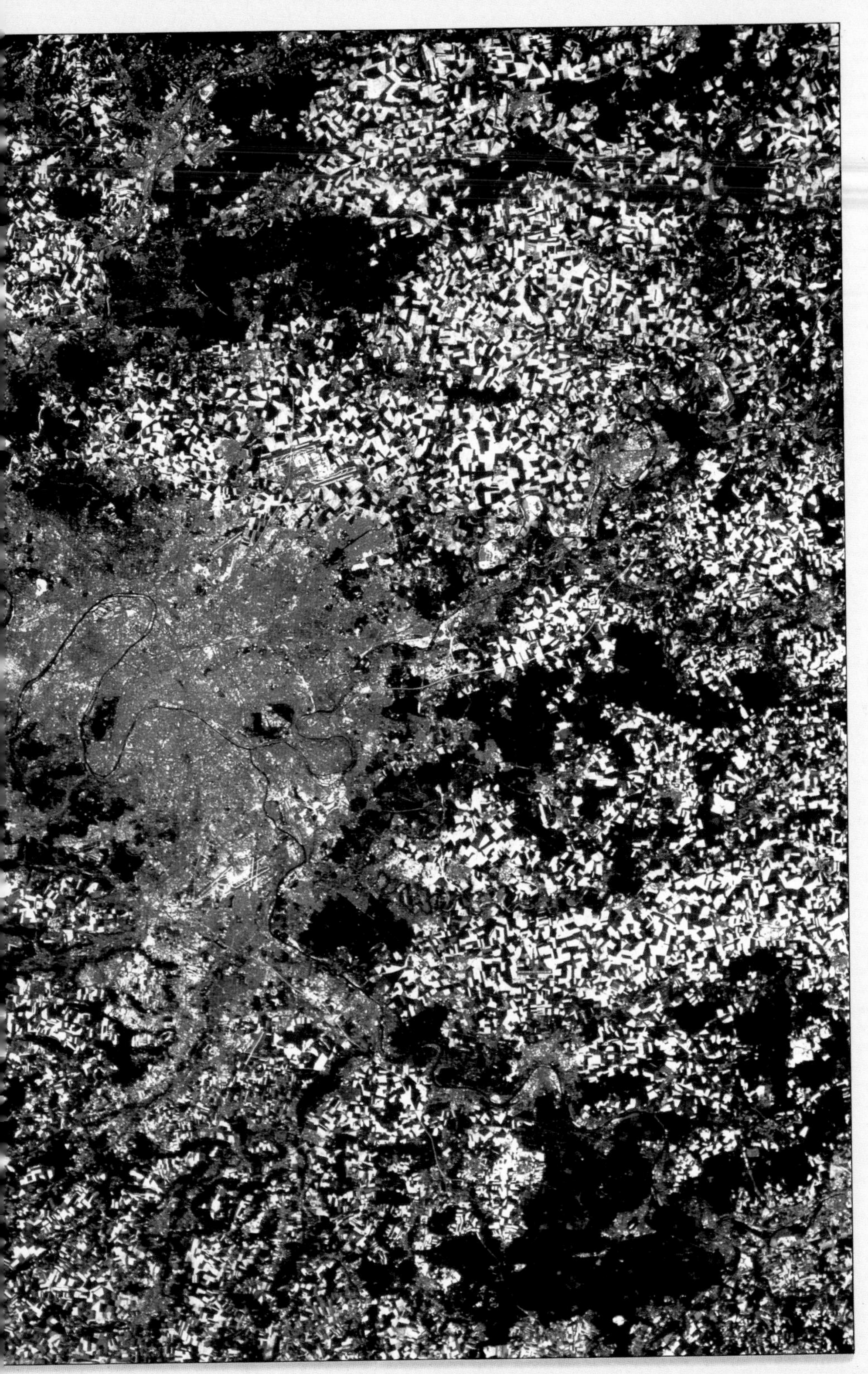

temperate climate, however, winters are seldom harsh, averaging 39°F (4°C). Summers are generally warm and sunny with an average of 65°F (18°C), including 10 days or so when temperatures can rise to over 86°F (30°C). Spring and fall are usually mild, averaging 52°F (11°C). Once or twice a year Paris enjoys a bit of snow, but rarely equaling the abundance seen in 1986, when, using the métro as their lift, skiers took to the slopes of Montmartre.

Paris is a city of reliefs. Starting from Grenelle, the lowest point at 85 feet (26 meters) above sea level, the banks of the Seine river swell gently north and south, forming two chains of hillocks. To the north, on the right bank (*la rive droite*), the tallest group includes **Montmartre**, the highest at 420 feet (128 meters), Ménilmontant, Belleville and the Buttes Chaumont. On the left bank (*la rive gauche*) Montsouris, the Montagne Ste.-Geneviéve, the Buttes aux Cailles and Maison Blanche at 256 feet (78 meters). **Mont Valérien** stands at 528 feet (161 meters). This is the highest point of the city's outskirts and provides an immense panoramic view of Paris from the west.

La banlieue, the suburbs, form two concentric rings around Paris. Wrapped tightly about the city, the inner ring is made up of three counties or *départements* (Hauts-de-Seine, Val-de-Marne and Seine-St.-Denis), and is itself enclosed by an outer ring of four counties (Seine-et-Marne, Essonne, Yvelines and Val-d'Oise). These *départements* together with Paris which constitute the greater Paris area (*Ile-de-France*), extend over 770 square miles (2,000 sq. km) and are linked by eight major highways, three RER lines, and an extensive railway network branching out in all directions from six train stations in Paris.

At the beginning of the 19th century, Napoléon Bonaparte imposed a special status on the city of Paris in order to maintain a firm hold on the capital's politics and willful populace. It wasn't until March 25, 1977 that Paris voted into office a city council which in turn elected the first mayor, Jacques Chirac. Today, each *arrondissement* also has its own council and mayor. Paris, with its double status as city and county, is represented nationally by 31 delegates and 12 senators in the two houses of Parliament.

***Fluctuat Nec Mergitur*:** "She is buffeted by the waves but sinks not": so reads the inscription on the city's coat-of-arms, symbol of Paris born on the flanks of the Seine river. The Gaulish village of Lutetia was indeed founded on the largest island, but today it is the Seine that's placed in the middle of the city. The capitol's widest avenue, spanned by a series of 34 bridges which provide some of the loveliest views of Paris, the Seine river is by far the city's calmest artery, barely ruffled by the daily trickle of tourist and commercial boat traffic. How hard it is to imagine this peaceful river encumbered by wash-houses, watermills and merchant ships hailing from every corner of France!

Equally difficult to picture are the 700 brightly painted Viking warships, invading from the north in the 9th century, or the thousands of floating bodies in 1572—victims of the Saint Bartholomew Day massacre. Today, barges and pleasure boats on their lazy way to Burgundy, source of the Seine 300 miles (500 km) away, use the St.-Martin and St.-Denis canals to shorten their trip, cutting across northeastern Paris. Stately and serene, the Seine now flows for tourists, poets and lovers.

On shore: Both divided and united by the Seine, Paris is a mosaic of 80 neighborhoods, each with its own distinctive character and activity: the Odéon quarter with its publishing houses, cabinet-makers in the Faubourg St.-Antoine, garment wholesalers at Sentier, colleges in the Latin Quarter, department stores at the Chaussée d'Antin, the business district around the Bourse (the Stock Exchange) and the Opéra or at La Defénse.

One of the most persistent images of Paris is its long avenues and boulevards graciously lined with chestnut and plane trees. Flowers and plants abound in a patchwork of 338 squares, parks and gardens, tended in the formal French tradition. Developed dur-

Sunning on the banks of the Seine.

ing the 17th century, the classical garden "*a la française*" is a flat stretch of land laid out geometrically in a simple landscaped succession of flowerbeds, lawns, hedges, terraces and pools.

Running from the Louvre to the place de la Concorde, the **Tuileries** was designed by Le Nôtre, creator of the Versailles gardens, and is a perfect example of this classical art of formal garden landscaping, with its paths, beds and innumerable statues. It is not surprising that the **Luxembourg Garden** in the sixth *arrondissement*, less symmetrical but more favorable to reverie, was frequented by poets at the turn of the century, and by students today—studying or even skipping their lessons.

To the east and west of Paris pump its two 'lungs'—the **Bois de Vincennes** and the **Bois de Boulogne**, which taken together represent 18 percent of the ancient forest surrounding Lutetia, later royal hunting grounds. Today the *bois* are a favorite haunt of joggers, horseback-riders, cyclists and canoeists.

At the request of Napoléon III, Baron Haussmann laid out the Bois de Boulogne like an English garden, more sinuous and disheveled than its rigorous French counterpart. But disheveled does not mean untamed. The Bois de Boulogne is very civilized, and many centers of interest attract crowds of locals and tourists, particularly on weekends: there are lakes, waterfalls, an amusement park for children (*le Jardin d'Acclimatation*), two racetracks (**Auteuil** and **Long-champs**), and the **Bagatelle Château** with its superb floral gardens. During summer Elizabethan plays are performed in English at the **Jardin Shakespeare**, an exquisite outdoor theater which is landscaped entirely with plants, trees and flowers named by the playwright in his works.

For the amateur necromancer, historian, art appreciator, celebrity chaser, sightseer or even dog lover, a visit to at least one of the 14 cemeteries is a must. The **Père-Lachaise** cemetery is one of the most frequented sites in Paris, notwithstanding its darker aspects; while **Montparnasse** is very rich in funerary structures and in celebrities; the most curious of all is the **Dog Cemetery** in Asniéres (a suburb to the northwest) where over 100,000 dogs, cats, birds and racehorses are buried!

From cemeteries to catacombs which are only one step down, underground Paris is a labyrinth of 100 miles (200 km) of métro lines, 2,000 miles (3,000 km) of sewers, scores of garages, and dozens of miles of ancient quarries. These Gallo-Roman stone quarries were converted into catacombs in the 18th century, when the remains of nearly six million individuals were brought together from several defunct graveyards, notably the Innocents Cemetery, a breeding ground of infection evacuated in 1785. Guided tours of the catacombs are given at 2 bis place Denfert Rochereau in the 14th *arrondissement*. Over the entrance the inscription reads: "Stop. Here lies death's empire," a warning largely unheeded by daring young explorers in search of clandestine nocturnal adventures.

Left, Bagatelle Gardens. Right, haze over the Champs-Elysées.

ARCHITECTURE THROUGH THE AGES

Two thousand years of history and seven centuries of artistic brilliance have made Paris a city rich in architecture. Yet invasions, sieges and insurrections have irreparably destroyed a great number of architectural masterpieces.

In 1944, as Allied troops were approaching, Hitler gave General Dietrich von Choltitz, Governor of Paris, the order to blast every single historical edifice so that the Allies' triumphant entry would be greeted by a field of smoking ruins. Charges of dynamite were laid under the Invalides, Notre Dame, the Madeleine, the Opéra, the Arc de Triomphe and even at the foot of the Eiffel Tower. But at the last minute, unable to perpetrate such sacrilege, von Choltitz refused to give the order and ultimately surrendered the city intact to General Leclerc, liberator of Paris.

Despite various devastations, Paris has maintained numerous examples of all ancient architectural styles in France, especially from the 12th century and the beginnings of the Gothic art era onwards. The city is a veritable textbook of architectural history, a living museum that requires little imagination to bring the past back to life. This explains the juxtaposition of different styles, complementary or contrasting.

These juxtapositions are never jarring or in bad taste. The architectural landscape always appears elegant and harmonious. The reason is because Paris has always had the best—the best architects, sculptors, masons and painters.

Roman remains: Nothing remains of the wooden huts occupied by the Gauls on the Ile de la Cité. However, as the Romans developed an extremely resistant concrete, their ruins can still be found in the Latin Quarter, the site of their settlement. Several streets like the rue St.-Jacques and the boule-

Upper chapel of the Ste. Chapelle.

vard St.-Michel are built on ancient Roman roads. Lutetia was not an important city at the time, but boasted, nevertheless, all the buildings necessary to Roman civic life—palace, forum, theater, arena, baths and temples.

The vestiges of one of these baths can be found in the garden at the Cluny Museum and the ruins of the arena have also survived. It is possible that early Christians were thrown to the lions in both the theater and circus here.

Gothic: Unfortunately, nothing is left of the Merovingian and Carolingian eras (6th to 9th centuries), the Vikings had burnt and pillaged Paris on three occasions during this period.

The Romanesque period, with its ponderous and gloomy structures hardly left a mark. The only remnant of this artistic and religious movement that spread throughout France at the turn of the first millenium is the St.-Germain-des-Prés church steeple.

Very early on, Paris and the Ile-de-France had turned to the newest rage in religious architecture: Gothic. Lighter, more slender and luminous, the birth of Gothic art coincided with the strengthening of the French crown and a fresh religious fervor inflamed by the Crusades. Gothic architecture is distinguished by the combined use of ribbed vaults with flying buttresses, a technique that allowed windows to replace walls, and walls to soar towards the heavens.

Perfection: The most beautiful religious edifice in Paris, Notre Dame, displays the perfection of this style. The cathedral was constructed on the site of a Romanesque church, which had been built on a Carolingian basilica, and before that a Roman temple. People have prayed here for at least 20 centuries!

Work on Notre Dame began in 1163 and took 200 years and several generations of

architects and craftsmen to finish it. The building began to decay during the 17th century. During the 19th century, its restoration was undertaken by Viollet-le-Duc, a salutory effort in keeping with the cathedral's spirit, if not with its form.

Notre Dame, like all medieval churches, was completely painted on the inside. The statues over the triple front doors were once multicolored on a gold background. The use of color was meant to glorify God and breathe life into the sculptures. These early paintings were the way medieval man learned the Bible stories.

Gothic's golden age, the flamboyant style, is represented by a fragile looking church, with all windows and stained glass (the oldest in Paris), supported by a thin framework of stone. Nestled within the walls of the Palais de Justice, the **Sainte Chapelle** was built by Saint Louis (King Louis IX) to shelter the crown of thorns and a fragment of the cross of Christ.

Renaissance: Imported from Italy in the 16th century, the Renaissance period is characterized by a contempt for Gothic forms, a rediscovery of antiquity and the development of a taste for the profane. In architecture, the ribbed vault disappeared in favor of flat ceilings with wooden beams. Medieval fortresses gave way to the genteel palaces and the Greek column of the earlier days made a comeback.

Architect Pierre Lescot and architect/sculptor, Jean Goujon, constructed the Hôtel Carnavalet in 1544 (23 rue de Sévigné, in the Marais district), then the west wing of the Louvre. Goujon also sculpted the bas-reliefs on the **Fontaine des Innocents**, a fine example of Renaissance sensuality jubilantly rejecting the sacred hierarchy of figures imposed by the Middle Ages.

Classicism: At the end of the 16th century, while all over Europe the Renaissance had succumbed to the baroque movement, French architects took a turn towards sobriety: classicism. A desire for strength and clarity, born of rationalism, dominated in architecture. The classical style is symmetry, simplicity of line and wide open perspectives. Constructed in 1606, the **Pont Neuf** (now the oldest bridge in Paris) was the first one built without houses on it! Thus, a view of the Seine was finally revealed.

To air the urban atmosphere, the first *places* were laid, ringed by uniform buildings with a statue of the king in the middle. The **place des Vosges** was the first and most elegant of the royal squares with its graceful arcades, a cool summer haven created by Henri IV, in 1612.

Another example is the **place de la Concorde**, designed by Gabriel in 1757. Its center was first occupied by a statue of Louis XV, then during the Revolution, by the guillotine, and finally in 1836, by an Egyptian obelisk from the temple of Ramses II in Thebes. The **Louvre** has been a continual

Left, place des Vosges. Above, the Opéra.

construction site since the Middle Ages, and looks nothing like its origins as a 13th-century keep.

Now you may be surprised by references to the "New Louvre" or *Le Grand Louvre*. That is the name given to the most recent restructuring of the huge palace and museum inside. I.M. Pei's **Pyramids** in the *Cour Napoléon* are already world-famous, an illusionistic "landscape" in stainless steel and specially created polished glass. Generally lauded for its beauty and efficiency as the musuem's main entrance, the Pyramids have entered the architectural legend of Paris.

Starting in 1760, the neoclassic movement turned back to forms grafted directly from antiquity, taking the utmost care to faithfully reproduce what recent progress in archeology had brought to light. Soufflot designed the **Panthéon**, originally, a church and, today, a secular temple where great patriots are buried. Copied from the ancient architectural repertory, the single column came into vogue (place Vendôme and place de la Bastille are examples), as well as colonnades (the Madeleine church), and the triumphal arch (place du Carrousel and place de l'Etoile).

Baron Haussmann's legacy: With the exception of a few elite neighborhoods, Paris was a squalid city during the 19th century. Poverty-stricken communities, with their filthy, narrow alleyways and miserable, overpopulated shacks, were constantly on the brink of revolt. For obvious sanitary reasons, but also to circumvent the risk of riots, Napoléon III and the Prefect Haussmann began a sweeping urbanization project in 1850.

Medieval Paris all but disappeared. Whole quarters were razed while wide, tree-lined avenues, more difficult to barricade as insurgents were wont to do, took the place of mucky backstreets.

The city of Paris today is still strongly marked by Haussman's plan. After clearing out slums and opening up the area around the Louvre, he concentrated on creating the *Grands Boulevards* ringing the city center. The central point was planned for a small hill then known as the *Butte Saint-Roche*, occupied by windmills, a gallows and a pig market. Joan of Arc led an attack on the city from that vantage point. It is hard to imagine all that today as you stand on the level, busy *place de l'Opéra*.

The Second Empire's most sumptuous construction was the Charles Garnier **Opéra House**, with its monumental staircase, its lavish auditorium almost dripping with red and gold, the ceiling by Chagall (painted in 1964), and a six-ton chandelier.

Mr Eiffel's Tower: The second half of this century was rich in creativity. Wrought-iron architecture made its début with the Grand Palais, the Alexandre III Bridge, and of course, the Eiffel Tower. Panned by critics during its construction in 1889, *la Tour Eiffel* is now the symbol of Paris.

The now-famous tower was orginally designed to be a temporary exhibit at the *Exposition Universelle* of 1900, along with "a grotesque city of plaster, staff and pasteboard...buildings from an Asian temple to a Swiss chalet, from Kanaka hut to medieval Paris, Chinese pagoda to Montmartre cabaret", as one contemporary visitor remarked on a trip to the city.

As Eiffel's controversial creation, symbolizing the uneasy relationship between science, industry and art, rose up higher and higher, bets were placed as to when it would topple over.

When Eiffel himself climbed up to plant the French flag atop his iron lattice-work fantasy, the cheering crowds were made up of ordinary Parisians who admired his vision; snobbish aesthetes stayed away. Finally, it was wireless radio that saved the Tower from demolition, and it is still used as a transmission station today.

This was also an eclectic period. The **Hôtel de Ville** (city hall) was rebuilt Renaissance-style, while the **Sacre-Coeur** was done in the antique tradition, and numerous churches along Gothic lines. Reacting against these academic approaches and inspired by Japanese art, Hector Guimard launched the *art nouveau* movement.

The sinuous plant forms and curving lines, natural and baroque at the same time, were decried by the new trend's detractors as "noodle style." Guimard designed several buildings in the 16th *arrondissement*, including the **Castel Béranger** (14 rue de la Fontaine) and also some lovely métro entrances of which Porte Dauphine and Abbesses are two.

Both the modern movement of the 1920s and 1930s and the art déco were born in the 16th *arrondissement* as well. Mallet-Stevens (rue Mallet-Stevens) and Le Corbusier (Maison Jeanneret, 8 square du Dr. Blanche) were the main artisans of this cubic style, all pure line and concrete. The **Palais de Chaillot** is a typical example of an architectural current that left its mark particularly on the Third Reich and Soviet Russia.

Paris has kept up with technical advances in architecture, building upward (La Défénce, Montparnasse Tower), expanding indoor space (Pompidou Center, La Villette, Bercy), and audaciously experimenting new materials that capture, reflect, and admit light. The new **Opéra de la Bastille**, like Pei's Pyramid or the **Géode** at La Villette, exemplifies the harmony of modern architecture in Paris by actually reflecting the neighbouring buildings and the changing Parisian sky. Gothic architecture, in its time, held a mirror to society in a similar way. But today's cathedrals are more often of a cultural, not religious, vocation.

Left, Montparnasse Tower. Above, art deco métro entrance.

CADEAUX

RARE BIRDS

The true *Parisien* (the male of the genus) or *Parisienne* (his counterpart) is a rare bird indeed. There are those who lay claim to the title by virtue of their families' history, whether noble or common, and those who are simply the embodiment of the city's spirit in one way or another.

The genus shares certain habits and traits which will help you distinguish the Parisian from the crowd of *provinciaux* (anyone born outside of a 31-mile or 50-km radius from Notre Dame) and *étrangers* (anyone who asks directions):

—They much prefer the urban environment; in the country, the sound of birds disturbs their morning sleep.

—Behind the wheel, they blithely assume that traffic will (and even should, by law) yield to them.

—They instinctively flock to the neighborhoods most recently deemed *à la mode*, which others only stumble on by chance.

—The plumage of the Parisian is always impeccable and harmonious. Seasonal moltings are greeted with great fanfare.

Blanc, black, beur: Past immigration policies led to the development of major communities from all the old French colonies and territories, especially Algeria, Tunisia, Senegal and the French West Indies. The progeny of these immigrant workers have lived most of their lives and attended school in France.

A genuine solidarity has grown between members of the younger generation who are *blanc* (white), *black*, and *beur* (a kind of pig-Latin variation of "Arab"). Youths who have been raised in the most multiracial areas of the city realize the true value of living in an environment influenced by cultures from around the world. In fact, that has always been a source of the strength of the Parisian character itself, beginning with the first meeting of southern Romans and northern Gauls.

Within the generic group *Homo sapiens Parisii* are several 'subspecies' easily identified in their usual habitat.

Vieille France: It's hard to be more royalist than the king, unless you are the *Comte de Paris*, currently leading the pack of contenders to the French throne. Yes, there are still monarchists roaming the streets, breathing more easily since the guillotine was removed from the place de la Concorde.

Les Bourges: Aptly celebrated by Jacques Brel in a popular song, *La Bourgeoisie Française* is made up of notaries, lawyers, landed gentry, and investment bankers. The young are recognizable by their clean-cut appearance, navy blue sailor outfits and perfectly white knee socks. Older members of the species are rarely seen on the streets, only seen coming in and out of churches, restaurants, and financial institutions

Les bureaucrats: If you have any intentions of doing business in Paris, you will run into

Preceding pages: the Latin Quarter. Left, a bird in hand at the market. Right, *Monsieur le gendarme.*

the *Administration Française,* where the term "bureaucracy" originated. Beware that it is considered an unforgivable slur to call a person "bureaucrat" to his face. The polite reference is *fonctionnaires* (civil servants), and they are more cooperative when you remember it.

Les Dragueurs: These nocturnal crawlers flock to the all-night districts like Montparnasse and Les Halles. Males are much more in evidence than females, stalking their prey in popular cafés, bars and clubs. Others operate in bookstores, post offices or cinemas. In fact, these birds are everywhere, in single-minded pursuit of romance, or just

hanky-panky, in Paris, capital of love. Two popular phrases also help to identify this particular Parisian: *Tu as de beaux yeux, tu sais* (What lovely eyes you have), and *Est-ce que tu habites chez tes parents?* (Do you live with your folks?). Forewarned is forearmed.

Baba Cool—This nearly extinct species flourished in Paris in the 1960s, and in 1968 played a major role in the disturbances and uprisings in the capital. The male of the species usually has long, graying locks and wears a full beard, while the female expresses herself with Indian cotton prints and folkart jewelry.

It is difficult to observe this species in Paris today; atmospheric changes have driven many of them south to the Larzac region, where they peacefully raise goats and make cheese.

BCBG (for *bon chic, bon genre*)—This species strongly resembles the North American *yuppie* or the British Isles *Sloane ranger*, in appearance, at least. They can be observed drinking hot chocolate in the tearooms of the Marais and Palais Royal districts.

Les beauf's—The term originates from the French word for brother-in-law—*beau-frère*. The term has come to replace *français moyen*, "average Frenchman," to describe a regular Joe with all the typical virtues and vices. A *beauf* is generally someone you are associated with by obligation rather than by choice, but good for a laugh, anyway.

Les artistes—Paris has always been a preferred nesting ground for this species. The rich beauty of the city, its history, the dark river, flowing wine and sleepless nights, all contribute to the proliferation of *artistes* in Paris.

Les bons vivants—The most celebrated Parisian species and certainly the most playful. You'll spot them, plumes in disarray, weaving through streets at midnight, seated at tables heaped with delicious food and wine, casually entering elegant shops and leaving with a package or two of something irresistible. This species will never disappear from Paris; it is truly indigenous.

The real thing: With such a diversity of color and habit, the Parisian is one of the most interesting *Homo sapiens* to observe. Camouflage is quite unnecessary, as most of the specimens you will encounter are not only indifferent to stares, but welcome them.

How can you be sure you're looking at the real 'things'? After all, the millions of foreigners who live here are adept at masquerade, too. Apply this acid test: at six o'clock on a Friday evening, true *Parisiens* are the only ones who can find a cab.

Left, near the Mosque. Right, love endures amid the roses, Bagatelle Gardens.

BON
ABARET
IT CLUB
SEXY

AGIC CLUB
Peep

Desserts

MOVEABLE FEAST

Hemingway captured one of the charms of the city in the title of his famous book, *A Moveable Feast*, where even the hardships had their aura of romantic adventure. Yet, if visitors have been taking part of Paris home with them for centuries, the city has not been one bit diminished and indeed, it changes and grows richer daily.

Yesterday's fashionable avenue is today's hoodlum hangout; a center-city train station holds a century of plastic arts; suddenly all the kids are wearing things you wouldn't dream of being seen in yesterday, but *plus ca change, plus c'est la même chose*. The standard tourist attractions have held up to the years: the Eiffel Tower, Montmartre, the Louvre, Notre Dame and the Latin Quarter, are all musts for the first-time visitor and well worth a gander for old hands, too. There are always new things happening, discoveries to be made.

The following pages include information on well-known highlights and under-appreciated nooks and crannies. A walking itinerary takes you through the different *quartiers*, each with its particular atmosphere and history. Museums—there are about 100 worth visiting—are in a separate chapter. Some visitors never see the inside of one and are no worse off for it, as the city itself is alive with the beauty of all the ages. Those with more than time to invest can visit the galleries mentioned here, and take home a little bit of Parisian style to hang on the wall.

People who are staying a little longer or who want to come into contact with the natives will find the items on various outdoor, sports and children's activities helpful. Or live out your dream of a bohemian life through some of the suggestions for longer term cultural and leisure activities.

Be sure to save enough energy for *Paris By Night*—besides the choice nightclubs, bars, glittershows, Paris has lately renewed the theater spirit and there is usually an excellent selection of old and new *spectacles* which will make your trip memorable. Needless to say, Paris is also a central showcase for unbeatable French food and wine, and you'll have no problem enjoying plenty of both.

Style is an important, if somewhat ambiguous factor in Parisian life. The rule used to be one good (and expensive) outfit for each season, and several accessories. Things are less formal now, but even if you want to pack light and practical, do bring along something dressy (and have it pressed) or plan to splurge on arrival. You will want to look your best, whether that means black leather or lemon chiffon—in some situations it's a ticket to better service and you will feel more comfortable. The essential thing is to carry it off. Be yourself with *panache* and you'll be a hit.

Preceding pages: art students in the Luxembourg Gardens; St. Eustache; view from Montmartre; Pigalle. Left, a weary visitor. Following pages: place du Tertre.

La Vie des Saisons: The biggest tourist season is from June through early September. The weather is generally warm then, and the days are magnificently long. In June, the sumptuous evenings linger on well past 10 p.m.; on July 14 the whole town is a party celebrating Bastille Day; in August, though a number of places close for vacation, the city enjoys an appreciable calm and good humor. August is also the month for special *fêtes et festivals* celebrating music, theater and wine. Be sure to check the newspapers and street posters for announcements.

The early fall season, known as *la rentrée* (return from vacation), is also a good time to visit. Everyone in the city is refreshed and excited about the new season's plays, exhibits and, of course, fashions.

Paris stays green and golden well into November and the weather is a mixture of balmy afternoons and sudden showers. The days are shorter and on an early evening stroll you can marvel at the million lights glistening on the wet streets.

Winters, cold and humid, are a source of endless complaints for Parisians. While not popular with tourists, winter is the most active season for business, and perhaps the best time to see the "real" Paris. You may even save enough on off-season plane fare to go in style enjoying taxis, fine restaurants, and a myriad of entertainment choices.

Christmas time is always festive and the decorations are stylish and bright. The shops are filled to overflowing, and the cosmopolitan hustle-bustle will sweep you off your feet.

Springtime in Paris is a legend in itself. After the long, dark days, Paris jumps up at the first unfurling of green. The weather is unpredictable, but when good fortune smiles on the heavy chestnut blossoms stretching along the wide avenues, when the young spring sun warms the old stone benches and the Seine comes bubbling up to the bridgetops...well, go ahead and fall in love.

D'INITIATIVE

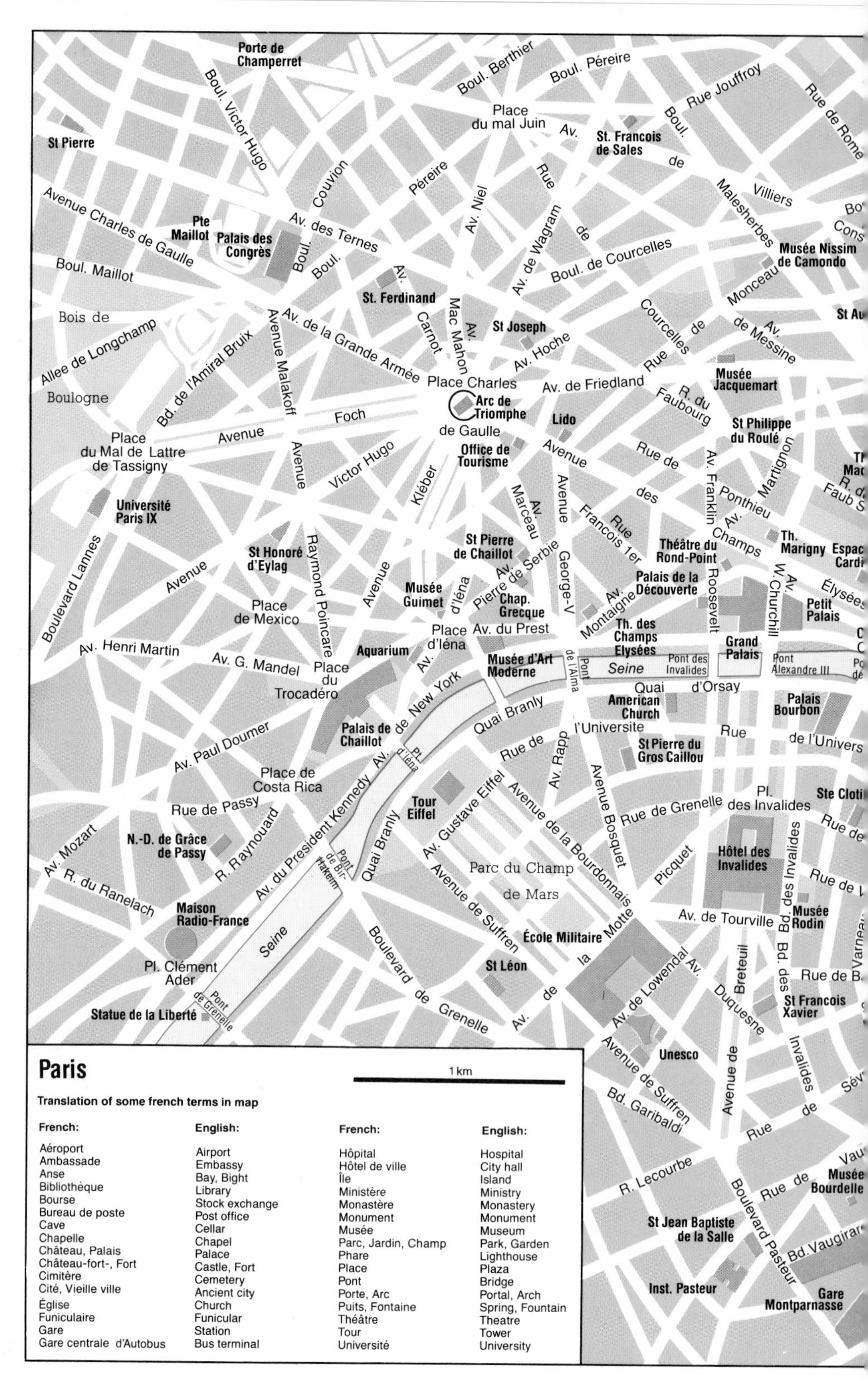
Porte de Champerret
Boul. Victor Hugo
Boul. Berthier
Boul. Péreire
Rue Jouffroy
Rue de Rome
St Pierre
Place du mal Juin
Av.
St. Francois de Sales
Boul. de Villiers
Rue de Wagram
Couvion
Péreire
Av. Niel
Malesherbes
Avenue Charles de Gaulle
Pte Maillot
Palais des Congrès
Av. des Ternes
Boul.
Av. de Wagram
Boul. de Courcelles
Musée Nissim de Camondo
Boul. Maillot
Monceau
St. Ferdinand
Av. Carnot
Av. Mac Mahon
Bois de Boulogne
Allee de Longchamp
Avenue Malakoff
Av. de la Grande Armée
St Joseph
Rue de Courcelles
Av. de Messine
Av. Hoche
Bd. de l'Amiral Bruix
Place Charles de Gaulle
Arc de Triomphe
Av. de Friedland
Musée Jacquemart
Avenue Foch
R. du Faubourg
Lido
St Philippe du Roulé
Place du Mal de Lattre de Tassigny
Avenue Victor Hugo
Office de Tourisme
Avenue
Rue de Ponthieu
Av. Franklin Roosevelt
Martignon
Kléber
Av. Marceau
Avenue George-V
Rue des Francois 1er
Université Paris IX
Av. Champs
Th. Marigny
Boulevard Lannes
St Honoré d'Eylag
Raymond Poincare
St Pierre de Chaillot
Théâtre du Rond-Point
Av. W. Churchill
Avenue
Av. Pierre de Serbie
Palais de la Découverte
Petit Palais
Place de Mexico
Musée Guimet
Av. d'Iéna
Chap. Grecque
Av. Montaigne
Av. Henri Martin
Place d'Iéna
Av. du Prest
Th. des Champs Elysées
Grand Palais
Av. G. Mandel
Aquarium
Musée d'Art Moderne
Pont de l'Alma
Seine
Pont des Invalides
Pont Alexandre III
Place du Trocadéro
Av. de New York
Quai d'Orsay
American Church
Palais Bourbon
Quai Branly
l'Universite
Palais de Chaillot
Rue de l'Univers
Av. Paul Doumer
Pt. d'Iéna
Rue de
Av. Rapp
St Pierre du Gros Caillou
Place de Costa Rica
Av. du President Kennedy
Avenue Bosquet
Pl. des Invalides
Tour Eiffel
Av. Gustave Eiffel
Rue de Grenelle
Ste Clotil
Rue de Passy
Avenue de la Bourdonnais
Av. Mozart
N.-D. de Grâce de Passy
R. Raynouard
Pont de Bir-Hakeim
Quai Branly
Parc du Champ de Mars
Picquet
Hôtel des Invalides
Bd. des Invalides
R. du Ranelach
Avenue de Suffren
Maison Radio-France
Av. de Tourville
Musée Rodin
École Militaire
Av. de la Motte
Seine
Pl. Clément Ader
St Léon
Av. de Lowendal
Breteuil
Bd. des
Rue de B
Duquesne
St Francois Xavier
Pont de Grenelle
Boulevard de Grenelle
Statue de la Liberté
Unesco
Avenue de Suffren
Avenue de
Invalides
Bd. Garibaldi
Rue de
R. Lecourbe
Rue de
Musée Bourdelle
Boulevard Pasteur
St Jean Baptiste de la Salle
Bd. Vaugirard
Inst. Pasteur
Gare Montparnasse
Paris
1 km
Translation of some french terms in map
French: | English:
Aéroport | Airport
Ambassade | Embassy
Anse | Bay, Bight
Bibliothèque | Library
Bourse | Stock exchange
Bureau de poste | Post office
Cave | Cellar
Chapelle | Chapel
Château, Palais | Palace
Château-fort-, Fort | Castle, Fort
Cimitère | Cemetery
Cité, Vieille ville | Ancient city
Église | Church
Funiculaire | Funicular
Gare | Station
Gare centrale d'Autobus | Bus terminal
Hôpital | Hospital
Hôtel de ville | City hall
Île | Island
Ministère | Ministry
Monastère | Monastery
Monument | Monument
Musée | Museum
Parc, Jardin, Champ | Park, Garden
Phare | Lighthouse
Place | Plaza
Pont | Bridge
Porte, Arc | Portal, Arch
Puits, Fontaine | Spring, Fountain
Théâtre | Theatre
Tour | Tower
Université | University

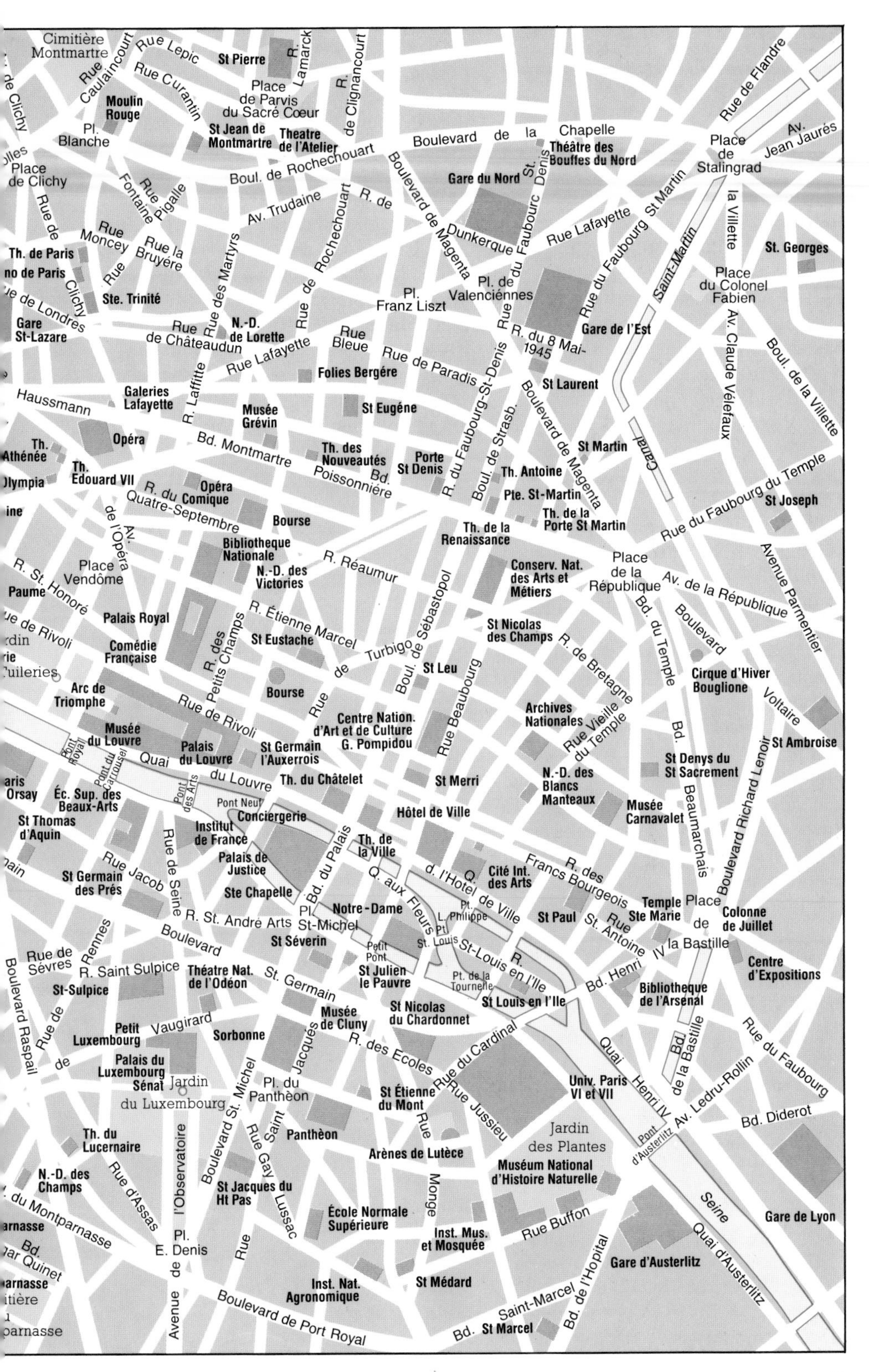

Cimitière Montmartre
Rue Lepic
St Pierre
R. Lamarck
Rue Caulaincourt
Rue Curantin
Place de Parvis du Sacré Cœur
R. de Clignancourt
Moulin Rouge
Pl. Blanche
St Jean de Montmartre
Theatre de l'Atelier
Boulevard de la Chapelle
Théâtre des Bouffes du Nord
Rue de Flandre
Place de Stalingrad
Av. Jean Jaurés
Place de Clichy
Boul. de Rochechouart
Gare du Nord
St. Denis
Rue Fontaine
Rue Pigalle
Av. Trudaine
R. de Rochechouart
R. de Dunkerque
Boulevard de Magenta
Rue du Faubourg St Denis
Rue Lafayette
Rue du Faubourg St Martin
Canal Saint-Martin
la Villette
St. Georges
Rue Moncey
Rue la Bruyére
Th. de Paris
no de Paris
Rue Clichy
Ste. Trinité
Rue des Martyrs
Pl. Franz Liszt
Pl. de Valenciénnes
Place du Colonel Fabien
Rue de Londres
Gare St-Lazare
Rue de Châteaudun
N.-D. de Lorette
Rue Bleue
Rue de Paradis
R. du 8 Mai-1945
Gare de l'Est
Av. Claude Vélefaux
Boul. de la Villette
Rue Lafayette
Folies Bergére
St Laurent
Galeries Lafayette
Haussmann
R. Laffitte
Musée Grévin
St Eugéne
R. du Faubourg-St-Denis
Boul. de Strasb.
Boulevard de Magenta
Th. Athénée
Opéra
Bd. Montmartre
Th. des Nouveautés
Porte St Denis
St Martin
Canal
Th. Edouard VII
Olympia
Opéra Comique
Bd. Poissonnière
Th. Antoine
Pte. St-Martin
Th. de la Porte St Martin
Rue du Faubourg du Temple
St Joseph
R. du Quatre-Septembre
Bourse
Th. de la Renaissance
Av. de l'Opéra
Bibliotheque Nationale
R. Réaumur
Place Vendôme
N.-D. des Victories
Conserv. Nat. des Arts et Métiers
Place de la République
Avenue Parmentier
R. St. Honoré
Paume
Boul. de Sebastopol
Av. de la République
Palais Royal
R. Étienne Marcel
R. des Petits Champs
St Nicolas des Champs
Bd. du Temple
Boulevard Voltaire
Rue de Rivoli
Comédie Française
St Eustache
Rue de Turbigo
R. de Bretagne
Tuileries
St Leu
Cirque d'Hiver Bouglione
Arc de Triomphe
Bourse
Rue Beaubourg
Archives Nationales
Rue Vieille du Temple
St Ambroise
Musée du Louvre
Rue de Rivoli
Centre Nation. d'Art et de Culture G. Pompidou
Pont Royal
Pont du Carrousel
Palais du Louvre
St Germain l'Auxerrois
Bd. Beaumarchais
St Denys du St Sacrement
Boulevard Richard Lenoir
Quai du Louvre
Pont des Arts
Th. du Châtelet
St Merri
N.-D. des Blancs Manteaux
Orsay
Éc. Sup. des Beaux-Arts
Pont Neuf
Musée Carnavalet
St Thomas d'Aquin
Conciergerie
Institut de France
Hôtel de Ville
Rue de Seine
Palais de Justice
Bd. du Palais
Th. de la Ville
Q. de l'Hotel de Ville
Cité Int. des Arts
R. des Francs Bourgeois
Rue Jacob
St Germain des Prés
Ste Chapelle
Q. aux Fleurs
Notre-Dame
Pt. L. Philippe
Temple Ste Marie
Place de la Bastille
Colonne de Juillet
R. St. André Arts
Pl. St-Michel
Pt St. Louis
St Paul
Rue St. Antoine
Boulevard St. Germain
St Séverin
Petit Pont
R. St-Louis en l'Ile
Rue de Rennes
Rue de Sèvres
R. Saint Sulpice
Théatre Nat. de l'Odéon
St Julien le Pauvre
Pt. de la Tournelle
Bd. Henri IV
Centre d'Expositions
St-Sulpice
St Louis en l'Ile
Bibliotheque de l'Arsenal
Boulevard Raspail
Musée de Cluny
St Nicolas du Chardonnet
Petit Luxembourg
Vaugirard
Sorbonne
Rue St Jacques
R. des Ecoles
Rue du Cardinal
Quai Henri IV
Bd. de la Bastille
Rue du Faubourg
Palais du Luxembourg
Sénat
Jardin du Luxembourg
Boulevard St. Michel
Pl. du Panthèon
St Étienne du Mont
Rue Jussieu
Univ. Paris VI et VII
Av. Ledru-Rollin
Bd. Diderot
Th. du Lucernaire
Avenue de l'Observatoire
Rue Gay Lussac
Panthèon
Rue Monge
Arènes de Lutèce
Jardin des Plantes
Pont d'Austerlitz
N.-D. des Champs
Rue d'Assas
St Jacques du Ht Pas
Muséum National d'Histoire Naturelle
Seine
Bd. du Montparnasse
École Normale Supérieure
Rue Buffon
Gare de Lyon
Pl. E. Denis
Inst. Mus. et Mosquée
Quai d'Austerlitz
Bd. Edgar Quinet
Bd. de l'Hopital
Gare d'Austerlitz
Inst. Nat. Agronomique
St Médard
Boulevard de Port Royal
Bd. Saint-Marcel
St Marcel

HEART OF PARIS

At first glance, the map of Paris will strike you by the cobweb-like intricacy of its more than 5,000 streets. Don't be timorous. Rather than keeping to the main thoroughfares for fear of getting lost, let yourself stroll along the by-paths. Some 430 métro stations will be your benevolent landmarks. If you can approach but one art in Paris, let it be that of dawdling.

The following itineraries will take you by major tourist attractions in addition to not-so-famous curiosities and places of interest.

Royal Paris: There is a place which is a showcase of what Paris has always stood for. It is harmonious, charged with history and wrapped in elegance, charm and luxury: the octagonal **place Vendôme**.

Following the course of historical events, it has changed names four times and the bronze column in its center has in turn supported the statues of Louis XIV, Liberty, Napoléon I, a *fleur-de-lys*, and Napoléon I again. The statue and the column were altogether pulled down during the Commune and were finally replaced by the present, identical monument.

It is surrounded by the luster of diamonds, rubies, sapphires and emeralds glowing behind the panes of jewelers like **Van Cleef** and **Arpels** and **Boucheron**. No doubt many of these jewels have ended up in the hands of some traveler putting up at the **Ritz** next door.

Down rue de Castiglione and on the other side of the arcades on the rue de Rivoli (where, if you are short of English or American literature, you can stop in at **Smith's** or **Galignani's** bookstore), go through the iron gates of the **Jardin des Tuileries**.

The garden extends partly over the former site of the royal palace which was razed in 1871. Two terraces run along each side of the garden, one along the Seine river and one along the *pétanque* grounds. At both ends, two ornamental ponds have seen generations of young sailors set their toy boats to sea there. The main alley between the chestnut and lime trees leads to the **Arc de Triomphe du Carrousel**. This monument was built in 1808 to celebrate Napoléon I's victories.

Turning back, you can admire the imposing historical perspective of the **place de la Concorde**, the **Champs-Elysées** and the **Arc de Triomphe** which is called *La Voie Triomphale* .

A new monument has now been inserted into that perspective opening from the walls of the **Louvre**: the pyramid designed by I.M. Pei, flanked by its two little sisters and which is the most recent, republican addition to the ever-evolving, royal and imperial Louvre.

The glass panels of the pyramid give light to the new and necessary underground services offered by the largest museum in the world, personified by its most famous and mysterious painting, the *Mona Lisa*.

Facing the colonnade and the moats of the palace, on the other side of the rue du Louvre, stands the church of **St.-Germain l'Auxerrois**, better known as the **Church of the Kings**. The late gothic bestiary on the outside is particularly extensive.

Kings and commerce: Halfway along the northern aisle of the Louvre, crossing rue de Rivoli again, you reach the place du **Palais Royal**. Across the adjacent **place Colette** (named after the popular and scandalous writer), take a look at the plays billed at **La Comédie Française**, the most prestigious classical theater in Paris.

The company was founded in 1680 by Louis XIV and united Molière's troupe with two others. Just follow the arcades which lead to the entrance of the **Gardens**.

Built in 1633, the Palais Royal was passed on by Louis XIV to his brother's family, the Orléans. During Louis XIV's reign, Philippe d'Orléans's lav-

Preceding pages: the Arc de Triomphe on the place de l'Etoile. Right, simply chic.

MODES
SERVAL
27

ishness had got him in a tight spot. In order to honor his debts, he hit upon the clever idea of setting up arcades around the garden. Philippe would then collect rent from boutiques which sheltered under his arcades. From the moment the construction was ended in 1784, to the revolution of 1830, the arcades became one of the most brilliant and animated spots in Paris: politicians, poets and novelists, as well as prostitutes, mingled and met here until late at night.

Today, books, miscellaneous articles like military decorations, coins and other antiques still catch the eye of the collector in the half-light behind the windows. A few cafés and restaurants used to resound with customers' political arguments which, during the Restoration, often burst into duels between supporters of Louis XVIII and Bonaparte. The royalist **Café de Chartres**, at the end of the galerie Montpensier, has become, under chef Raymond Oliver's management, one of the finest restaurants in Paris—**Le Grand Véfour**.

Nowadays, part of the Palais Royal is occupied by governmental institutions. From their windows, the officials overlook the mirrored fountains and new columns designed by Buren, spectacularly lit at night.

Above the boutiques, the palace is divided into luxury apartments, where celebrities such as poet Louis Aragon, Colette and artist Jean Cocteau lived at different times.

Haute couture—nouveau!: At the other end of the garden, cross the little, well-named rue de Beaujolais and take the picturesque passage des Deux Pavillons to get to the **place des Victoires**. It was built by one of Louis XIV's subjects in order to show off his beloved King's statue. The stately residence around the monument has been converted into fashion houses held by new couturiers like **Kenzo** and **Thierry Mugler**. In the adjacent rue Etienne Marcel, other shops opened recently have become famous in a matter of weeks: among them are Junko Shimada, Kabuki, M.T. & F. Gibault and Comme des Garçons. The geographical gathering of new talents in *haute couture* gives this part of Paris a specially chic look.

At the back of the place des Victoires, the narrow rue du Vide-Gousset bears the name of a charming habit which involved rifling the reckless passerby's pockets. The street leads to the pious **place des Petits-Pères** and the church of **Notre Dame des Victoires**, where the Virgin Mary, according to the ex-votos covering the walls, has already answered more than 30,000 prayers!

Mysterious Paris: The passage des Petits-Pères, across rue de la Banque, opens onto one of the mysterious galleries of Paris which gives its peculiar aura to the whole second district in which it is situated. Built during the first half of the 19th century, their rotundas and soft, hazy light cascading from glass roofs attracted a majority of idlers then. A delicious hint of nostalgia hangs around their corridors today.

Left, Galerie Vivienne. Right, "Just looking thanks."

Galerie Vivienne might very well be Paris's most characteristic museum, with its monumental staircase and geometrical mosaics. Enjoy a tasty cake in the cane chairs of the quaint tearoom, after poking about in the dark, second-hand bookshops or vintage wine stalls.

The adjacent **Galerie Colbert** has been recently restored; the statue in the center of its rotunda as well as the marble columns make it a model of elegance. Not surprising then that Jean-Paul Gaultier chose this spot for his extravagant *haute couture* boutique. Across from the large café and the **Musée des Arts du Spectacle**, the **Bibliothèque Nationale** (National Library) has opened two exhibition rooms and a bookshop.

Turmoil and tranquility: At the end of rue de Richelieu, a building dating from 1808 supported by 128 Corinthian columns sets the area astir. It is the temple of finance, **La Bourse** (stock exchange), surrounded by the head offices of insurance companies, banks and brokers, auction rooms, newspaper offices and news agencies. To flee this turmoil head for the quiet labyrinth of galleries at the corner of boulevard and rue Montmartre.

The **Galerie des Variétés**, where old protectors met young extras, is still imbued with Offenbach's operetta arias which marked the best years of the Théâter des Variétés. The passage des Panoramas brings to mind the very origin of the word panorama. The submarine inventor, an American named Fulton, created painted canvasses to cover the walls of the rotundas. They have long vanished, but the charm is still preserved. The **passage Jouffroy**, across the boulevard, is philatelists' bliss, while the continuing **passage Verdeau** is a favorite spot for musical instruments and antique cameras.

Le Sentier: The wild agitation of the neighborhood will fall upon you in rue de Faubourg-Montmartre as you retrace your steps to the boulevard and go down rue Montmartre. Jean Jaurés,

The newest fashion center: place des Victoires.

French socialist, humanist and pacifist leader, was assassinated in the **Chope du Croissant** café at the corner of rue du Croissant on the eve of World War I.

At the end of rue du Sentier is the heart of the **garment district**. The narrow streets here are always obstructed by delivery trucks and ears suffer an almost continual concert of horns. The city workers bustle about in an Egyptian enclave: in fact, rues Damiette, d'Aboukir, du Nil, d'Alexandrie and du Caire owe their names to Napoléon I's Egyptian campaign.

On place du Caire, a strange façade displays the heads of sphinxes and hieroglyphs. All day the entire area bursts with vitality, but at night, when it is totally deserted, it is shivers time: you are standing on the very site of what used to be called *La Cour des Miracles*. Those who wandered in here seldom got out alive, as Victor Hugo recounted in his novel *Notre Dame de Paris*.

The street called Mont Orgueil (Mount of Pride) bears an ironic name: it rose up from the 10th to the 16th centuries atop layers of garbage. If you are still in want of delightful frights, follow the dark, narrow and winding stairs of the passage opening at No. 20. Otherwise, you can also take the 5-foot (1½-meter) long rue des Degrés, the smallest street in Paris, which is, in fact, a stairway.

The royal way: Proceed on to the former Roman road to Normandy. Earlier it was known as *La Voie Royale* (The Royal Way); today it is just plainly called rue St.-Denis. At each coronation, the kings of France used to make their solemn entry into Paris by going down the street to Notre Dame. The street was not only a witness to royal glory, but also to royal passings when they traveled in the opposite direction to be buried at the **St.-Denis Basilica**.

The southern half of the street has now been contaminated by the new look of Les Halles, and the northern part, with its little perpendicular alleys like passage Blondel is devoted to a

erious usiness at a Bourse.

profitable though not prestigious trade. In this quarter, prostitution goes back to St.-Louis's reign in the 13th century. Only the decor, with its neon signs, peepshows and sexshops has changed.

In the wee hours: Mont Orgueil meets up with rue Tiquetonne where a very popular and abundant **food market** held every day except Mondays still provides a great animation. Delivery vans start arriving as early as 3 a.m., so if you happen to be a nightowl or, on the contrary, an early bird, you can either have a last drink or a café-croissant at a bar nearby. The century-old pastry shop **Sthorer**, 51, rue Mont Orgueil, is sure to make your mouth water.

On your way down the street, you will cross rue Etienne Marcel. The oldest, medieval vestige of Paris, at No. 20, is the 1408 **Tower of Jean-sans-Peur**, the duke of Burgundy who murdered Louis d'Orléans in rue des Francs-Bourgeois.

St.-Eustache and Les Halles: At the end of rue Mont Orgueil, what certainly is the most beautiful religious monument in Paris, after Notre Dame, raises its 100-foot (34-meter) high vault to the sky. **St.-Eustache** was at first a little chapel built in 1214. It became a church between 1532 and 1637. The proportions of the gothic structures are considerable and are embellished with Renaissance decoration. Both Liszt and Berlioz had their work premiered there.

Les Halles, the central food market was created in the 12th century. Both Baltard's pavilions, built in the 1850s, and their noisy population inspired Zola's title for one of his best novels, *Le Ventre de Paris* (The Belly of Paris).

By 1969, the market had grown too vast for the space and the buildings had become dangerously dilapidated. The market has been moved to Rungis and the **Forum des Halles** has replaced the pavilions.

Square des Innocents: The **Square des Innocents** has always been a favorite meeting place, notwithstanding its environment. Indeed, this lively place served as the cemetery of the neighboring parishes and welcomed two million Parisians from the 10th to the 18th centuries. Later, the corpses were piled up in charnel-houses set upon vaulted galleries surrounding the cemetery. Despite the stench, the galleries were visited by small traders, letter-writers, strollers, and mourners' "comforters." Among others, the *Fables'* great author, La Fontaine, was buried there. After a communal grave collapsed into a cellar, the cemetery was closed, the medieval church razed, and the skeletons carried to the Catacombs.

A market settled on the empty space, around the Renaissance fountain built in 1549 against the church. It will be very hard for you to guess which façade was later added together with the dome. The market became a popular square, and you can check the comings and goings from the **Café Costes**.

Artistic Paris: If you pass under the last remaining arcades of the charnel-house, 11 and 13 rue des Innocents, you

In the Marais.

get to the little **rue de la Ferronnerie**. This is where the iron merchants used to carry on their trade.

Cross boulevard de Sébastopol and proceed to the church of **St.-Merri**, at the corner of rue St.-Martin and rue de La Verrerie. It was erected between 1515 and 1612 and houses the oldest bell of Paris (1331). On Saturday afternoons and Sunday evenings you can enjoy a free classical concert.

The new **place Georges Pompidou**, also called plateau **Beaubourg**, used to be a no man's land haunted by the memory of the poet, Gérard de Nerval, a precursor of Baudelaire who frequented the local bars at night and was found hanged one day at dawn.

Culture and controversy: In 1977, a project conceived by President Georges Pompidou in 1969 came to fruition. The cultural center bearing his name was inaugurated amidst murmurs of amazement, unbelief, incomprehension, and enthusiastic or disparaging comments. Time goes past but the **Arts and Cultural Center Georges Pompidou** remains a favorite subject for debates on architecture or cultural policy, and is the most visited place in Paris. "The building with the bowels outside" attracts hundreds of idlers attending the shows of medieval jugglers, fire-eaters and mimes, listening to the speeches of pseudo-philosophers and poets, watching the electronic clock draining the seconds left until the year 2,000, and buying the unique postcard witnessing the exact time of their visit—all even before entering the museum!

For those under 30 who haven't yet found an affordable place to stay, help is at hand at the A.J.F. (**Accueil des Jeunes en France**), 119 rue St.-Martin. On the southern side of the Center, rue St.-Merri, view the colorful and humoristic Tinguely and Nicky de **St.-Phalle Fountain**.

Le Marais: And now, more than ever, take time to stroll along the little streets leading to the historical quarter of **Le Marais**. This is one of the most beauti-

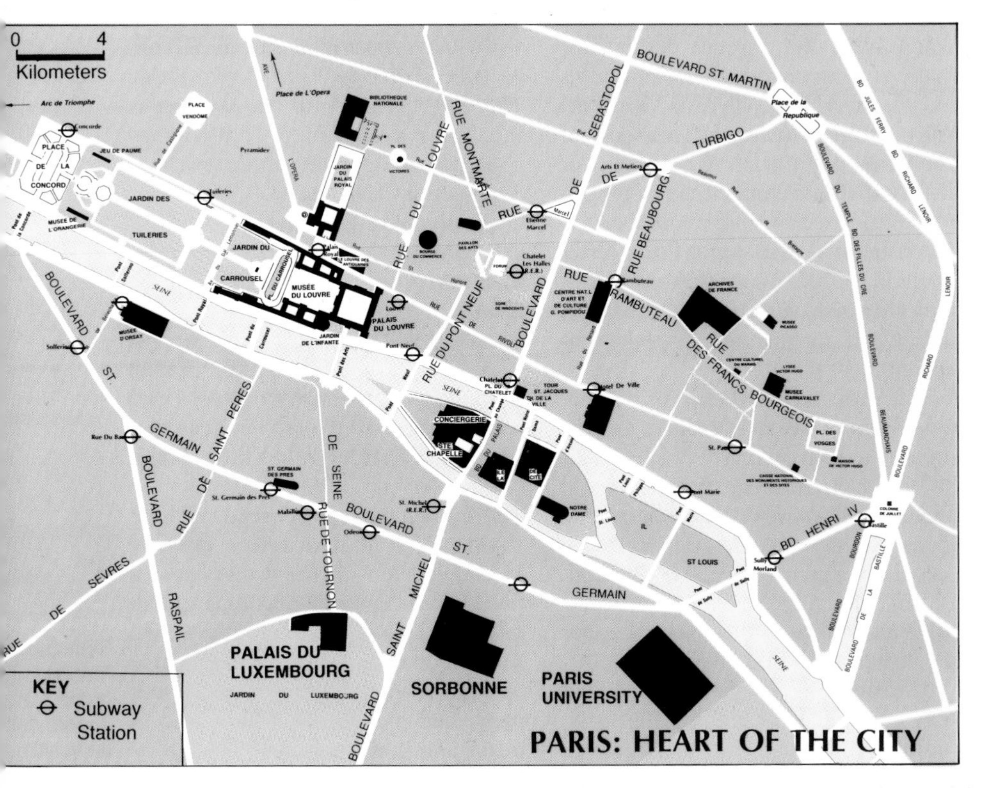

ful parts of Paris. Every street or lane has a residential *hôtel*, a paved court or an inner garden, and a huge gateway.

The **Hôtel de Sully** is the central headquarters for the National Historical Monuments administration and there you will find information about excellent guided walking tours of the Marais. Most of the renowned contemporary art galleries on the rightbank have settled in this area. Cafés, restaurants and shops have multiplied alongside traditional trades.

A good start for a visit on your own is **rue de Quincampoix**, displaying its 17th- and 18th-century ornamented façades and wrought iron balconies.

At the corner of rue des Archives, opposite an 18th-century fountain, the sumptuous **Palais Soubise** on rue des Francs-Bourgeois, and the **Hôtel de Rohan-Strasbourg** contain the **National Archives**.

Ancient mysteries, modern art: Roaming about **rue de Thorigny**, **rue Payenne**, **rue des Francs-Bourgeois** and **rue Vieille-du-Temple**, discover the magnificent Renaissance residences, many of them turned into art museums like the **Hôtel Salé (Picasso Museum)** and the **Hôtel Carnavalet (Museum of the History of Paris)**. At the corner of rue Vieille-du-Temple stands a typical medieval house bearing a corner turret. If you are short of shopping ideas, ferret about in the little shops on your way—they are sure to surprise you with original objects such as curios, trinkets or ancient books.

The gem of Le Marais is without contest the **place des Vosges**, erected during the 16th century. Between 1832 and 1848, Victor Hugo lived at No. 6, and most of *Les Misérables* was written there. The house is now a museum dedicated to the great writer and politician. Prestigious and specialized book, antique and art shops have settled under the arcades all around the place.

The little door at No. 7 opens on the back of the beautiful **Hôtel de Sully**, built in 1624. (Its main entrance is 62, **rue St.-Antoine**). At No. 5 of rue St.-Antoine, a plaque reminds the passerby that he is stepping over the former threshold of what was and is still the symbol of the absolute power of the monarchy—the **prison of the Bastille**.

This is the edge of the **Jewish quarter**, with its synagogue in rue Pavée and a stirring **Memorial to the Unknown Jewish Martyr** in rue Geoffroy-l'Asnier. The main street is rue des Rosiers, but the roses of the 12th-century have long disappeared. The Jewish community, despite periods of persecution, is deeply rooted around rue des Rosiers and sees to it that it is presently one of the liveliest streets in Paris, except on Saturdays when everything is closed. Under the Hebrew signs which are sometimes half-erased (reminders of World War II anti-semitism), the shops abound in kosher products from central Europe or from the East. The most famous delicatessen is **Jo Goldenberg's**, open until late at night.

On the way back, you can either stick to the little narrow streets or walk up the wide and commercial **rue de Rivoli**, past the **Hôtel de Ville** (Town Hall). The neighboring **Tour St.-Jacques** is the last remnant of a 16th-century church standing on the pilgrims' way to Santiago of Compostella.

On **place du Châtelet**, the spirit of entertainment has replaced an ominous medieval prison. Two theaters flank the fountain: the **Théâter Musical de Paris** specializes in classical concerts; while the theater where Sarah Bernhardt met so many triumphs and where her dressing room has been preserved, the **Théâter de la Ville** has multicultural events.

If you want to enjoy concerts without paying a dime, the **chickens** of **Quai de la Mégisserie** will charm your ears for free. Their unusual accompaniment includes an orchestra of dogs, cats, squirrels and monkeys making faces at cayman, fish, guinea pigs and company, half-hidden behind curtains of plants and flowerpots.

Renaissanc fountain in the Square des Innocents.

50 F
120 F
80 F
1980
50 F
43 F
60 F
Chateau
GARAUDIERES
140 F

A Word On Wine

"The shortest road to heaven is down the cellar stairs."

Of course, French wines are legendary—unsurpassed in quality, and integral to the country's culture, "the blood of the earth and the children of the sun." Happily, and despite occasional crises (bad weather, management scandals, vineyards bought up by foreign investors), a great deal of the snobbishness that surrounded the enjoyment of wines both great and ordinary has disappeared. Whether it is a glass of Beaujolais with a sandwich at lunchtime, or a fine white, red, or bubbly nectar carefully selected to accompany a traditional French meal, one can now take the time to sample and savor them all.

The wines of France have changed with the centuries, as have tastes and culinary styles. Greek merchants planted vineyards in the Marseilles region more than 2,000 years ago, and when the Romans spread through Gaul, they brought their grapes with them. The Gauls introduced the use of wooden wine casks, which represented an important step forward for improved fermentation, aging and transportation of wine. Medieval monks who perfected the fine art of winemaking had the best vineyards at their disposal, as well as a significant body of accumulated knowledge and the time to pursue their studies.

Today, over 300 varieties of grape are used in winemaking, both singly and in mixtures. Beaujolais, for example, is made only with Gamay grapes, while some Côtes du Rhone use up to 13 different kinds. A strict order of classification defines quality: *VVC* (*Vins de consommation courante*), *vins de pays* and *vins de table* are common wines and are, variously, awful, palatable or quite good; *VDQS* (*Vin délimité de qualité superieure*) are wines which have achieved some distinction; *AOC* (*Appellation de' origine contrôlée*) is marked on select bottles. *Vins de Pays* are a good bet in general, especially if the label says "*mis en bouteille a la proprieté*" (bottled at the vineyard). Usually when fine wines are offered in a respectable restaurant, it is rare indeed that they do not satisfy.

Selecting and savoring: Wines begin with a meal, but if you enjoy a glass beforehand, order a *vin doux apéritif* like **Banyuls**, **Muscat** or **Rivesaltes**, which are richly colored, with the aroma of the sunny southern region they come from; or a **Pineau de Charentes**, a heady blend of wine and cognac. If you plan to drink several bottles during a meal, the rule of thumb is that the vintage you are drinking should never make you nostalgic for its predecessor: begin with light, young fruity wines served chilled (whites and rosés), and continue with strong, aged wines with a rich bouquet, served at room temperature. Avoid drinking white wine with red meats, roasts, game and strong cheeses. Likewise, red wines don't go with oysters, shellfish, dishes in white sauce, soft young cheeses, creams and desserts. Champagne may be served at any time, especially the drier (less sweet) vintages.

Wines are judged on various aspects of their qualities. First is "character": a wine may be a frivolous tease; biting and alert, or aging, friendly, tender and proud. Next is the "body" which relates to the strength, acidity and tannin level: wines are muscular, two-fisted, virile; light, silky, seductive; ample and full; flimsy and weak. The "robe" defines color, clarity and elegance: with age, reds fade from royal-purple towards the orange hues of sunset, whites go to deep yellow and amber. Finally, the "bouquet" is the complex, subtle and changing aroma that the wine exudes as you roll it gently over your palate. The first "grapey" bouquet is slowly overtaken by the secondary bouquet, the flavor of

eceding ges: café front of e Pompi- u Center. ft, some of ance's est.

the landscape, and its soil and flowers. A secondary bouquet may recall violets, raspberries, nuts and cinnamon, or gravel, limestone and flint. Though the first is detectable in the youngest wines, the secondary bouquet develops only after two or three years. The best wines, aged first in the cask and then in the bottle, have a rich final bouquet when enjoyed at their apogee—a unique savor recalling forest growth crushed underfoot, mushrooms, wild animals...

A rosé by any other name: About one-third of the finest wines in France are **Bordeaux**. Though the red is better known, an equal amount of white wine is produced in the region. From vintage red *Medoc*, *Graves*, and *St. Emillion* (it's hard to make a mistake with these), to popular young clarets (light-colored reds) and gooey white *Sauternes*. There is a Bordeaux for every occasion: even "bad years" are reasonably good, while some of the more obscure vintners produce excellent results, and rarely will you hear a guest object that he doesn't care for Bordeaux.

The wines commonly take the name of one of the 3,500 châteaux which have long lent a touch of nobility to the landscape. These aristocratic appellations now refer to the specific climatic conditions affecting the vintage in question, for indeed, some of the castles are completely ruined, or have been reclaimed by nature.

Most commonly served in café carafes or by the glass are **Côtes du Rhone** and **Beaujolais** red wines. The latter is best young and chilled; every year the arrival of *le Beaujolais nouveau* is celebrated expansively in cafés and bars. Both wines are generally inexpensive. However, some Côtes de Rhone are quite distinguished, like the **Côte-Rôtie** which is France's oldest vintage wine with a price tag to match.

Bourgogne (Burgundy) wines, like Bordeaux, include some celebrated vintages such as *Nuits-St.-Georges Pommerand*, *Chassagne-Montrachet* and other excellent selections: *Côte de Beaune*, *Côte de Nuit*, *Chablis* and *Mâcon*—red and white. These wines are identified with one of the 1,200 strictly defined micro-climates found in the region between Dijon and Lyon, which are less than 100 miles apart.

Although the abundance of appellations may be confusing, the wines themselves are hearty, rich and good-natured, just like the wonderful people who make them.

Vins de Provence are humbler reds and rosés to be enjoyed with seafood and grilled foods, especially prepared "*provençal*" style with fresh herbs.

You will also enjoy the light wines from **Tourraine**, and their cousins, **Vin D'Anjou**, **Muscadet** and **Gros-Plant**. The sharp white wines of **Alsace** and **Savoie** are especially good with the favorite regional dishes, sauerkraut and cheese fondu.

More vigorous, stouter wines include deep red **Cahors**, excellent with red meat and often a bargain, and wines from **Languedoc** and **Minervois**. Though their reputation is for strength without nobility, they are very enjoyable and satisfying and will leave you feeling warm and happy.

The choice of table wines is as extensive as their history. Your own taste can guide you to reds, whites, or rosés, then let your pocketbook and the *sommelier* (wine steward) take over. In obviously cheap places, avoid the *vin maison* (house wine), which may be a mixture of different European wines which have traveled a dubious road in truck-loaded tanks. In better establishments, the *cuveé du patron* is generally a good buy.

Don't be shy about giving the *sommelier* a price range, and do check the label when the bottle is delivered. The person who selected the wine should taste it and and make sure it is being served at the correct temperature.

Queen of the grape: The sparkling queen of the fermented grape is **Champagne**. Dom Perignon, a 17th-century Benedictine monk, made important contributions to the development of this naturally carbonated delight, including experiment with blends of different grapes, a technique still used today. A Champagne wine with the year marked on the label is *millésimé*, made with the best vintages of a good year.

The aging process is very delicate and tedious: it involves rotating the bottles around an eighth of a turn daily, and gradually tilting them until the cork points downwards. It is best chilled in an ice bucket (six to eight degrees Celsius), recorked after service (to keep it from "fainting") and poured gently into tulip-shaped *flûtes* which hold the bubbles longer.

Some less illustrious bubblies are also enjoyable with dessert or as a cocktail: *Clairette*, *Café de Paris*, *Blanquette de Limoux* and *Saumur Mousseux*. Top off a delicious meal with a strong black coffee accompanied by a *digestif* liquor.

The most famous is **Cognac**, from the region of the same name. A truly excellent, aged cognac should be warmed in the hands as long as 20 minutes, allowing the harsher vapors to evaporate, leaving a super-smooth elixir in your snifter. The vapor given off this way is known as "the angels' share". Heavenly.

Traditions, old and new: Paris still boasts one vineyard, on the **Montmartre** hillside; it produces 500 bottles in a good year. The drinking of Montmartre wine is recorded as early as the 15th century. Today the wine is mostly purchased for sentimental reasons, and the first Saturday of October is devoted to a festival celebrating the symbolic vestige of a long tradition.

The wine bar is a relative newcomer to town. In fact, the modern local version is actually an upscale *bistro*, serving light meals or daily specials, and offering a wide selection of wines by the glass and by the bottle.

A few addresses for wine bars are: ***L' Ecluse***, the granddaddy of wine bars, now with three locations (15 quai des Grands-Augustins, rue Francois I and place de la Madeleine); ***Le Coude Fou***, near the Pompidou Center (12 rue du Bourg-Tibourg), has a warm, relaxed atmosphere and good food at reasonable prices; **Willi's**, off the place des Victoires on rue de Petits-Champs, has an excellent selection of Côtes du Rhône from good vintage years.

Remember, wine is not only intrinsically good, it is also good for your health, (when taken in moderation and with food). It contains essential vitamins, yeasts, organic acids, sugar, glycerine, tannin and minerals like iron, copper, magnesium and zinc.

Wine is claimed to stimulate the appetite, help digestion, calm the nerves, and promote a state of overall well being and sometimes euphoria.

It puts a spot of sunshine in your heart and is commonly prescribed by doctors in the treatment of circulatory, nervous and intestinal disorders. It's not surprising that the usual toast proffered in France is Santé!—to your health!

resh French aves to ccompany ny wine.

NATIONAL
RESSE
BAR L'ANNEXE
le pot de fer
pot de Terre
L'APRES-BAC
où
s'inscrire en
HAUTE COUTURE

COIFFURE
GLADYS 43-31-87-50
Schwarzkopf
L'ATLANTIDE

INTELLECTUAL PARIS

When crossing the Seine towards the left bank and the islands—the intellectual nest of Paris—you will journey back through the centuries to the origins of the city, named Lutèce until the 3rd century. At the end of quai de la Megisserie, the massive **Pont Neuf**, built in 1607, is the oldest and the most famous bridge in Paris. The bridge, a popular meeting place long ago, was spectacularly wrapped by the artist, Christo, in 1985. Right in the middle, the statue of Henri IV on horseback rises above the Square du Vert-Galant.

La Cité: Settled on 2,000 years ago by a tribe of fishermen, the Parisii, **La Cité** was stirring with life during the Middle Ages but has since mellowed. It is now a ground of cohabitation for both spiritual and temporal powers: the courts of justice and the police headquarters surround one of the most prestigious religious monuments in the world.

Enter the island by turning your back to Henri IV, and proceed to the charming, shaded **place Dauphine**, introduced by two red houses dating back to Louis XIII. Once the trees growing on the river's edge were part of the royal orchard.

On quai de l' Horloge, walk along the walls of the Gothic **Palais de Justice**, where the kings of France lived until the 14th century. **La Conciergerie,** opening between two round towers, is filled with souvenirs of the Revolution, since this is where the parties involved were, in turn, imprisoned before being beheaded during the years of *la terreur*. Thus, after the splendid *gens d' armes'* room, you can visit the neighboring cells of Queen Marie-Antoinette and of two of her main accusers, the revolutionaries Danton and Robespierre.

Turn around the corner of boulevard du Palais, below the gilded 14th-century clock of **La Tour de L' Horloge**. A little farther on the boulevard, at the

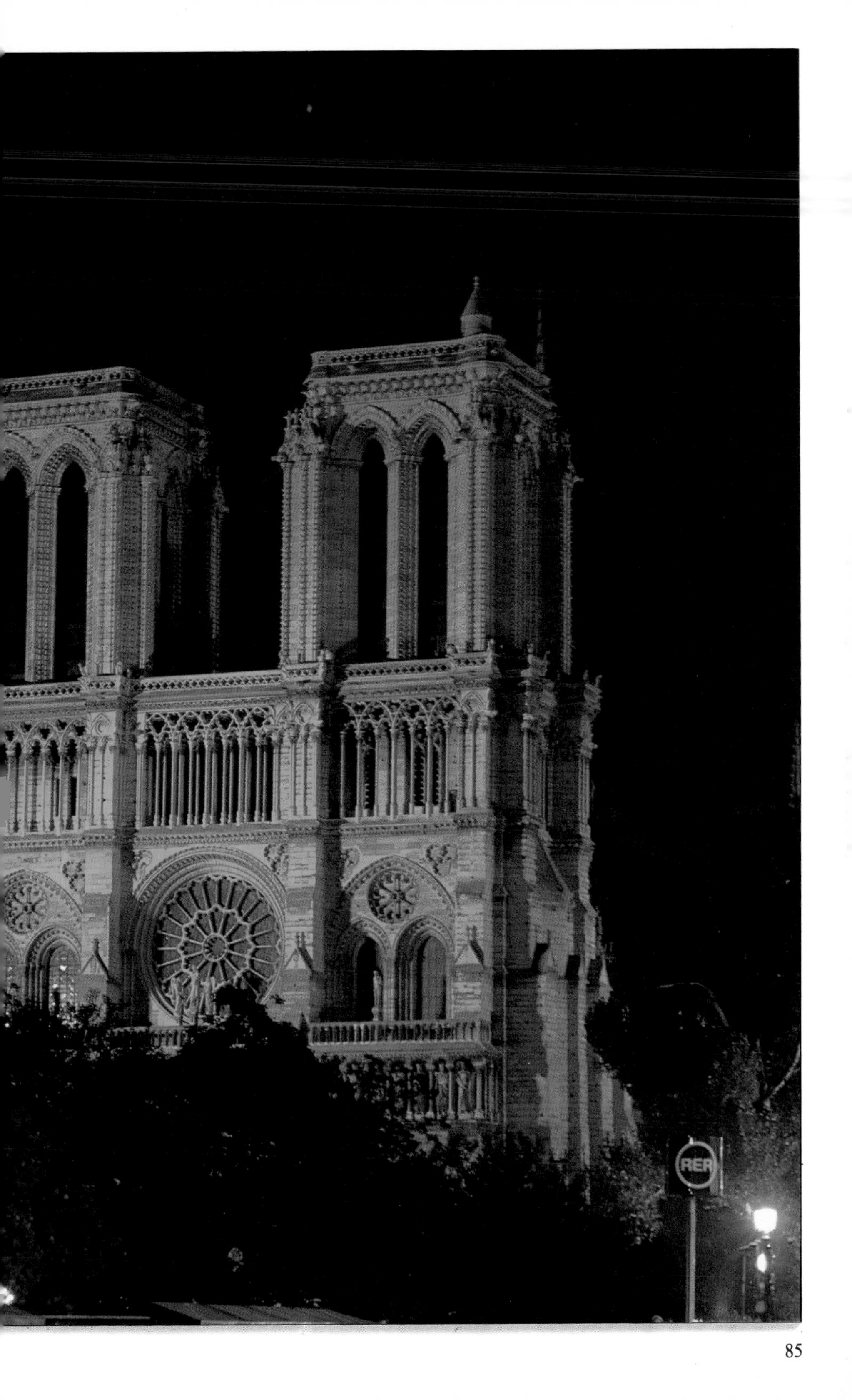
RER

bottom of the steps of the Cour du Mai, lawyers in black robes fly past the monumental 18th-century wrought-iron gates, leaving aside the **Sainte-Chapelle.**

This jewel of Gothic art—a miracle of balance—was built by Saint Louis in 1246 in order to shelter the Crown of Thorns. The height is due to the superpositions of two chapels: one for the servants, and one for the royal family lit by sparkling stained glass windows.

On the other side of the law courts, the **quai des Orfèvres** is a favorite film scenery, since it is the police headquarters. If you go up along the Seine, the quays will lead you to the open space in front of **Notre Dame Cathedral.**

The Cathedral's foundation-stone was laid in 1163, but construction ended only in 1330, making Notre Dame a good example of the transition from romanesque to Gothic art. Unfortunately, it suffered extensive damage, especially during the Revolution,when it served as a wine store. Only the original stained glass of its three, wide rose windows has been partly preserved. The cathedral was in a state of total neglect when the moving story of a hunchbacked bell-ringer named Quasimodo brought on its restoration.

The great events in the history of France went through the doors of Notre Dame, including Napoléon I's coronation and the *te deum* of the Liberation in 1944. You can ascend the towers to get a splendid view of the Cité, visit the T*résor,* or attend the free organ concert given every Sunday at 5 p.m. Unlike other neighborhoods, this one is lively on Sundays with cathedral visitors and visitors to the **Flower and Bird Market** around the corner. Behind the cathedral and the rows of tour buses there, a striking sunken monument is set into the earth, the **Memorial de la Déportation**, in homage to deportees who perished in World War II.

The island of peace: The Pont St.-Louis welcomes you to the peaceful, provincial **Ile St.-Louis**, where anglers still linger, shaded by the walls of the 17th-century patrician hotels. As the historical plaques testify, the first residents of the island were financiers, lords or magistrates, but they were gradually replaced by artists and writers like André Breton. Long before him, in 1845, Théophile Gautier and Baudelaire had founded the Club des Haschischins in the **Hôtel de Lauzun**, 17, quai d'Anjou, where they experimented *paradis artificiels.*

Certainly the most beautiful building is the **Hôtel Lambert**, 2, rue St.-Louis-en-l'Ile, which belongs to the Rothschild family. This street is the main street of the island and, on hot summer days, is filled with ice-cream devotees, surrounding the **Berthillon** temple, hesitating over a selection of more than 100 flavors.

The Latin quarter and the quays: From rue St.-Louis-en-l'Ile, you will head towards the part of the left bank which used to be the scholars' quarter, where Latin was spoken until 1793. It is still

Preceding pages: afternoon in the 5th arrondissement; Notre Dame by moonlight. **Below,** Gothic art in the Ste. Chapelle.

the site of prestigious schools and universities, but at night you may find its academic ambience somewhat drowned by the flood of tourism.

Sunrise is the best time for a walk along the misty quays, browsing through the *bouquinistes'* stalls in which you can find old publications, prints and secondhand books. From the **Pont de Sully**, Notre Dame rises majestically above the water. Under the bridge, there used to be a beach which Henri IV frequented before he learnt how to use a fork in the famous restaurant, **La Tour d'Argent** (15, quai de la Tournelle). Even if you cannot afford the restaurant's sumptuous meals, you can buy a souvenir in the shop across the street.

If old books are up your alley, don't miss the legendary **Shakespeare and Company bookstore**, along the quai St.-Michel. Founded by Sylvia Beach, the bookshop stands near Square Viviani and the country-style church, St.-Julien-le-Pauvre. There used to be many wooden houses lining both the Petit-Pont and the Pont-St.-Michel, but they burnt down so many times that they have long since been eradicated.

Around the Boul' Mich': During the day, students invade the bookstores on **boulevard St.-Michel**, and at night, they mingle with tourists around the winding mall, and at the entrance of cinemas or jazz-vaults, amid wafts of grilled meat coming from American, Greek and North-African fastfood restaurants. In rue de la Huchette, the **Hôtel du Mont-Blanc** has housed generations of Americans and famous personalities including Hemingway, Henry Miller and later, the Chilean ambassador and poet, Pablo Neruda. Unknowns, like the GIs of the Liberation, also stayed in this hotel. The young Napoléon Bonaparte lived at No. 10. The beautiful **St.-Séverin** church, with its splendid organ is also sited along this street.

The fountain representing Saint Michel slaying the dragon, on **place**

nch tcards in ookstall ng the ine by tre Dame.

St.-Michel, is a meeting place for students, tourists, and tramps alike. The Latin quarter exits in the neighboring, medieval **rue St.-André-des-Arts**, where most of the famous revolutionaries lived. The dreadfully famous Dr. Guillotin lived at 9, cour du Commerce-St.-André-des-Arts, close to the beautiful **Cour de Rohan** where a wrought-iron step designed for stout horsemen can still be seen.

The busy boulevard St.-Michel crosses the intellectual St.-Germain by the site of the **Thermes de Cluny**, built during the Roman occupation of the left bank. The medieval museum contains famous tapestries.

But the true intellectual crossroads of the area is **La Sorbonne,** the university of Paris. Created in 1253, it reflected historical changes throughout the centuries. Lately, the paving stones have been covered up, in retort to the active role they played during the events of May 1968. Even though they are reconstructions, the galleries, the amphitheaters, the main courtyard, and Richelieu's grave are worth a look.

On the way to the Mouffe: At the back of La Sorbonne, an imposing 18th-century church built in Roman style was transformed during the Revolution in order to welcome the remains of great defenders of French freedom. Since then, Voltaire, Rousseau, Victor Hugo, Emile Zola, Jean Jaurés, and Resistance leader, Jean Moulin, have been laid down in the crypt, under the high cupola of the **Panthéon**.

Going down mount Ste-Geneviève, the legendary lamps of **place de la Contrescarpe** will greet you at the bottom of **rue Mouffetard**. This is one of the oldest, most animated market streets in Paris. Behind the colorful and scented stalls, you can glance in ancient shops, Nos. 122 and 134, or venture into picturesque passages starting at Nos. 101 and 104.

Discover the mysteries of the Arab world in the **Mosque**, raising its minaret over white buildings. The decora-

The Paris Mosque.

tion of the patio, arcades and the prayer-hall is sumptuous, and after the visit you can enjoy a hot, mint tea under the wainscoted ceiling of the café. While relaxing on a mattress in the *hammam* (steam baths), you can also dream of Rita Hayworth's wedding with Aga Khan, which took place in the library.

Nearby, a greenhouse, dusty botanical and mineralogical galleries and a paleontological gallery, renovated thanks to singer Renaud's generosity, surround the **Jardin des Plantes**, popularized by Tardi's *bandes dessinées* (comic books). Its most remarkable trees are a cedar of Lebanon dating back to 1734, and the oldest tree in Paris, planted in 1636. Near the zoo, a cut of a 2,000-year-old American sequoia also bears historical reference marks.

And if you want to enjoy a typical, national game of *pétanque* in an outstanding setting, you will be delighted by the **Arènes de Lutèce**, built in the second century.

Paris of the 1920s: Throughout decades, the fashionable turmoil of Paris has moved from one place to another. Lately, it has latched on to the right bank. But there used to be a time when, in order to be up-to-date, one had to dwell on the left bank. In the 1920s, Montparnasse was **the** place.

At the border of the Latin quarter, the elegant garden *à la française* of **Le Luxembourg** is favored by students, young children and their mothers, and tennis players. The palace, built by Marie de Médicis in 1615, has become the **Senate House**, which the Germans made their general headquarters during the Occupation.

Near the romantic fountain of Médicis surrounded with foliage, one can recall the shadows of the "lost generation" which still linger on: F. Scott Fitzgerald, who lived in rue de Vaugirard, T.S. Eliot, Ezra Pound, Hemingway, Sinclair Lewis and Gertrude Stein used to call at Sylvia Beach's bookstore and the café Voltaire, place de l'Odéon, which later became the American library. Then, Hemingway would proceed to the fountain, which marks the end of the gardens prolonging Le Luxembourg and offers a splendid view of the palace and the basilica of Montmartre. He would sit at a table at **Closerie des Lilas** and there return to writing *The Sun Also Rises*. At the next table, French writer, André Gide, would compose—perhaps sitting on the same the chair as that of his predecessors, Baudelaire or Verlaine.

This list of literary luminaries, however, wouldn't impress the bronze **Lion** commemorating the resistance of the town of Belfort against the German invasion of 1870-1871. It goes on observing the traffic on place Denfert-Rochereau and marks the entrance to the **Catacombs**.

In the dark of this small part of the quarries, perforating the Parisian underground like a gruyère cheese, six million skeletons were piled up at the end of the 19th century, in order to clear the cemeteries. The decoration may be

uffetard
rket.

somewhat gruesome, but one can draw philosophical conclusions, knowing that these were the mixed remnants of revolutionaries, nobles and defenders of the commune. Although the quarries are sometimes enlivened by clandestine night parties, nocturnal explorations have proven to be dangerous. Outside, the joyful market on **rue Daguerre**, where both sculptor Calder and the Russian revolutionary Trotsky lived, is sure to jolt you back to life.

This cheerful sight is transient if you are heading on a pilgrimage to the **Cemetery of Montparnasse**, where the most famous 'guests' are Baudelaire, Jean-Paul Sartre, Simone de Beauvoir and Samuel Beckett to name a few.

Intellectual enjoyments: The **Montparnasse** quarter developed at the turn of the century when artists began settling there. Then, Modigliani, Miro, Giacometti and Chagall would emerge from their studios to have lunch at **La Coupole** or **Le Dôme**. There, they could meet with artists like Picasso, Man Ray and Matisse, political exiles such as Trotsky and Lenin, composer Stravinsky, poets André Breton and Cocteau, American writers Scott Fitzgerald, Hemingway, Dos Passos and Henry Miller, and director Eisenstein.

This incredible concentration of talents brought fame to Montparnasse, but didn't save it from the trauma of renovations. In 1973, amid murmurs of disapproval, the business and commercial center of the **Tour Montparnasse** was inaugurated. From the panoramic bar-restaurant on the 56th floor, more innovative architectural realizations such as the place de Catalogne—set between the blocks of rue du Château and rue Pernety, which still fight against demolition and shelter new artists' studios—can be seen. At night, the lights glitter around the cabarets and theaters of **rue de la Gaîté** and **rue Vavin**, adding to the frenzy surrounding the cinemas in this Breton stronghold. Only Rodin's controversial statue

The art of café life.

of Balzac remains impervious.

Paris of the 1950s: World War II shattered the intellectual life of Montparnasse, and it emigrated down the busy rue de Rennes. A last vestige of the intellectual concentration which Montparnasse enjoyed remains at 27, rue de Fleurus, where Gertrude Stein used to live.

A little farther on, sculptor Visconti designed a majestic fountain at the harmonious **place St.-Sulpice.** From her windows, Catherine Deneuve can overlook the imposing proportions of the church, rebuilt in the 17th and 18th centuries in classical style. Its walls were painted by romantic Delacroix, and its superb organ played at Victor Hugo's wedding. Starting from place St.-Sulpice, smaller streets lined with elegant shops, will take you to the place which succeeded Montparnasse.

Jazz and literature: At first, **St.-Germain-des-Prés** was just a place where existentialists Jean-Paul Satre, Simone de Beauvoir and Albert Camus came to work and for discussions, keeping aloof from the German occupiers. Unclassifiable writer Jean Genet later joined them for conversations and drinks. Their favorite meeting places were **Le Flore** and **Les Deux-Magots**.

Under the walls of the former St.-Germain-des-Prés abbey, the oldest church in Paris was originally built in the 11th and 12th centuries in the middle of fields. The atmosphere remained rather peaceful until the outburst of life and enjoyment following the end of the war flooded the area. Non-conformist disciples looking for their gurus invaded cafés and cellars like The Blue Note, listening and dancing to new music from the United States called jazz.

Today, the turmoil is over and most writers prefer the secrecy of luxurious bars, in hotels such as the **Pont-Royal**. Politicians hide behind the tinted windows of the selective **Brasserie Lipp**. Even **La Rhumerie** has become quite fashionable.

tertainment place rstenburg. llowing ges: emorial la portation hind tre Dame.

But the little street and **place de Fürstenberg** have not changed, and peace remains under the chestnut trees and old street lamps. Painter Delacroix lived and worked at No. 6, which has been turned into a museum.

Only the Seine remains the same: Little streets, bordered with residential hotels covered with ivy, at the back of quiet, paved courtyards, lead to the Seine. Most jazz clubs have disappeared and art galleries, antique dealers and bookshops have now settled around the **Ecole** and **rue des Beaux-Arts**, where Oscar Wilde used to live, along rue Bonaparte, rue des Sts.-Pères or quai Voltaire. The benches of the romantic **Pont-des-Arts**, set between big flowerpots, are a refuge for lovers and painters. Artists catch the reflections of light in the water here, at the end of the island of La Cité. The bridge offers a pleasant view of the spectacular **Institut de France** and the sober **Hôtel de la Monnaie**. Under the cupola of the institute, five academies hold their meetings—the most famous of which is the Académie Française, which sets the rules for the French language. French currency is printed at the Hôtel de la Monnaie, which also has a small museum to interest coin collectors.

The noble Faubourg St.-Germain: Descendants of nobles who, in the 18th century, used to hide behind the high walls of the streets between the river and rue de Sèvres, continue to entertain their guests in the alleys of wide and private gardens. But their 20th-century neighbors are ministers and ambassadors. For instance, the Hôtel Matignon, 57, rue de Varenne, is the residence of the French prime minister. A little farther down the street, the **Rodin Museum** occupies the magnificent Hôtel Biron, where Isadora Duncan and Matisse lived before the sculptor. Take time to go through the *salons* and the delightful landscape garden. In fact, the whole area is peaceful, and on Sundays, when civil servants stay at home, it is almost totally deserted.

Play And Stay

What more delightful way to extend a Paris trip than to play and stay awhile, by taking advantage of the amazing selection of activities open to both tourists and the French public.

From becoming a wine connoisseur or a grand chef to becoming proficient in the French language, Paris offers endless cultural and intellectual opportunities for those who stay. As Josephine Baker put it, "*j'ai deux amours, mon pays et Paris*".

Whether or not a long-term student visa or *carte de séjour* is necessary depends on the duration of the activity you choose. Many of the following suggestions could be taken up spontaneously, without much advance planning and without dealing with administrative details.

For long-term stays and to see how the French really live, you could organize a house or apartment exchange with a French family. Several organizations located in Paris and other parts of France as well as London and the United States offer this service.

The next question is whether or not a certain knowledge of the French language is necessary to fully appreciate staying awhile. Some knowledge may be necessary for some of the activities suggested below, while others (particularly in the artistic fields) can be done without a word in French, using your palette, your body language or your physical strength. Some activities and workshops are actually carried out in English. Although these types of programs are usually more expensive, they may be more worthwhile and in the long run and more fulfilling.

receding ages: ainter on ie Pont des rts. **Left**, dvice from connois-eur. **Right**, orso at the ouvre.

French Classes

The **Sorbonne**, France's most famous university was founded in 1253 and first housed 16 theology students. At the turn of the century, there were already 15,000 students, studying under masters such as Saint Thomas Aquinas and Roger Bacon. The school has also been known for its authority and audacity in its relationship with the French Government.

During the Hundred Years' War, the Sorbonne was on England's side, against France. In 1624, the college was restored by Jacques Lemercier, under Cardinal Richelieu's supervision and then was closed down during the French Revolution in 1792. Napoléon opened it again in 1806 and founded the *Académie de Paris* there. This was also the site of the 1968 student demonstrations where barricades were set up and hundreds were arrested and injured.

The best alternative is the month-long French language crash course for foreigners. The school is open to the public at all times and you can walk in, feel the atmosphere, gaze at the domed ceilings, sit on the wooden benches and dream of scholars past.

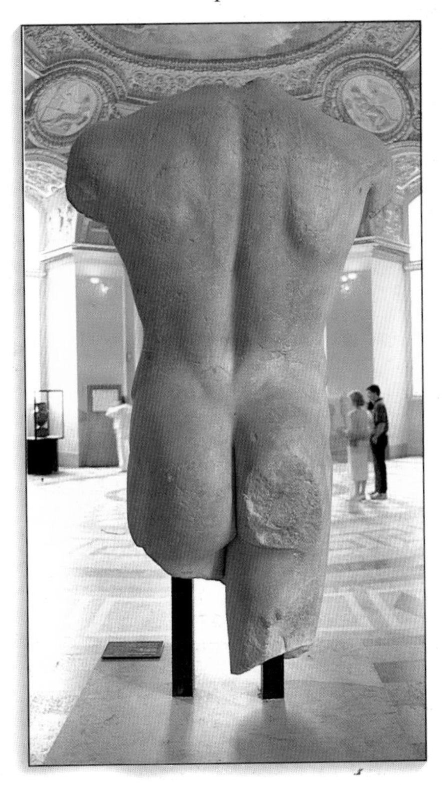

Another alternative in the national university system is the **Académie de Creteil**, known as France's "open" university, as there are very few prerequisites to becoming a student. Just outside of town in St. Denis, easily accessible by subway, taking classes or even becoming an *auditeur libre* and sitting in on classes will give you a real taste of the French academic system.

The other advantage here is the presence of French students and the chance to meet the local people and other foreign students. A good knowledge of French is required and classes are offered in all areas of liberal arts.

The **École du Louvre** gives classes in art history and culture, on both a long-term and short-term basis. Being an *auditeur libre* is also possible here.

The **Alliance Française** offers French language, civilization and business classes for all levels. There are two main systems, one for 8½ hours of classes per week and another for 17½ hours per week. The place is friendly, full of international students and offers all kinds of other activities, including films and lectures for those who are interested.

The **Institut de Langue et de Culture Française**, which is the Catholic Academic Institution in Paris, also offers French language and business courses for both students and French teachers. These classes are held for a minimum six-month period.

The **Amicale Culturelle Internationale** has information on travel-study groups, exchanges and holds informal foreign language conversational meetings to improve both your English and French, accompanied by a good glass of French wine for a minimal charge.

The **Centre Odéon Franco-Américain** is another good place to look for French contacts. The Centre offers French classes, shows films and has many other activities, as well as a good bulletin board to check what is happening in the Franco-American community around town.

Teaching Opportunities

For teachers or students interested in working in the French school system, the **Service de Placement Enseignement Privé** and the **Comité National de l'Enseignement Catholique** can lead you in the right direction. There are possibilities of student teaching in the English departments for those with less experience or guest teaching for a year if you are qualified.

Artistic Adventures

The **Fédération Française de Danse, d'Art Chorégraphique et d'Expression Corporelle** is a good place to go for a start. They can supply you with basic information on the various dance schools in town, the level of proficiency necessary and the career opportunities which may result.

The **Institut d'Art Théâtral** in Les Halles is one of the most modern artistic institutes, offering theater, dance and singing classes.

For less glittery and more experimental work, try the **Atelier Expérimental de Théâtre** or the **Atelier Théâtre d'Aujourd'hui**. The latter also offers classes in photography, film, video, script and technical design.

For those interested in following in the footsteps of Marcel Marceau, the best place in town for mime classes is the renown **École Jacques LeCoq**, where language ability is secondary to true artistic expression. Marcel's alma mater is the **École Internationale de Mimodrame de Paris**, which is a bit more serious. The school accepts students up to age 25 and they are admitted by audition.

For English alternatives, check **Théâtre et Anglais** or **Le Petit Atelier**, which offer theater classes in English for professional and semi-professional actors.

Finally, for an original and unforgettable workshop, check with the **Théâtre de l'Opprimé** (Theater of the

Oppressed), founded by Augusto Boal which has a school in Paris offering a taste of this unique South American theatrical technique.

Drawing and Painting

Inspired by the artists on the *quais* of the Seine? No need to speak French to express your feelings for the city on canvas. **Martine Moisan** offers one-week and weekend summer workshops on painting the city.

The **École Supérieure des Arts Appliqués** offers low cost drawing and painting classes with live models. The **Paris American Academy** gives workshops and half-day classes in drawing, painting, fashion design, fashion history and textiles.

A fun place to go for a large variety of classes and workshops is the **MJC St.-Michel**. The *Maison des Jeunes et de la Culture* are scattered around Paris and are usually present in each *arrondissement*. This one is really the best, located in an ancient building behind the Fontaine St.-Michel, with a great view over the entire Latin Quarter. Here you'll find everything from rock 'n roll and ballet lessons, to drawing, painting and photography courses. The other advantage here is the possibility of paying for just one class. Stop by and check the schedule outside or step in, take a look around and ask the friendly teachers and receptionists about their work.

A unique alternative is organized by the **Association pour le Développement de l'Animation Culturelle**, which offers workshops on a French *péniche* (barge), all the while traveling down the Seine. The world renown **Schola Cantorum** (music and dance), and the **Centre de Danse due Marais** are typical and housed in ancient quarter of the city

For those interested in cinema, contact Mr. Renault at the **Ciné Amateur Club Montmartrois**, which offers beginning as well as advanced classes in film.

...idents and ...ef at ... Varenne.

French Cuisine

Wouldn't it be fun to treat your friends to a great (and authentic) French meal when you get back? Paris has got to be the ideal place to try your hand at cooking or improve your skills.

The top on the list is **La Varenne**, which offers courses to become a French chef, as well as daily demonstrations and short summer sessions. The reputation of the school is well established on both sides of the Atlantic. The chefs all speak French, but an interpreter is on hand during the classes to translate questions and answers.

For the 25-week class leading to a diploma, the student visa is necessary. Short-term summer classes and cooking demonstrations, require advance registration. The demonstrations take place at 2:30 p.m. daily and every Tuesday a guest chef from a local restaurant comes in to share his knowledge and *savoir-faire*.

All the classes are small, with a maximum of ten students. The demonstrations are bigger, with a 45 person limit. The place is warm and friendly, English is the main language and the smells coming from the kitchen are heavenly.

For more serious artists of French cuisine, the **École Supérieur de Cuisine Française**, known as the **École Ferrandi** has recently opened its doors to English speaking students. They now offer classes both in French and in English (much more expensive), but the professional quality of the teaching cannot be beat.

The academic year classes lead to the French C.A.P. diploma, recognized both in France and in the United States. A treat for all is the Tuesday night student-made dinners, where a seven course *nouvelle cuisine* meal is offered for a mere 150 Francs. Call in advance for reservations.

Other cooking schools include **Le Pot au Feu** and **Le Cordon Blue**.

If you'd rather delve in wine, try the **Académie du Vin**, located in the Cité Berryer, in the heart of ancient Paris. Courses, lectures and luncheons are organized with the accent on wining and dining. Learn to appreciate and savor wines selected to accompany certain foods and all occasions.

Les Vendanges

Picking grapes or gathering fruits and vegetables in the French countryside can be a rewarding vacation and a chance to meet people from all over the world, not to mention a possibility to sample great country wine.

The *vendanges* take place between mid-July to the end of October, depending on the vegetable or grape and the region. Most of the organizational offices for finding this type of work are in Paris and buses are organized to take you to the region.

Foreign students are welcome, as well as all E.E.C. nationals. For Americans, it may be a bit trickier, but usually

Clowning around in Montmartre

it is possible to find a vineyard which will be more than happy to receive you. Pay is minimal, but enough to get by and the benefits to your health and the pleasure of having an original vacation more than compensate for your work.

If you want to work in the city, even for a short period, PROMATT and UNETT are two organizations representing over 400 temporary work agencies in Paris. However, you must be a resident of the E.E.C. These organizations can give you the low down on the various agencies and the addresses of the branches by specialization.

National Treasures

Interested in helping France preserve its history? The **Associations de Chantiers de Travail Volontaire** (Volunteer Restoration Work) may be just the thing. The Associations work on helping in case of natural disasters, in the development of rural areas, in preserving natural treasures and monuments, in archeology and in protecting the environment.

The majority of the workshops take place during the summer from the end of June until September. Shorter opportunities do exist during the school vacation periods and even for weekends.

All nationalities are welcome and no remuneration is involved. Many *chantiers* (work sites) take place outside of Paris or in the Paris region.

If restoring old *chateâux* inspires you, write or call one of the Associations listed in the Guide in Brief section for more details. Check the French magazines *Archéologia* and *Site*s for more ideas.

You may end up like Josephine Baker or so many other expatriate connoisseurs, artists and scholars who have elected to live in the city of lights.

Whether you stay forever or play and stay for a summer vacation or school year, extending your visit through any of the many activities available will make Paris your own "moveable feast".

piration the xembourg rdens.

CARICATURE
"FRIS"...
C'EST DANS UN STYLE
"B.D.", AVEC GAG
AU CHOIX
...

AROUND TOWN

The *grognards*, veterans of Napoléon's Old Guard, no longer rest under the lime trees of the **Esplanade des Invalides**, but the memory of two French emperors still lingers around quai d'Orsay and on the opposite bank. Both have left traces behind them to remind the visitor either of their glory or the awe they inspired.

Imperial Paris: The **Hôtel des Invalides** was founded as a veterans' home by Louis XIV, once housing as many as 4,000 retired or disabled soldiers. Now it is closely associated with Emperor Napoléon I. His remains rest beneath the splendid 18th-century dome. They were brought back to Paris in 1840. Six coffins shroud him, hidden under the majestic sarcophagus in dark red porphyry stone designed by Visconti. The crypt also shelters the tombs of great generals of the French army, and that of Napoléon's young son, who was called the King of Rome.

The **Musée de l'Armée** is now installed in the Hôtel des Invalides, near the cold and severe church **St.-Louis-des-Invalides**. Its only decoration, apart from the 17th-century organ, consists of flags seized from the enemies of the imperial army.

So as not to awake Napoléon, proceed down the esplanade, past the Air France terminal to the pretty **place du Palais-Bourbon**, surrounded by residential hotels built during Louis XVI's reign. Go round the palace built in 1722 by Louis XIV's daughter, and from the bridge you can see the typical Napoléonic façade imitating a Greek peristyle. This building has been the **Assemblée Nationale** since 1827. It leans against the Hôtel de Lassay, which is the residence of the president of the Assemblée.

In summer, you can watch the frolics of the very fashionable sun lovers showing off at the **Piscine Deligny**, on the other side of the bridge.

Opposite the Tuileries, the **Palais de la Légion d'Honneur** is overwhelmed by the **Musée d'Orsay**, a former railway station inaugurated at the universal exhibition of 1900, and became a musuem for 19th-century art in 1986. Before it welcomed the Impressionists, movie director Orson Welles used it for his film based on Kafka's story, *The Trial*.

The **Pont de la Concorde,** erected with stones of the fallen Bastille, so that the people could trample them underfoot, connects the Assemblée Nationale to the octagonal, 18th-century **place de la Concorde**. It was previously called *place de la Révolution* in 1792, and in turn Louis XVI, the queen Marie Antoinette, and the revolutionaries were guillotined there. After that bloody period, it was given its present, more hopeful name.

Since royal statutes would unceasingly undergo changes of government, they were replaced by the present-day

ceding es: ntmartre caturist. t, St.- is-des- alides. ht, lisk at ce de la corde.

Obelisk, from the Egyptian temple of Luxor. Drivers stuck in the frequent traffic jams here have ample time to decipher the hieroglyphs. The Obelisk stands in the middle of *La Voie Triomphale*, overlooking Roman-inspired fountains, while at night, the view from the terraces of the Tuileries Gardens is magnificent. The museum of **Le Jeu de Paume** has lately been deserted by the impressionists, but in the **Orangerie**, also dating back to the Second Empire, the *Nymphéas* painted by Monet are enhanced by the oval disposition of the rooms.

Champagne and caviar: Two twin buildings with colonnades flank the entrance to rue Royale. One is the prestigious **Hôtel Crillon**, beside the American embassy. The rue Royale and the streets around are the realm of luxury, either displayed behind windows like silversmith **Christofle's**, or hidden behind the bullet-proof glass of **Maxim's**. The street is most splendid under Christmas lights.

The church of **La Madeleine** echoes the Palais Bourbon, directly across the river. It all but became a railway station, then a temple dedicated to Napoléon I's soldiers, before welcoming official ceremonies. Nonetheless you can visit **Fauchon**, the temple of exquisite and sophisticated food, where clients in mink coats buy caviar, chocolate, truffles and exotic fruits in all seasons.

If you are interested in theater, you can get a 50 percent reduction at the kiosk in the center of the square. Your chances of getting a good ticket (for performances on the same night) are best before noon.

Join the elegant idlers watching the windows of **Yves Saint-Laurent**, **Hermés**, **Lanvin** or **Gucci**, on rue de Faubourg-St.-Honoré. Sentries guard the entrance to the **Palais de l'Elysée,** where Napoléon I signed his abdication after the Battle of Waterloo, and which is now the official residence of the President of the French Republic (open to the public once a year, on July 14).

Gardens at the end of the Champs Elysées.

La Voie Triomphale: Back to place de la Concorde, the group of horses by the prolific French sculptor Guillaume Coustou, known as the *Chevaux de Marly* (originally from the château of the same name), opens up the most famous Parisian avenue, the ever-entertaining **Champs-Elysées**. Although it used to be more aristocratic in the 19th century, its present commercial aspect doesn't deprive the avenue of the glory of its past charms as an elegant bridal path, its military grandeur on Bastille Day, or the final sprint of the *Tour de France* bike race. First, beyond gardens and curtains of chestnut trees, you catch sight of imposing stone and iron-work buildings covered by glass roofs. They were built for the universal exhibition of 1900, just like the impressive **Pont Alexandre III** bridge, and shelter temporary exhibitions. The *Palais de la Découverte* has settled in the **Grand Palais**, while the museum of fine arts of Paris is in the **Petit Palais.**

The impressive **Arc de Triomphe**, erected by Napoléon I to honor the French armies, closes up the avenue on **place de l'Etoile**, also named *place Charles-de-Gaulle*. In fact, Napoléon never saw the completion of the monument which now rises above the tomb of an unknown soldier from the World War I, but his remains passed under it when they came back from his last exile, in 1840. The platform overlooks the 12 avenues springing out, and the new **Arch of La Défense** welcoming businessmen and inhabitants to that "French Manhattan."

Paris modern style—the Trocadéro: A whole part of Paris was marked by the universal exhibitions of 1889, 1900 and 1937. Smart avenues lined with luxurious hotels lead to place d'Iéna, around which a group of museums concentrate: they are the oriental **Musée Guimet**, the **Palais de Tokyo** which house the **Centre National de la Photographie** and the **Musée d'Art Moderne de la Ville de Paris,** and the **Musée de la**

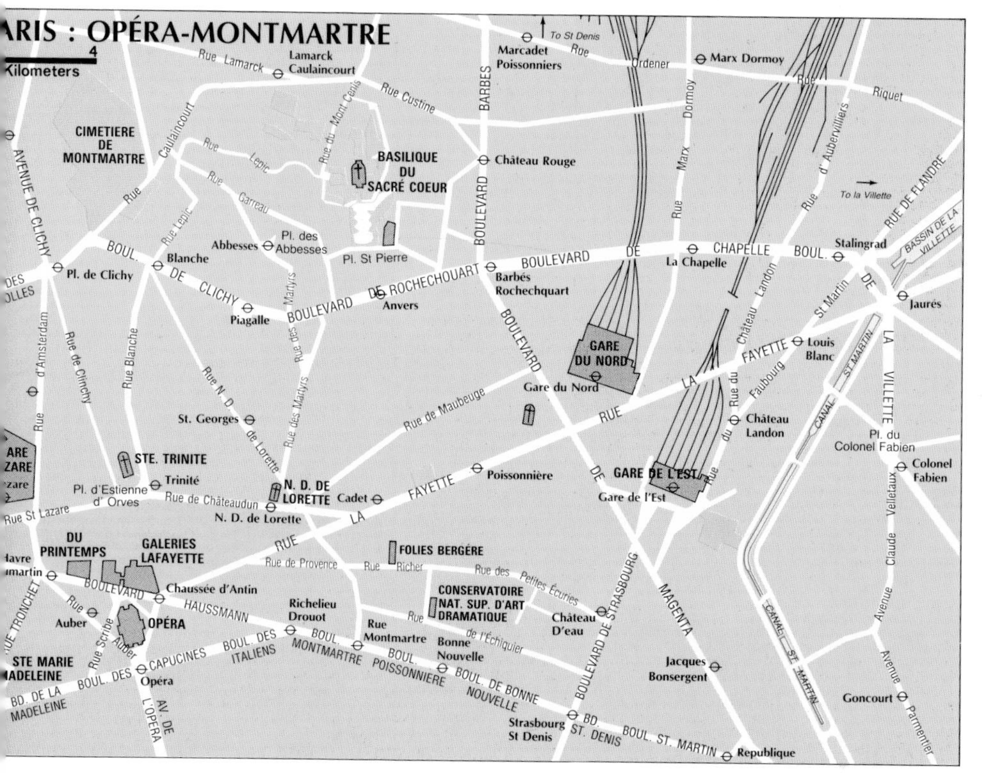

Mode et du Costume of the Palais Galliéra.

A large terrace, watched over by golden bronze statutes, parts the two curved aisles of the majestic **Palais de Chaillot**, adorned with inscriptions in golden letters by poet Paul Valéry. Lean on the stone parapet and survey the gardens sloping down to the Seine and the most famous Parisian monument, the Eiffel Tower. A lively fountain, merry roller skaters and colorful street vendors fill the gardens with music and color.

Otherwise, you can visit the **Musée de la Marine**, the **Musée des Monuments Français**, the **Musée de l'Homme**, the **Aquarium**, or the **Musée du Cinéma**. Then, take time to stroll along the powerful waterspouts. And if you are definitely on a slow beat, why not saunter on to **Passy**? Have a sip on the way at the **Musée du Vin**, and enter the **Maison de Balzac** in the rich and quiet rue Raynouard. If the spirit of the writer is absent, it may be that he slipped through the back door, like he used to when creditors came to claim their dues.

The French Iron Lady: Across the Seine again, the symbol of Paris rises up to 1,000 feet (300 meters), silhouetted in light at nightfall. The **Eiffel Tower**, despite early disputes, was the chief attraction of the 1889 and 1900 world's fairs. The view from the platforms and restaurants, over the river and towards the École Militaire, is spectacular at sunset. To the southwest, you can catch sight of a large, circular building, the **Maison de Radio-France**.

Starting below the tower and extending in the direction of the Tour Montparnasse, the **Champ-de-Mars** welcomed the first anniversary celebration of the fall of the Bastille on July 14. It was later used as a launching ground for balloons, and then a drill-ground for the **École Militaire** at the far end. Built in the 18th century and surprisingly magnificent, the school was intended for promising but poor officers like

École Militaire from the Eiffel Tower

Bonaparte, who was told there that he would go far if circumstances allowed. The most international building of Paris, the **UNESCO**, stands in the background.

***The Grands Boulevards*:** Under Napoléon III, the controversial administrator Baron Haussmann literally upturned Paris. On the ancient walls of the city, he opened up avenues, large squares and boulevards, both for traffic and riot control.

Former promenades were flooded with cars a half-a-century later, and thousands of shops and cafés jutted out on the pavement. Cinemas took over the many popular theaters which once gave the area of place de la République the name of *boulevard du Crime*. Today, the western part of the boulevards remains the most elegant.

Department stores are concentrated on boulevard **Haussmann**, and at Christmas, the windows of **Le Printemps** and **Les Galeries Lafayette** are an attraction for kids and parents alike.

At the end of boulevard Bonne-Nouvelle and boulevard St.-Denis, the **Porte St.-Denis** and the **Porte St.-Martin** commemorating Louis XIV's victories were erected on the site of the medieval gates.

Boulevard des Italiens, where the *incroyables*, *merveilleuses*, *dandys* and *lions* displayed the fashion excesses of the 19th century, leads to **place de l'Opéra**. Relax with a drink at the smart, international **Café de la Paix**, looking out on the opera building designed by Garnier, built in the typical, wedding cake-style of Napoléon III's reign. Film lovers will be glad to know that the very first movie projection by the Lumiére brothers took place on boulevard des Capucines.

Cancan and Rock 'n Roll: A certain image of Paris still lingers around the nightly wanton cabarets such as the **Folies-Bergéres**, the **Crazy-Horse**, the **Lido**, or the **Moulin-Rouge**. At the turn of the century, French cancan infatuated male audiences and inspired painter Toulouse-Lautrec. The Moulin-Rouge used to enliven an area on the loose. Today, **Pigalle** has become rather hard, and under the neon lights of sexshops and peepshows, the affable ladies have turned into transvestites.

But a new Pigalle is emerging, a Pigalle yielded to rock music. Clubs have opened one after another in former strip joints, and the **Locomotive**, the **Cigale**, the **New Moon**, **Megatown** and the **Martial** shake up late at night with various groups. **Place Clichy** retains some of the past atmosphere in the anachronic *Académie de billard,* Jean Genet's bar Le Cyrano, and Henry Miller's restaurant Wepler.

The village: There is no doubt that **Montmartre** has remained the most picturesque part of Paris, probably because of its hilly shape. Studios hide behind the little, tree-lined squares at the top of several flights of stairs. Artists settled here long ago, both because of the beauty and the relative cheapness of life on the hill. Montmartre was the

ric ladies
the Opéra.

Jesuits' cradle, but it is also here that the revolt of the Commune first started in 1871.

Walk up rue des Martyrs, owing its name to Saint Denis' martyrdom. You can rest on the old benches of the typical **place Charles-Dullin**, on which the *Théâtre de l'Atelier* has settled, or on **place des Abbesses**, with its splendid art deco métro station designed by Guimard. Then proceed to the charming **place Emile-Goudeau**, whose trees shaded so many artists, including Picasso, Matisse and Von Dongen, as they entered and left **Le Bateau Lavoir** restaurant (still in business). At the top of rue Poulbot, stop in the **Wax Museum** for a good collection of camp souvenirs

Walking along the panoramic terrace, you may wish to have your portrait made in the most famous, commercial section of Montmartre, the **place du Tertre**, somewhat over-animated at night—crowded with painters and musicians, ringed by noisy restaurants and cafés. Otherwise, go around the old St.-Pierre church to get to the terrace of the **Sacré-Coeur**, towering over Paris and always crowded with tourist coaches. The basilica was highly criticized, both for its affected style and its purpose, which was to atone for "the sins" of the Commune. But nowadays, the white dome and cupolas are irremovable from the Parisian scenery.

You can either go down hill by funicular railway or yield to the charm of the narrow rue St-Rustique. Turn right on rue St.-Vincent for a glimpse of the last vineyards of Montmartre. The traditional cabaret, **le Lapin Agile**, is in the cozy, painted house on the corner.

Lovers will fall for the allée des Brouillards and the Square Suzanne-Buisson. Going down rue Lepic, don't miss the Moulin de la Galette on your right, the last remaining windmill immortalized by painter Renoir when it was a dance hall. Farther down, the street becomes a lively market place. About halfway down, you'll surely notice the precious little house on the corner, where painter Vincent Van Gogh lived with his brother.

***Paris populaire*:** On the morning of July 14, 1789, 600 rioters rushed through the main door to assault a prison. By the afternoon, 300 guards joined them, and the governor surrendered and was killed. Only seven prisoners were actually found in the prison. The next day demolition started. Although July 14 was to become the National Day, the fall of the **Bastille** didn't seem to impress Louis XVI very much; he had been hunting at Versailles and in the evening he wrote in his notebook: "Today, nothing." The bronze column topped by a symbolic figure of Liberty breaking her chains and rising up was completed in 1840.

The New Bastille: At the corner of rue de Lyon, the construction of the new **Opéra** has given a lift to the development of a quarter where activities used to concentrate on the Faubourg St.-Antoine, one of the most picturesque

School's out in Montmartre. Right, Sacré-Coeur

parts of Paris. Whereas other craftsmen in Paris have lost their strongholds, the joiners, inlayers, varnishers, and cabinet, bronze and mirror makers here have remained since Louis XI allowed them to settled there in 1471. But the recent cultural outburst of the Bastille has recovered the former workshops in the courtyards and turned them into artists' lofts and galleries.

To perceive this evolution, start from **place de la Bastille**. Go down the **passage du Cheval-Blanc**, a labyrinth of little courts bearing the names of the months of the year. At the end of the **passage de la Main-d'Or**, discover **Chez Marius**, one of the last *bougnats*, i.e., a shop selling wood, coal, wine and spirits. On rue de Charonne, the **Cour Delépine** at No. 37, is a perfect summary of the changes brought into the area. In the cobbled courtyard, old gilding workshops keep going beside fashionable lofts, while other lodgings are country-style.

If during the day the area is jammed by delivery vans, at night the place de la Bastille is filled with the roars of motorbikes assembling for their ritual meeting, and the streets overflow with young revelers rushing towards the cosmopolitan bars and clubs of rue de Lappe, which have flourished next to the ballrooms dating back to the turn of the century.

Paris at a slow pace: Between boulevard Bourdon and boulevard de la Bastille, the dock of the **Arsenal** can harbor hundreds of yachts and is a starting point for an excursion along the canals or down the Seine to the Palais Bourbon. The **Canal St.-Martin** is first hidden up to place de la République, and the boat, *La Patache*, slowly glides under light shafts. It gets back to the surface between the trees and gardens of quai de Jemmapes and quai de Valmy. Barges wait patiently at the locks, beneath airy footbridges, and in autumn, the hazy light adds a poetic touch to the scenery. Watch for the **Hôtel du Nord** on the left bank, a leg-

Jim Morrison's grave in Père-Lachaise.

endary setting and title in French cinema. The **Bassin de la Villette**, dating back to the 19th century and bordered with old cafés and warehouses, brings to mind the docks of London. It is closed up by the last drawbridge, the **Pont de Crimée**. There, the canal divides into the Canal St.-Denis and Canal de l'Ourcq.

The Parc de La Villette: On the former location of slaughter-house, a huge cultural site was created in 1986. The cattle market, which is a beautiful sample of 19th-century architecture, was turned into an exhibition hall called **La Grande Halle.** The **Géode** is an impressive sphere of polished steel containing a cinema with a hemispheric screen of 3,300 square feet (1,000 square meters). As for the **Cité des Sciences et de l'Industrie**, the visitor plays an active role in discovering man's technical, scientific, and industrial adventures.

Ménilmuche: On the way to Maurice Chevalier's beloved neighborhood, cross the hilliest park in Paris, the enchanting **Buttes-Chaumont**, from whose suspended bridge and little temple on the top of an island you get a pleasant view of Montmartre.

ternoon
p.

Belleville used to be an area of *guinguettes* (taverns), known as a shelter for immigrants. Lately, the North African majority has made room for the Asiatic community, and now the quarter looks just as Chinese as Arabic.

Ménilmontant has undergone similar transmutations and in those popular areas, the ballrooms have been pulled down and replaced by monotonous buildings. Nonetheless, workers' houses of one or two storeys remain in a few lanes like the **passage Notre-Dame de la Croix.**

Where all arts and politics meet: The **Pére-Lachaise Cemetery** is the largest and most interesting cemetery in Paris, and the impression given by the hills and greenery is not too ominous. You can purchase a map indicating the most famous tombs at the entrance on boulevard de Ménilmontant. Among the well-known ones are Chopin and Rossini for music, Colette, Balzac and Oscar Wilde for literature. Painter Modigliani rests beside the great singer, Edith Piaf, not far from the most venerated tomb of Allan Kardec, the founder of spiritualism. The tomb of Jim Morrison, *Doors* bandleader is still incredibly decorated by his fans. To conclude this historical pilgrimage, you should include the **Mur des Fédérés,** where the last *Communards* were shot down in May 1891.

Many of the old tombs are tiny chapels, like miniature houses in a strange, still city. Standing before the resting place of medieval lovers, Abélard and Héloise, or before the stark memorial to those who perished in World War II, the weight of history settles like a shawl around your shoulders, and draws you into the heart of Paris, in communion with the men and women, both great and unknown, who have loved her before you.

hamon quatre saisons
hamon
PLATS CUISINES

6698 PK 92

A Word On Convenience

Some sorry travelers spend a good bit of their time discovering, like Dorothy in *Oz*, that "there's no place like home." Certainly not, and *vive la differénce*! But even the most adaptable or adventurous traveler meets an unwelcome surprise on occasion, giving him cause to wish he had a pair of ruby slippers to trade, or had spent his airfare on an illustrated encyclopedia instead.

Don't let minor inconveniences get you down: remember Henry IV, who took the trouble to convert to Catholicism in order to stay on and rule? If Paris, as he said, is "well worth a Mass," it is certainly worth making a few concessions to the local style of living and doing business.

Getting around: The most economical and, arguably, the quickest way to get around is by the *Métro*. The Parisian system is world-famous, and rightly so, for most often the trains are clean, frequent and will carry you within a few blocks of your destination. Large maps in every station help you plot your course and pocketsize versions, including a bus map, are distributed free-of-charge at all ticket booths. Avoid weekday rush hours as much as possible and do keep wallets well out of harm's way.

In the day, buses are a great way to see the city and get off your feet. The latest models, with an accordion-pleat section that makes them look like big caterpillars, are very quiet and comfortable. Most drivers are courteous and helpful. *Métro* tickets are good on the bus or you can buy them, at a higher rate, on board.

Taxi drivers are not such an amiable lot, although they are generally honest. Any surcharges (like those in effect at night, for extra luggage, suburban destinations, radio call, etc.) are posted on the window. Cabbies start picking and choosing passengers late at night when the *métro* shuts down and when their cars are in demand. They don't have the right to refuse a customer, but it's hard to argue a point when the doors are locked and you can't get in.

At taxi-stands or in crowded neighborhoods, the competition gets fierce. Defend your place in line vigorously, with elbows or pointed umbrellas if necessary. Loud comments concerning certain people who think they can get away with pushing ahead in line may hit home, though sometimes you may never know as Parisians are true masters of indifference.

Garçon! Garçon!: Leaders at this game are waiters in cafés, who can stare unperturbed over a sea of waving hands as though they were gazing at foam tossed in the wind. It is useless to become annoyed when service is slow. If repeated shouts of '*s'il vous plait!*' do not bring your waiter running, try standing up and putting on your jacket.

On the other end of the spectrum are over solicitous shop women who plant their painted claws in you as soon as

Preceding pages: business as usual on rue Lepic. Below, 365 stations for your convenience.

you enter the boutique. They have some high pressure techniques that make you feel like a real clod if you walk out empty-handed. One way to avoid them is by shopping in large stores where browsers are tolerated if not overly welcome, unless you know exactly what you want to buy. This and other Parisian attitudes towards commerce may be baffling at best, akin to rudeness at worst.

Don't call us...: The French telephone system is still notoriously unreliable, though major improvements have been made. Old coin-operated phones suffered such vandalism that now when you use a public phone you must have a *Télécarte*, a plastic card you insert in the slot. They are sold in *tabac* stores and in the post office (if they haven't run out). Cafés generally have phones, though sometimes reserved for paying customers only.

In the *tabac*, according to French law, the phone (as well as the restroom for that matter) is at public disposal but in practice it depends on the owner's goodwill. International calls can be made from a public booth with the *Télécarte*, or in a post office. There you leave identification at the window, make your call, and pay afterwards. Collect calls can be made to foreign countries only, or your correspondent can ring you back at a public phone with the number posted on it.

Of course, *La Poste* is the place to mail cards, letters and small packages. Any overseas package heavier than 11 pounds (5 kg) requires special arrangements, and must be mailed from a main post office, not a branch, or the S.E.R.N.A.M. package delivery service. Packages up to 2.2 pounds (1 kg) can be sent *petit paquet* rate, and arrive almost as soon as a letter. Otherwise, air rates are prohibitive, and surface mail takes a slow boat to its destination.

There is a special rate for books, which are only handled at the Central Post Office on rue du Louvre (open 24 hours a day). If you have picked up

-Lazare tion, lpture Arman.

everything on your reading list for the next five years while visiting Paris, this is the only way to send it back—in giant canvas bags with the characteristic *PTT* logo. Doing anything at the post office seems to take ages, so try to limit the number of trips you make by planning ahead and buying stamps or picking up a phone card if you plan to make many local calls.

There is one aspect of the French character to keep in mind when exasperated by Paris: every French person believes that he or she is always right. There are certain cultural phenomena on which they fall more or less into agreement (such as how to open an oyster or the correct way to address the mayor), but in matters of politics, politeness and service, each member of the species is fiercely individualistic, and most have taken lessons at 'The School of The Withering Look.' This is a part of the Paris costume that never goes out of style—but it's like the emperor's new suit, too—a little bit of honest laughter can turn almost any situation around.

On the brighter side: Paris has been host to legions of tourists and the trend is not slowing. The city offers many services and despite minor inconveniences caused by oddities of business hours and holidays and certain inadequacies, visitors will be grateful.

It is very easy to change foreign currencies and traveler's checks. American Express has a large office behind the Opéra with exchange and tour services, travel reservations, car rental, telephones, and special cardholder services including mail and personal check cashing. Lost or stolen traveler's checks really are replaced immediately (if you have your receipts).

The Tourist Office on the Champs-Elysées is stocked with brochures and staffed with helpful, multi-lingual employees. Other offices are located in train stations, and there you can find a hotel room, pick up a subway, or get directions to your destination.

There are many categories of hotels, from international chains to quaint family *pensions*. One thing most have in common is good service and a friendly welcome.

The smaller mid-town hotels, though not equipped in the most modern fashion, have more charm and certain advantages. Along with your café-croissant in the morning, you're likely to get some good advice on neighborhood restaurants or a quick French lesson. Of course, you must remember to reserve in the busy summer season, but at other times it's easy enough to find a room that suits you.

Finally, you may find the most convenient thing in Paris to be the many cafés. To Parisians, the café is a kind of home-away-from-home, for making rendezvous, conducting business, warming up, cooling off, or just watching the world go by. Parisians would be lost without them, and tourists, lost or not, will relish this simple, Parisian pleasure.

Left, a family outing. Right, the natives can be friendly.

SI VOUS
POUR
A MANGER
NO FOOD
YOU.
Olu-Olu

Museums

The array of museums in Paris is a little like the variety of enticing pastries in *pâtisserie* windows; there are so many delectable things to choose from, you'd want to nibble at them all. There are museums for every era, from prehistory into the future, and for every specialized interest—whether it's the intricacies of Chinese calligraphy or the charms of French wines.

For opening hours of museums, take a quick glance at the thorough listing in the *Pariscope*. In general, national museums are open from 9:45 a.m.-5 p.m. every day except Tuesdays, and municipal museums except Mondays. Take advantage of a Sunday visit, when some museums charge either half-price or are free.

You will not want to miss the four major museums: the Louvre, the Musée d'Orsay, the Center Pompidou and La Villette. Their exhibits transport you from ancient art to the latest leaps in artificial intelligence.

Whether you're making a hurried dash through the Louvre, or ferreting out a little-known sculptor's studio, take time to admire the architecture and the *ambiance*, and to get a taste for the *quartier*. Paris museums are a feast for all the senses.

Major museums: Alas, no one could leave the **Louvre** alone: Philip Augustus started building a fortified castle in 1200 and since then, 10 kings and emperors have demolished, added on or transformed wings and gardens; and the process continues today with the completion of Pei's controversial glass pyramid in the central courtyard. For seven centuries, the Louvre has served as royal residence, barracks, prison, academy, administrative office, art school and finally, museum.

Pei's pyramid, in the center of the **Cour Napoleon**, now serves as the main entrance and reception area of the

Louvre. While digging the underground services site, construction crews unearthed a myriad of relics, from Roman ruins to royal garbage.

They also uncovered the ancient walls of the early fortress, and towers that were once city gates. Drawings and scale models reveal the many transformations of the palace. The discreet interior design sets off the stone foundations perfectly. In the Saint Louis room, admire the golden helmet of Charles IV, discovered by archeologists

The breadth of the museum's important and varied collection is astounding. It is advisable to buy a guide-book or rent a cassette in English. Wear your most comfortable shoes for this visit along slick marble floors, past statues in alcoves and imposing paintings in gilt frames.

The Louvre is best visited on a sunny day; on a gray day, the museum may appear dark, drafty and gloomy. There are no electric lights as natural light illuminates the works through numerous skylights and windows, offering pleasant views of the Seine.

eceding ges: asso seum; ience seum at Villette; ntain tside aubourg. **ft**, yptian art the uvre. **low**, nus de lo.

Originally, the collection of **Oriental**, **Egyptian**, **Greek** and **Roman Antiquities** was the first set up in the early 1800s and is quite comprehensive, if somewhat dusty. Many of the items (some dating back to about 2500 B.C.) were brought to Paris at the time of Napoléon's various campaigns. In the Oriental section, a representation of **Hammurabi's Code**, from the ancient city of Babylon, is one of the most remarkable pieces in the Museum.

The Egyptian section has some illustrious inhabitants, including Rames III (whose obelisk is now in the center of the nearby place de la Concorde), Zet the Serpent King, and Amenhotep IV, whose gigantic sandstone bust reigning over the top of a staircase was given to France by Egypt in 1972 in appreciation for the country's efforts to preserve Nubian monuments.

Two very famous ladies grace the Greek and Roman rooms: **Venus de Milo** and **Winged Victory**. Their celebrity has helped them overshadow the rest of the collection, which is very rich and varied in sculptures and also contains frescoes, marbles, bronzes, ceramics, jewelry, ivories, glass and mosaic.

Greek vases, spread through the nine rooms of the Galerie Campana, represent art from the origins of Hellenism to the last hours of the Roman Empire. Each one is both a historical document and a work of art, as the lithe figures upon them relate the myths and legends of a lost civilization.

Paintings from all the European schools—French, Italian, Flemish, Dutch, German, Spanish and English—from the 13th to the 17th centuries, occupy the upper floors. In the immense halls, glide past Rembrandt and de la Tour to the Salle Rubens with 20 magnificent paintings commissioned by Marie de Medecis. Later, follow the clearly-marked signs to the **Mona Lisa**, still smiling after centuries.

A full two-thirds of the paintings in the collections are French. Such 17th and 18th century greats as de la Tour, Poussin, Watteau and Fragonard hang in the Grande Galerie. Among the works of a later period that never fail to catch the visitor's eye are **Napoléon Crowning Josephine** (David), **The Great Odalisque** (Ingres), **The Raft of the Medusa** (Géricault), and the revolutionary and inspiring **Liberty Guiding the People** (Delacroix)—this spirited *dame* has been leading the people on, flag raised and breasts bared, since 1830.

Another major section of the Louvre is devoted to **Objets d'Art**, including precious objects and furniture, much of it acquired from the Royal Collection and confiscations made during the Revolution. Royal treasures are exhibited in Apollo's Gallery, under a decorative ceiling painted by Delacroix. Glass cases contain all that remain of the Crown Jewels of France, regal headgear and invaluable bric-a-brac.

The collection also displays statuary and objects from early medieval times through the First Empire. Later periods are especially interesting for beautifully crafted tapestries, wooden furniture, jewelry and clocks. The rooms are set up to illustrate a period style or genre (the Chinese room), particular tastes (Marie Antoinette rooms), or the work of one artist.

Louvre lovers waited many years before the Ministry of Finance was cajoled from its treasured office space in the wing facing the rue de Rivoli. Adding to the improved access and service areas provided by the Pyramid and the new underground archeological section, the expanded space will allow the fabulous collection to breathe.

The Orsay train station, on the banks of the Seine in central Paris was imaginatively transformed into an art museum. The **Musée d'Orsay** offers a panorama of the art—including paintings, sculptures, architecture, furniture and art objects—of the second half of

Orsay Museum, main floor.

the 19th century.

With the building's 1900s exterior in mind, architect Gae Aulenti turned Orsay's wide, open space into a beautiful and unique multi-leveled interior. Tours and an excellent guide in English are available at the entrance.

Orsay's painting exhibits can be divided into two major categories: from the late 1840s to the birth of impressionism in the early 1870s, and from impressionism to the birth of modern art around 1905. On the ground floor, you can follow the influences of Ingres and Delacroix through to the changing aesthetics of the early works of Monet, Manet and Renoir. On the upper level, wander through entire rooms devoted to Van Gogh and Cézanne. At the far end of the museum, two towers rise majestically on either side of the huge semi-circular window. Both Towers are devoted to sleek *art nouveau.*

From the towers, take the platform to the big, transparent clock. Instead of telling harried train passengers the time as in the past, it now offers a beautiful view across the tree-lined Seine to the front gardens of the Louvre. Not far away, there is also a reasonably-priced restaurant and rooftop café.

An inside-out museum: The **Center Pompidou**, affectionately known as **Beaubourg**, is Paris' *enfant terrible*—hyperactive and still causing controversy after nearly 15 years. Though sometimes referred to as "that hideous refinery", it is a popular, vibrant cultural center. The area's intriguing history and unusual architecture combine to make Beaubourg one of the most lively arts centers in Paris.

The sprawling, old market district known as *Les Halles* was razed to accommodate Beaubourg's construction. Now, instead of finding rows of produce stalls and vendors, there is a never-ending vaudeville show of jugglers, acrobats, comedians and fire-eaters on the sloping cobbled terrace. After winding your way past the various entertainers in the square, stop at the

mptuous cor inside say.

welcome desk at the foot of the escalators to find friendly guides and informative brochures.

This dynamic center houses an Industrial Design area (**CCI**), a public library, the **Musée National d'Art Moderne**, a center for musical research and performance (**IRCAM**), a cinema, rooms for theater, dance and video, a rooftop café and a great bookstore.

The **Industrial Design** area has several exhibits and hosts debates on architecture, furniture, urbanism and visual communication.

The visitor won't want to miss the prestigious collection of the **Musée National d'Art Moderne** on the fourth floor. You can sink into one of the soft, black leather armchairs and admire the well-displayed paintings and sculptures, including works from Fauvism to the present day, from the graceful colors of Matisse's paintings through cubism, to Kandinsky, Mondrian and Brancusi. The latter willed his lifework to the French government, and a reconstruction of his *atelier* is open to the public in front of Beaubourg.

For music or movies, it would be wise to consult Beaubourg's weekly program. IRCAM has weekly concerts and musical debates, and rare films are often shown in the **Salle Garance**, at reasonable prices.

Inch your way up the glass escalators to the cafeteria on the top floor, offering one of the best rooftop views of Paris.

Outer space in the city: The **Cité des Sciences et de l'Industrie** in the **Parc de la Villette**, is a fantastic technological playground. This immense 137-acre (55-hectare) park was designed as a cultural and communication center specially dedicated to science, technology and industry. At first glance, the futuristic architecture appears otherworldly and slightly unreal—a delirious architect's Lego experiment with gray, blue and black metals, greenhouses and water.

The entire complex will eventually include the Science and Technology

The Georges Pompidou Center is affectionately known as "Beaubourg".

Center, the City of Music, the Exhibition Hall, a park studded with cafés, restaurants and gardens, and finally the Géode. There is so much to see, the visitor might want to devote an entire afternoon to exploring the multidisciplinary exhibits and surrounding park.

The Science and Technology Center is one of the most well-organized museums in Paris and one could spend as long as three hours in it alone. The numerous guards are friendly and helpful, and brochures and cassettes are available in English.

In its lobby—the Science Center is the main building—are satellites and astronauts dangling from the ceiling, while computer and video displays flicker at every turn. This building houses permanent exhibits called **Explora**, some temporary exhibits, an **Inventorium** for children and a Multi-Media Library.

Experience weightlessness on a brief excursion into outer space, or travel back in time in the **Theater of the Universe** to the Big Bang. Brush up on your particle theory in the **Valley of the Isotypes**, before cavorting with robots in the **Cybernetic Zoo**.

The **Planetarium** offers a simulated sky with 10,000 stars and a complete view of the solar system. For researchers, or just the curious, books, periodicals and audio-visual presentations are available in the Multi-Media Library.

Saunter outside into the park behind the Science Center to the enormous **Géode**, one of the most striking attractions at La Villette. This dazzling, mirrored hemispherical structure is a space-age theater, containing the largest screen in the world. Visitors are immersed in images and six-track stereo sound, with special effects added by lasers, mirrors and holograms.

Continuing through the park, you can't help but notice the **Zenith Concert Hall** with an airplane teetering on its roof, the **Exhibition Hall** in the renovated *halles* and the giant dragon winding through the playground.

éodesic here at a Villette.

Medieval memories: Discover the middle ages at the **Musée de Cluny** where the medieval *Hôtel* of the Benedictine Abbeys of Cluny adjoins the ruins of 2nd-century Roman baths. The museum is renowned for its collection of Flemish tapestries, ivory, stained glass and furniture, spanning from the 12th to the 15th centuries.

A step inside is a leap back across time: gargoyles greet you in the Cour d'Honneur, lined with 15th-century arcades, delicate balustrades and elaborate cornices.

Duck through the low doorways into the rooms with painted beams, crude chandeliers and small windows of tiny colored panes. On display are enormous chests, religious reliquaries, fabric remnants and even shoes from the 12th century.

In the airy room, Notre Dame de Paris, light pours through the skylight, illuminating the 21 heads of the Kings of Judah. Originally a part of Notre Dame's decoration, they were vandalized during the Revolution, and recently unearthed at a construction site.

Before heading down the hallway to the Roman baths, stop in the small, dark room on the right. Here you can see stained-glass windows of devils, beasts, saints and kings which are beautifully illuminated from behind.

The Roman thermal baths, especially the vast **Frigidarium**, are remarkably well-preserved, due to their continued use into the 1400s.

Upstairs, the famous **Lady and the Unicorn** tapestry series is displayed in a round, skylit room. The tapestries were woven at the end of the 15th century for Jean Le Visite, whose coat-of-arms with three golden crescents recurs throughout the design. Five of the six gracious tapestries represent the senses: sight, hearing, taste, smell and touch. The sixth, *A Mon Seul Désir*, still remains unexplained.

Royalty and revolution: To understand Parisian life better, immerse yourself in the history of Paris at the **Musée Car-**

Outer Space at La Villette.

navalet, a beautiful 16th-century mansion in the Marais. The exhibits help you to envision Parisian life from the late Middle Ages through the Revolution. The building was also the home of **Madame de Sevigny**, a famous 17th-century character, renowned for her intellectual correspondence and not-so-intellectual gossip.

The first room plunges you into the early Renaissance: artisans' wrought-iron shop signs hang from the walls, inviting you to buy bread, candy, wine, tobacco and other sundries. An apothecary's façade occupies an entire wall, complete with small vials and bizarre taxidermy.

Take the marble staircase upstairs to the private apartments of Madame de Sevigny. Her paintings, embroidered armchairs and ornate Chinese-lacquered desk still remain. You can also peruse some of her personal correspondence, including her marriage contract with the Count de Grignon.

The benches in the back garden offer a tranquil respite, among the carefully tended hedges, before heading back into the darker rooms featuring the French Revolution. Displayed in glass cases are swords, drums, enormous keys—perhaps, for locking unfortunate souls in dungeons—and more personal relics such as hand-held fans, gloves and embroidered wallets.

For visitors who want for a more in-depth look at history and affairs of state, the **Archives Nationales** are just a few blocks away in the splendid **Hôtel Soubise.** Changing exhibits as well as genealogies, letters and historical documents are on display.

For a change from political history, see centuries of French interior design at the **Musée des Arts Decoratifs**, recently reopened on the rue de Rivoli. Good taste glimmers from every display case in this varied collection of porcelain, glass, gold-plate, furniture, sculpture and paintings.

Men and monuments: The sparkling **Palais de Chaillot** was constructed at

e history Paris is e theme the rnavalet useum.

Trocadéro for the 1937 World Fair. Among other things, it now houses two museums of historical interest: natural history at the Musée de l'Homme, and architectural history at the Musée des Monuments Français.

The terrace between the two wings of the Palais offers one of the most magnificent views of Paris. Across the gardens and the Seine, the Eiffel Tower rises above the Champs de Mars and the École Militaire, which is almost 2 miles (3 km) away.

A gigantic head from the mysterious Easter Island greets visitors to the **Musée de l'Homme**. This popular museum's collection covers the entire globe in three galleries: Biological anthropology, Paleo-anthropology and Prehistory.

You can skip from mummies to genetics, to Eskimos, to tattoos, to primates and to the precursers of modern man. If you tire of skeletal remains, head to the **Salon de Musique**, featuring a wonderful collection of old string, wind and percussion instruments.

Just across the terrace, in the left wing of the Palais, is the **Musée des Monuments Français**. Contrary to what its name suggests, it is not full of equestrian statues of Napoléon and the like, but rather examples of Roman, Gothic and Renaissance architecture and frescoes from all over France.

Touring this museum is like a private drive through the French countryside, passing small 12th-century chapels or more ornate Renaissance cathedrals, with occasional stops to peer at the frescoes and statues inside.

The **Musée de l'Armée** is located in the grandiose 17th-century **Hôtel des Invalides**. The world's largest military history museum features armor and weaponry from the Middle Ages to World War II, as well as a collection of Oriental arms from China, Japan and Turkey. You can follow troop movements and decisive battles on the well-displayed maps, slides and films.

Adjoining the Musée de l'Armée is

Left, Rodin's "Thinker". Right, Alexandre III bridge and the Dome of the Invalides.

the **Musée des Plan-Reliefs** with unique and minutely detailed topographical maps and models of important strategic fortifications between 1668 and 1870.

Napoléon's final resting place is in the magnificent **Église du Dôme**, also adjoining the military museum. Ornate walls and columns, bas-reliefs and polished marble surround the Emperor's tomb, located under the impressive painted dome.

Advertising and film: The reserves of the **Musée de l'Affiche et de la Publicité** contain over 50,000 posters, covering the world history of poster design from its beginnings to the present day. Small temporary exhibits are also on display in the skylit galleries.

This fun and varied poster collection advertises everything from cars to plays and sardines. In the **Montmartre** corner, Toulouse-Lautrec's dancers invite you to the Moulin Rouge; others invite you to even more dubious spots: the questionable *Café des Incohérents* or the infamous *Cabaret des Décadents*.

Old advertisements—animated or filmed—are constantly projected in a small cinema in the back. Great cards, books and, of course, posters are on sale in the bookstore near the exit.

Paris has always been the "City of Cinema," with more movie theaters per capita than any other city in the world. The **Musée du Cinéma**, in the Palais de Chaillot, houses over 5,000 objects from all over the world, progressing from shadow puppets, to early animation, to modern film techniques and lore. Henri Langlois founded this museum and dictated that it be visited only by guided tours. Tours in English, lasting around 90 minutes, are available but must be booked well in advance.

The tour is imaginatively presented by guides obsessed by all aspects of the "seventh art." It's more like a fanciful history lesson, touching on late 18th-century caricature, 19th-century inventions, and the development of present-day cinematographic technology. Old

ft, Military useum the valides. ght, aillot lace and o towers; ffel and ontpar-sse.

lenses, cameras and projectors abound, as well as costumes and model decors.

If you think westerns originated in America, take another look at the early frames of Frenchmen playing cowboys and Indians in the Bois de Vincennes housed here. Film paraphernalia include costumes worn by Louise Brooks, Bette Davis and Liz Taylor, as well as a less-refined, personal gift from Alfred Hitchcock: the head of Norman Bates's mother in *Psycho*.

For enthusiasts: Enthusiasts of things Eastern will find Oriental art and artifacts at the Musée Guimet and the Musée Cernushi. The **Musée Guimet** has a varied collection of statues, paintings, ceramics and masks from the Orient. For those interested in China, the **Musée Cernushi**, offers ancient Chinese artifacts in bronze, jade and ceramics in a beautiful 19th-century building near the serene Parc Monceau.

Other collections are devoted entirely to one artist's work. You can trod the wooden floors in the intimate environment of such great artists as Rodin, Moreau and Balzac. Many of these museums adjoin peaceful, private gardens, inviting you for a leisurely stroll.

The **Musée Rodin** is one of the most pleasant and inviting museums in Paris. Cross the front courtyard under the gaze of the celebrated *Thinker*, with *Balzac* majestically glaring behind him. To the left are the *Burghers of Calais* with their marvelous hands, and the monumental *Gates of Hell*. Inside, Rodin's large sculptures share the light and airy rooms with his smaller works and studies. The white marble of *The Kiss* glows with sensuality in the light. In the two round rooms in the wings, large gilt mirrors reflect light onto *Adam*, who is facing *Eve*, as she flees the garden.

Interspersed among the sculptures are works by other artists, notably Camille Claudel, Rodin's mistress and assistant for 15 years, until she sadly sank into madness.

After the museum, treat yourself to a

Medieval times at Cluny.

stroll through the formal garden. Serenity reigns. Grapes hang from the low walls; the tree-lined paths are shaded.

Relax on one of the many benches, or have a cool drink in the pleasant, outdoor café until dusk, when a cloaked guard wanders slowly down the alleys, ringing a bell for closing time.

A jewel: For more contemporary sculpture, the visitor shouldn't miss the **Musée Zadkine**, where the Russian-born, cubist sculptor lived and worked for 40 years.

You might have some trouble locating the museum but don't be daunted! It's down an alley off the rue D'Assas, easily accessible after a Sunday walk through the Luxembourg gardens.

The alley leads to a cluster of private residences; ring the bell to be admitted, and enter the enchanting sculpture garden. Sculptures straddle flowerbeds, a cubist woman with a guitar reclines by the walkway, and a fragmented couple peers from behind the rhododendrons.

The Zadkine is a jewel of a museum, and so rarely visited that you risk waking the guards upon arrival. Once awake, however, they are friendly, attentive and helpful.

In the cluttered rooms, light filters through the garden trees and enormous windows, teasing the angles and hollows of the sculptures in marble, bronze and wood.

In Zadkine's studio in the back, personal paraphernalia line the walls: saws, picks and chisels, photos, even his accordion. It's a delightful glimpse into the private world of this inexplicably unappreciated sculptor.

Moreau, Monet, Picasso: On a small street in the ninth *arondissement* is an unassuming building housing the **Musée Gustave Moreau**. An unusual 19th-century character, Moreau lived there with his deaf mother all his life, and counted such modern masters as Matisse and Rouault among his pupils.

His high-ceilinged *ateliers* are crammed with so many huge symbolist paintings that the visitor is completely

Rodin seum is he Hôtel on.

overwhelmed by the fantastic palatial decors and mythical figures. Joining the two floors of his *ateliers* is a graceful spiral staircase—a little easier to focus on than the paintings—and itself worth the price of admission.

After the rigors of symbolism, a visit to the Monet collection at the **Musée Marmottan** is just the thing. It is beautifully situated in the chic and well-manicured **Parc Ranelagh**.

The museum contains the best collection of Monet's deliriously colorful impressionist works, spanning the last 20 years of his life. Downstairs, dive into the **Water Lillies**; upstairs is the collection of the Marmottan family, including their furniture and medieval, illuminated manuscripts.

It's just a short leap of the imagination from Monet's delicate impressionism to Picasso's striking cubism. Opened in 1985, the **Musée Picasso** in the 17th-century **Hôtel Salé**, is a delicious feast for the eyes.

The name *Salé* comes from the French word for salt. The 17th-century proprietor had the lucrative job of collecting salt taxes. He earned both a great deal of money, and the wrath of the *quartier's* residents, who disdainfully deemed him "Salé."

The Hôtel has been beautifully renovated and now houses a lifetime of Picasso's paintings, sculptures and souvenirs. As you climb the majestic marble stairs and enter the exhibition rooms, look up at the chandeliers, and around at the benches and chairs, all designed by Picasso's contemporary and friend, Alberto Giacometti. The rooms are arranged chronologically, with helpful explanations in English.

Vins extraordinaires: The **Maison de Balzac** is tucked away in the posh 16th *arrondissement*. Stairs lead down to the charming and shaded front garden of the house Balzac occupied from 1840-1847. In these rooms, he revised his monumental work *La Comédie Humaine*. On display are caricatures, some original furniture, family souvenirs and personal objects of this gargantuan literary personality.

The most interesting room is his study, furnished with the original chest, desk and armchair. His ever-present coffee-maker and inkwell are displayed next to some surprisingly small finger-puppets, apparently indispensable to his creative process.

Downstairs, you can see his jottings and marginal corrections on original manuscripts, as well as the genealogy of the hundreds of characters in his epic work, *La Comédie Humaine*.

Balzac's house was also equipped with secret underground passageways; he used them frequently to flee his creditors. One passageway led to what is now the **Musée du Vin**. There, you can see a wax figure of Balzac sneaking down the cellar stairs, perhaps for an escape, perhaps merely a nightcap.

The Musée du Vin displays the lifeblood of French culture, *intelligentsia*, high society and dereliction: wine.

Located in what used to be the Passy Abbey of the Franciscans, the vaulted cellars of the Musée date from the 13th century. Sip your complimentary glass of wine while wandering past dusty bottles in alcoves, lewd statues of Dionysus and Bacchus and pictures of dancing grape-pressers. There are exhibits of different wine glasses and bottles, wooden tools and scientific instruments used in wine-making and bottle-corking. Wax Frenchmen, all wearing neat berets, illustrate various techniques for making wine, champagne and cognac. At the exit is a well-stocked wine boutique and an expensive bistro.

So, perhaps, the museums of Paris are more aptly compared to that distinguished and so thoroughly French product—wine. Like wines and liqueurs, museums settle with age and many are sublimely refined. Others are young and sparkling, or tender and warm. Something is sure to meet your fancy as you sip and savor the fine collection of Paris museums.

Picasso and friend.

CONTEMPORARY ART

The impressionists and the cubists hung their paintings along the smart avenues near La Madeleine; the surrealists scattered in the Montparnasse quarter, while in the 1950s the defenders of abstraction landed on the Seine's left bank, around St.-Germain-des-Prés. With the opening of the "art refinery" of Beaubourg, in 1977, the center of Paris was invaded by new art galleries. The latest movement, dating back to the early 1980s, is once again taking hold of the Bastille.

Although it is not exhaustive, the list of galleries below offers a good survey of the present art trends in Paris, and will enable you to see a little more of the Parisian cultural life. Since the settings of the galleries are themselves a matter of interest, both profane and initiated visitors will be gratified. If you can, include visits to these galleries in your itinerary, and remember that galleries are generally open every afternoon except on Sundays and Mondays.

If you are fortunate enough to buy a work of art—either because you have fallen in love with it, or because you bet on the artist's future, or, perhaps, because it's not one of those items subject to the stock exchange turbulences—notice that red dots indicate works already sold. A listing of the exhibitions is available in any gallery or in the **Center Georges Pompidou**.

Art on the right bank: When talking about contemporary art in Paris, it is impossible not to mention the **Lelong Gallery**, which is a reference for excellence. Works by most international and famous contemporary artists, including the German expressionist F. Bacon's tortured and distorted portraits; J. Brown's embroidered and stained sheets; N. De Maria's bright colors; and A. Tapiès' personal calligraphy, are represented by Lelong, 13, rue de Téhéran.

The lofts of Beaubourg and Le Marais: A good place to start on the right bank in the Beaubourg area, is **Samia Saouma**'s painting and fashionable photograph gallery. G. Baxter's drawings, underlined by captions filled with absurd humor, and D. Michaels' dreamlike photos, are regularly exhibited here (2, Impasse des Bourdonnais).

The New York painting, photography, and sculpture **Zabriskie Gallery** has settled at 37, rue Quincampoix, and shows photographer W. Klein's urban and international shots.

The new realists at the **Beaubourg Gallery**, 23, rue du Renard, are already well-known. Among them are sculptor César's compressed materials and the sensual painter, Fassianos, who refers to Greek myths.

Two international and prestigious art dealers have settled in the Beauborg area. One of them is **Daniel Templon**, whose two galleries face one another. The works of great New York artists and stars of figurative art, such as graf-

receding ages: laire Burrus her allery. Left, C. Blais nd his ork. Right, budding rtist on the ft bank.

fiti painters J.M. Basquiat and K. Haring, and nostalgic J. Le Gac may be admired at 30, rue Beaubourg; and 1, Impasse Beaubourg.

Templon's rival and friend, **Yvon Lambert**, owns two galleries. Lambert's artists, whether figurative or abstract, are world stars: J.C. Blais paints over layers of posters; Christo wraps monuments and stages natural sites; J. Schnabel paints on velvet or tarpaulin; and D. Buren is a linear artist. Lambert's smaller gallery is at 5, rue du Grenier-St.-Lazare, while the more spacious and prominent one is at 108, rue Vieille-du-Temple.

The **Ghislaine Hussenot** and **Liliane et Michel Durand-Dessert** loft galleries, 5 bis and 3, rue des Haudriettes, specialize in conceptual art, such as B. Nauman's zen-inspired collections of pollen. The **Farideh Cadot Gallery**, 77 rue des Archives, also specializes in conceptual art, including Georges Rousse.

Further in Le Marais, at 9, rue St.-Gilles, **Gilbert Brownstone** has opened a new gallery for established artists like Erro, who excels in collages; and the optical conjurer, Soto, whose work you can admire in the hall of the Center Georges Pompidou. Another very famous German Gallery, **Karsten Greve**, recently opened at 5 rue de Belleyme, and displays the creations of well-known artists such as Willem de Kooning and Lucio Fontana.

Finally, **Nikki Diana Marquardt** owns what may be the most beautiful gallery in the area, at the back of a hotel courtyard in a residential area (9, place des Vosges). Sculptures and neons are often exhibited under the glass roof.

The studios of La Bastille: Today, **La Bastille** is what *Le Moulin de la Galette* or *Le Bateau-Lavoir* in Montmartre used to be at the beginning of the century. Due to its relatively limited number of artists, La Bastille opens the doors of its studios every season and draws itineraries on the pavements.

Otherwise, **Michel Vidal**, at 56 rue

Yvon Lambert.

du Faubourg St.-Antoine, exhibits Duchamp's humorous followers such as Ben or Willem. The **Claire Burrus** gallery, 30, rue de Lappe, specializes in minimalist art. On the same, dynamic street, at No. 47, the welcoming **Gutharc-Ballin Gallery** dares to discover and display new talents.

The largest gallery, set on three levels, is **Lavignes-Bastille**, 27, rue de Charonne. Andy Warhol, and the "lacerator of posters," Rotella, have been its distinguished guests.

The Swedish director of the Art Fair of Stockholm, **Leif Stähle**, defends pure abstraction in Cour Delépine, 37, rue de Charonne.

A few other galleries in rue Keller, such as **Keller** or **Antoine Candeau** offer their walls to young, conceptual artists, and will bring you back to rue de la Roquette where, at No. 57, **J. et J. Donguy** bills new and daring illustrators, photographers and performers.

On the way back to Beaubourg, **Agathe Gaillard** keeps renewing her famous team of photographers like A. Kertesz, with young artists like B. Faucon, who stages and photographs dummies of young boys. The gallery is at 3, rue du Pont-Louis-Philippe.

The large **Galerie de France**, 50-52, rue de la Verrerie, hosts famous artists, abstract and figurative, such as H. Hartung and Matta, whose large paintings are pervaded with the strength of celestial phenomena.

Beau Lézard, 7, rue Pecquay, concocts a new and fresh *cuisine*, whether figurative or abstract.

You can end your visit of the new, artistic right bank with the **Laage-Salomon Gallery**, 57, rue du Temple, which devotes much space to German expressionists like G. Baselitz.

Art on the left bank: The generally more traditional left bank has a few galleries which are really up-to-date. For instance, the **Galerie de Paris**, 6, rue du Pont-de-Lodi, stages installations with music in the background.

Jean Briance, 23-25, rue Guéné-

et J.
ngy
thers.
llowing
ges:
niel
mplon.

gaud, has chosen a humoristic line with figurative artists like Topor, while the promising artist M. Bastow is inspired by both Gauguin and E. Shiele.

Just across the street, at No. 14, **Caroline Corre**'s gallery is also filled with the humor pervading its multi-colored *livres-objets* (books-objects). At No. 35, **Isy Brachot** is the final stop on rue Guánégaud. In an original setting, Brachot presents surrealists like P. Delvaux and R. Magritte, but also creations of hyper-realists such as J. de Andrea's nude and very human looking wax ladies.

On rue Mazarine, other galleries are worth a look: among them the smart **Krief-Raymond Gallery**, No. 50, as well as **Lucien Durand** (No. 19), which was the first to exhibit the famous, monochrome painter, Y. Klein, and **Montenay** (No. 13), which also discovered new talents.

Rue de Seine offers another concentration of galleries. **Jeanne Bucher's** historical gallery exhibits J. Dubuffet's strange, little characters with pointed noses, while **Lara Vincy**, at No. 47, has preserved some of the spirit of the Dada school and of the 1970s.

Claude Bernard, 7-9, rue des Beaux-Arts, is an important gallery for established, realist artists such as David Hockney.

An art mammoth would be a good end to your day's promenade. **Adrien Maeght** used to work with Lelong, and exhibited celebrities like Picasso, Miro and Matisse. His successor is renewing his gallery with young, but already famous artists like H. Delprat, who covers her dark paintings with cabalistic signs and figures of death. Maeght's gallery is at 46, rue du Bac.

Finally, those who want to see something totally new and surprising, should head for the bookshop, **Les Yeux Fertiles**, 3, rue Danton. Here you can see the French graphic art of B. Richard, P. Doury, Placid and Muzo, which may, sometimes, be very aggressive but is always interesting.

HERMÈS
ULTIMA II
CHANEL

LANVIN
Beverly Hills

SHOPPING

Paris—the indisputable capital of high fashion, fine wines, beauty, food and luxury products. From the classic to the unusual, everyone can find something in the city to suit his or her taste to take back home.

To help you get around, Paris has been divided into areas of shopping interest, highlighting the major streets and squares where you'll discover your own treasures: the **Islands**, the **Latin Quarter, St.-Germain-des-Près**, **Le Marais**, **Les Halles**, the **Louvre**, the **Champs-Elysées** and **St.-Honoré.** Some of the more famous, chic or original shops have been specifically mentioned, the addresses for which can be found in the "Travel Tips" section.

The Islands: The Islands in the heart of the city will take you back to times of shopping past. No luxury designer shops and department stores here, but original souvenir shops, or the flower and bird market at **place Louis Lépine**. Small boutiques and classy *épiceries* on the ancient side streets have loads to offer, especially on the *Ile St.-Louis*. Walking down the main street, **rue St.-Louis en l'Ile**, you'll see some of the oldest and most historic boutiques which still line the streets of Paris.

For a touch of the exotic, stop by at **A l'Olivier**, founded in 1860, still selling every oil on earth—nut and grape seed for salads; beauty oils (hazelnut, tortoise, apricot); special beauty products, as well as all types of French mustard, pickles and vinegars (even raspberry and pear). The classic bottles are half the beauty, as well as the giant pottery casks for olive oil.

Visit with **Madame Pierre Fain**, the owner of a toy and school supplies store, where faithful children have left their mark by crayoning an entire autograph book all over the walls. Great gifts for kids and original postcards.

Stop by the tiny chocolate factory

Preceding pages: Galeries Lafayette department store. Below: something for everyone.

when arriving from the Pont St.-Louis, **Au Pain de Sucre**. Try the *florentines* (chocolate coated grilled almonds), truffles and some monogramed sugar cubes for presents!

The Latin Quarter: The **boulevard St.-Michel** and the neighboring side streets have loads of shops, most catering to students' tastes. You'll find artsy clothing and jewelry boutiques, book and record stores and an exotic, open-air market on the **rue Mouffetard**.

For more serious shoppers, there is the **Comptoirs de la Tour D'Argent,** the gourmet boutique, across the street from the restaurant of the same name. Here you can buy the trademark blue and white Limoges plates, champagne glasses, coffee spoons and ashtrays, instead of paying for the 100 dollar dinner in what is reputedly the best restaurant in town. Fresh *foie gras* is on sale and even a $2,500 bottle of Fine Clos du Griffier cognac from 1788.

Try the very authentic **Village Africain**, where the African population of Paris goes to buy exotic spices, dried fish, flours and grains.

ci Market.

And for the traditional, visit **Jean Baptiste Besse** and his 16th-century wine cellar. He's got 50 years of wine experience under that *béret*. One of Paris' best known and most typical wine merchants, Papa Besse will dig that dusty old bottle out of the cellar and offer you friendly and knowledgeable advice on wines for all occasions.

Walking from the place St.-Michel, head towards the **quai de Montebello Booksellers**. The *bouquinistes* offer you a wide variety of books, postcards, posters and rare first editions. Across the *Ile de la Cité* on the corner of *Pont Notre Dame* is Mr. Lelue at stall No. 102, who restores old manuscripts and has a private collection of 18th-century leather-bound books.

St.-Germain-des-Près: This area bordering the Latin Quarter is a bustling, trendy shopping section. The tree-lined **boulevard St.-Germain** will take you past alleys and side streets overflowing with bookshops, antique dealers and chic clothing stores. At No. 34, stop in at **Diptyque**, a boutique founded by three English artists, specializing in homemade crafts, antique bead necklaces, sachets and scented candles. Next door is **HG Thomas**, a store with the best in gifts for men—luggage, hunting knives, bar as well as designer accessories.

In the middle of the boulevard is a lively, late-night bookstore called **La Hune**, snuggled between the *Café Duex Magots* and the *Flore*, where Simone de Beauvoir and Jean-Paul Sartre used to discuss their existentialist theories. Browsing in this place can make you feel like one of the current literary crowd.

For a real taste of the Paris alternative fashion scene, which this quarter is also known for, see **Issey Miyake**, the Tokyo designer who creates his own dresses, as well as the fabrics.

Off the boulevard, stop by the **Cabinet de Curiosité**, an 18th-century pharmacy, now an unusual boutique, offering scientific instruments, brass hourglasses and even shoes from Louis the XVI's days! Next door is **La Danse**, the only bookstore in Paris specializing in dance, with books in all languages, etchings and sculptures. **Lefebvres Fils** is the famous hundred-year old china store where Victor Hugo used to shop. Here you'll find animal and vegetable-shaped dishes to take home.

The **Reunion des Musées Nationaux** offers all the Paris museums' catalogs and posters since 1966. You'll also find jewelry, handbags and scarves crafted under the inspiration of famous pieces from antiquity.

Porcelain plate designs from 18th-century China are used as *motifs* for *crêpe de chine* scarves and the rings patterned after those from European goldsmiths' art of 1100-1200 B.C. make very special gifts and look as modern as those made today.

Don't miss the **rue Jacob** and the **place de Fürstenberg**, where little antique galleries and book shops are hidden, with rare first editions and famous autographs. In a corner of the place you will find **Yveline**, an antique dealer with quite original tastes.

At **Manuel Canovas Boutique**, the fabric designer and interior decorator offers shoes, scarves, bags and linen made from his original fabrics sold in the decorating shop next door.

Across the boulevard, is the **Odéon**, a large square with some of the hottest, newest and craziest boutiques.

Ancient Paris is never far away and on the **rue de Seine** is the traditional **Buci Market**, along with an array of small art galleries and shops. Gaze in the windows at **Au Beau Noir**, an antique doll shop with authentic *guignols* and wind-up toys.

Pay a call next door on **Alain Vian**, Boris' brother, who runs an antique musical instruments store.

A few more steps towards the river is the **rue St.-André des Arts** which leads down to the Place St.-Michel. This little, crooked street is more like a pedestrian mall, with an amazing variety of shops left and right.

At No. 59, the **Cour du Commerce St.-André**, built in 1776, was Paris' first covered shopping mall and is overflowing with history.

This was where a German carpenter called Schmidt worked on perfecting the guillotine and where meetings were held before the French Revolution took place. Step inside and breathe in the history of the city and browse the antique shops and bookstores.

The **place St.-Sulpice**, once the major religious relic center is now flanked by two **Yves Saint Laurent** boutiques and during the summer months, you'll find an antique and book fair here.

The neighborhood **FNAC** (there are several in Paris) has the largest selection of books, records, maps and photo equipment in town.

Finally, in the mood for a fancy French *négligé* at a reasonable price? Not far is the rue St.-Placide, and a shop called **Comme des Femmes**, where you can find a large selection of last seasons' wear from Barbara, Chantelle and Simone Pérèle at 50 to 60 percent off. Current season's wear is discounted and offered 20 to 25 percent off regular prices.

And if you're adventurous, get off the beaten boulevard and call on the **Artisanat Monastique**, near Montparnasse. Open afternoons, you'll find a calm boutique run by the *Couvent de la Visitation*. The nuns offer hand embroidered items, smocking, handmade scarves, painted silks, lamps, leather goods, pottery, porcelain (hand-painted) and book-binding leather.

Le Marais: Walking around the maze of small cobblestoned streets in the Marais, you'll discover unsuspected treasures of shopping pleasure. Visit the **place des Vosges** boutiques, especially **Mythes et Légendes**, where you will find a veritable museum of antiques and tapestries for sale.

Stop by in the afternoon (only), at the **Jardin de Flore**, a small publishing house specializing in reissues of antique manuscripts, rare first editions and maps. Ancient Renaissance bookmaking techniques are used: handmade paper, gold-leaf leather and hand-colored illustrations.

At **A L'Image du Grenier sur l'eau,** you have over one million postcards to choose from, and great cinema and old advertising posters.

Nearby, check out French health food at **Diététique Régime**, one of the oldest natural health food stores in Paris. On the impressive *rue des Francs-Bourgeois* is **SMART** (**Société des Métiers d'Art**), where craftsmen from all over France have gathered to sell their handpainted tiles and ceramics. The *pièces de résistance* are the miniature clay puzzles of the *place des Vosges* or 17th-century houses, bakeries, butcher shops, churches and *cafés.*

The big auctions in Paris take place regularly at the **Crédit Municipal de Paris,** where particularly good deals in jewelry may be found. Call in advance for the dates or check the board outside.

This is also the heart of the Jewish quarter, where window shopping will transport you to another world (due to the Jewish Sabbath, remember that many shops are closed Saturdays).

Les Halles: As for the modern glass four-story mall of the **Forum des Halles**, here you will find the latest fashions all under one roof. The Forum boasts 180 different boutiques, which get classier as you go up each level. Just next door, take a trip back to the past and walk through the **passage Molière**, between the **rue St.-Martin** and the **rue Quincampoix,** a tiny 19th-century alley, where you'll find old tailor shops and antique stores.

Trot down the rue Montorgueil, a market street in the heart of the city. Outside, near the **place des Innocents**, stroll along the pedestrian walkways to find new-wave, retro and fashionable little shops, with reasonable prices.

t, pping ers. ht, rug rchant, overhead.

Pick up an original Paris souvenir in the form of French street or store sign at **Papeterie Moderne**, which has hundreds to choose from. Right behind *St.-Eustache*, **Marithe et François Girbaud**, two young designers, have their own lines of clothes and especially trendy sportswear displayed in a three-story modern clothing palace.

If you're bargain hunting, check **Halle By's**, a *hôtel particulier* with sales on clothes from Pierre d'Alby, Plein Sud, Incognito, Dior, Yves Saint Laurent and Guy Laroche. Designer **Pierre Cardin** also has a half price factory outlet nearby.

Heading to the more fashionable West, don't miss the **place des Victoires**, where you will get an idea of the fashions to come. On a small side street, **Tokio Kumagai** has the most original shoe store in town.

Tired of walking? Both men and women alike can take a break at **Magic Beauty**, right on the **rue du Rivoli**—the only *institut de beauté* in town *sans rendezvous* (no appointment necessary). Just stop in and let Madame Lefebvre and her competent staff offer you "the works", including lessons in Paris makeup techniques. Try the Carole Franck line of French natural beauty care or *balneo* and vitamin therapy treatment.

For your hair, **Jean Philippe Pages** has to be the most *avant-garde* of all the Parisian hairdressers. Here you'll walk out not just with a new cut, but with a work of art. Mr. Pages is a veritable head sculptor and even sells postcards of his creations.

The Louvre and the Champs-Elysées: Start your day with coffee at the rooftop café on the top floor of the **Samaritaine** and savor one of the best views of Paris. Then stop by the colorful plant and pet shops along the **quai de la Mégisserie** or the stamp market on **avenue Matignon** and **avenue Gabriel** (open Thursdays, Saturdays and Sundays).

Everyone's heard of the *Champs-Elysées* and surprisingly enough, some

Browsing at the Stamp Market.

good deals and sale prices can be found in the *Galleries* leading off this ritzy avenue. A lot of the shops remain open late in the evening along this 24-hour street.

A bit to the North lies **Chez Androuet,** where you'll find nearly every cheese made in France in this fragrant boutique, along with other gourmet specialities. The only thing on the menu of the restaurant upstairs are delicious cheese-based dishes.

Peek in at the **Rene Gerard Saint Ouen** bakery. These loaves are works of art. Variety abounds and there is everything from turtle- to bicycle-shaped breads. The loaves can also be varnished and hung on the wall as souvenirs or purchased as a unique gift.

Closer to the Louvre, walk down the **rue de Rivoli**, where you will find reasonably priced dress shops. The **Louvre des Antiquaires**, however impressive, is not so reasonable. Visit the 250 different shops under the arcades, but ask the dealers for their cards, as they often have less expensive shops in other parts of town.

The top French names in *haute couture* are on **avenue Montaigne: Chanel**, with Karl Lagerfeld's collections, has a beautiful boutique with more mirrors than walls. **Nina Ricci** displays sumptuous styles and perfumes and the most refined lingerie around (check the "bargain" basement). **Christian Dior** has got a different Dior boutique for every member of the family, even "*Bébé Dior*" (infant wear), as well as one shop entirely devoted to shoes and stockings, some with diamond studded Eiffel Tower seams. **Louis Vuitton, Ungaro, Valentino** and fine jewelry stores (**Cartier**, **Gerard**) are here too.

St.-Honoré: This is it—the most fashionable shopping section in town, the **Faubourg St.-Honoré**. All the famous designers are here, and the best names in furs, jewelry, crystal and caviar.

At the top of the line in French clothing is *haute couture*. The only thing

rstyling
ıon-
tion at
Halles.

holding you back will be your pocketbook—the price of a woman's suit usually starts around $3,000 or $4,000. *Haute couture* shows are held at the end of January for the spring and summer lines and at the end of July for the fall and winter collections.

Second best is *prêt-à-porter* (ready to wear) and the related accessory lines. Clothes from the majority of *couture* houses can also be found in the *Grands Magasins*.

In general, the big sales (*soldes*) take place towards the end of the year and throughout January and at the end of June through the month of July. You may be lucky though, and run into a shop displaying *liquidation* in the window, which is a French excuse to revamp the store and offer great prices.

The most exciting section of St.-Honoré runs from **avenue Matignon** to the **rue Royale**. **Lanvin**, for perfume and accessories and **Hermès**, whose original 1837 saddle shop has turned into one of the best in designer fashion. Their collection of 200 silk scarves (*carrés*) is world-renown. The Paris store stocks all the scarves back to the original blues and if you change your mind (or buy them on the airplane with the duty-free discount), they will exchange them for the new scarf of your choice at any Hermès boutique around the world.

There are bargains to be found one floor above the "real" **Gucci** boutique, where last year's collections sell at 30 to 40 percent off. **Honore 316** is one of the few duty free stores in town to offer Americans 40 percent off.

Stop by the flower market at **place de la Madeleine** and sample at **Fauchon**, the place the billionaires come to shop with every possible fruit and vegetable in the world. The presentation of the items is as much of an art as stocking the food itself. No self service here, a hands-off policy is *de rigueur* and a smiling salesperson will be delighted to help you pick and choose. There's a delicatessen of the same name across

Left, shopping i the Latin Quarter. Right, the newest fashions a found at place des Victoires.

the street, where you can sample the Fauchon *cuisine*.

A nice side street behind the Madeleine is **rue Vignon**. Stop by the **Maison du Miel** (since 1908), for some lavender honey and miniature gift pots; at the **Victoria** for good buys in leatherwear or at the **Flirt** for fantastic cashmere sweaters. The open-air market in the **Cité Berryer** is held Tuesdays and Fridays from 8 a.m. to 1 p.m. at 25, **rue Royale**.

Le Sphinx is the place for Napoléon fans, offering Paris' widest collection of antique weapons and memorabilia. A bottle of Napoléon's cognac, portraits of Josephine and even one of his famous hats are for sale if you're ready to pay up to $75,000 (the price of the hat!) for the memories.

See the wealthiest square in Paris at the **place Vendôme** and the new mall where dignitaries shop while in Paris at 62, **Faubourg St.-Honoré**, home for some of the city's newest and upcoming designers.

The *Grands Boulevards* are here to stroll along, between the *Opéra* and the *place de la République* and the *Bastille*. At the **Hôtel Drouot**—the Sotheby's of Paris, auctions are held almost every afternoon. Go early to check the merchandise, which is a sight to behold.

Finally, for rainy days, get out a map of Paris and discover the turn-of-the-century **Galeries**. These glass-roofed shopping malls are where you can find everything from walking sticks to antique cameras.

Les Grands Magasins: The *Grands Magasins* are the very Parisian department stores of the last century. Learn the *art d'acheter* by descending the wide wooden staircases, gazing at the fancy metal beams and domed ceilings and leaning against the huge wooden counters of eras past. Going shopping here is an outing in itself and makeup demonstrations and fashion shows are daily events. But don't let their convenience keep you from discovering the small neighborhood boutiques, where

xury
opping
ly.

service is often more personalized (even if the salespeople can be a little pushy at times).

Au Bon Marché is Paris' oldest department store dating back to 1869 and quite a bit calmer than the *Grands Magasins.* Au Bon Marche is located on the other side of the river. You'll find a very impressive collection of oriental rugs and the famous *Trois Hibous* section catering to children—a goldmine for the kids, as well as the city's biggest *épicerie fine*, recently entirely remodeled and open daily (after the store closes) until 7:30 p.m.

La Samaritaine is one of Paris' largest *art-nouveau* department stores. Legend has it that Emile Zola had the original idea of creating this store and commissioned the initial design, which inspired him to write *Au Bonheur des Dames*. The main attraction is the rooftop café in Store No. 2. The store itself is usually mobbed and poorly organized, although the sports section is quite good.

Le Printemps was founded in 1865 and was the first Grand Magasin to use electric lighting, rather than gas. The huge domed ceiling built in 1923 by Brière is now classified as a historic monument. The perfume department has the largest selection in Paris and the store offers a V.I.P. fashion advice service free of charge (call 42.82.64.23 for an appointment).

Galeries Lafayette, inaugurated in 1895, is mainly known for its devotion to high fashion. A new *Avant Scene* section was recently created, complete with a fashion show stage, fashion video clips and a bar. The lingerie department has the widest selection in town. Check with Jacqueline Muray, an international American fashion consultant who recently started a free fashion advisory service here at the store called *Mode Plus*. Interested in getting a new French look? (Call 48.74.50.13 for an appointment.)

Markets: *Les Marchés de Paris* are central to the lives of millions of inhabi-

Local artist works are available a place du Tertre.

tants: housewives who go daily for vegetables and news, friends who meet there on the weekend and spend Sunday eating together, lovers who wake up in the morning and go to gather their breakfast. The explosive colors of rows and rows of fruits, game and seafood, the sweet smell of flowers and cheeses, the hidden treasures to be found in old racks of clothing, boxes of books... *faire son marché* is an authentic Parisian pleasure. No one needs to be told how to enjoy, the minute you walk by one, you'll be inexorably drawn in.

Birds of Paradise: The year-round **Flower and Bird Market** is a feast for the eyes and the nose, with everything from lemon trees to birds of paradise.

Ernest Hemingway and Josephine Baker shopped at the **Mouffetard Market** (started in 1350). You can find fresh produce from around the world, baskets, flowers, artistic cards, old clothing and jewelry. Get a taste of Africa by stopping at the **African bazaar** on the **rue de l'Arbalète**.

ven
tired
oppers.

Everything your heart desires: In the heart of the Latin quarter is the **Buci Market**, one of the most colorful and traditional markets.

The **Marché St.-Pierre**, in the garment district at the foot of Montmartre, has an amazing selection of fabrics, lace and trinkets from all over the world.

The **Marché d'Aligre**, however, is mainly known for fruit and flowers. It has both an open-air and a covered market. In the middle of the square, there is a small and quaint flea market selling old books, clothes, glassware, lace and jewelry. Plan to avoid the weekend crowds.

The biggest **flea market** in town is the **Puces de St.-Ouen** with 3,000 marketeers and five separate individual markets on the adjoining streets.

Wherever you choose to shop, from the glittering boulevards with their famous boutiques to the traditional markets, Paris offers you everything your heart desires.

Sports and Games

From January 1 to December 31, holidays included, Paris offers a complete calendar of national and international sporting events. From international tennis championships to a day at the races, from a peaceful game of *pétanque* to a gallop through the woods—the choice of events or activities to include in your Paris agenda is wide, indeed. Visitors may also enjoy a trip to one of the fairs organized regularly in or on the edge of the city. Some are state-of-the-art professional exhibitions and others are more nifty-gadget oriented. Finally, there are many activities and parks that children will especially enjoy, making their experience memorable, too.

Spectator sports: Everyday, millions of French place their bets of five francs or more on their favorite horse. They don't all go to the major racetracks to do it, however, but often wager at a café which serves the **Paris Mutuel Urbain** (PMU). Certain races are world-famous, like the *Prix de l'Arc de Triomphe* held the first Sunday in October at the **Longchamp Racetrack** in the bois de Boulogne. In autumn, show jumping takes place at **Auteuil**, also in the bois, and *cavaliers* compete for the *Prix du Prèsident de la République* on Easter Sunday. The *Prix de l'Amérique* runs on the first Sunday in January; trotters and sulkies compete at the **Vincennes Racetrack**. On the third Sunday of June, the *Grand Steeplechase* takes place at Auteuil. This colorful affair gathers all that Paris has to offer in the way of elegance and wealth. The show is as much in the grandstands as it is on the track.

A new arena: Since its construction in 1985, the **Palais Omnisport de Bercy** (known simply as *Bercy* to Parisians) has become the latest Mecca of world-class athletes. Thanks to its modular design, it can host some 20 different sports, from judo to figure-skating, tennis, cross-country motorcycling, rugby, horse shows, not to mention rock concerts and an occasional opera or blockbuster theater piece. The main events here include the Paris Tennis Open in November and the *Six Jours Cycliste de Paris*, an international bike race that goes on nonstop for nearly one week. Tickets run from 80 to 300 francs per seat.

But the biggest cycling event occurs at the end of July, when riders participating in the *Tour de France* cross the finish line on the Champs-Elysées, where the French president awards the legendary *maillot jaune* (yellow biking shirt) to the winner.

Like London, New York, Beijing and Tokyo, Paris welcomes nearly 15,000 runners for the May marathon, with a first prize of 350,000 francs. Spring is also the season for the *Coupe de France de Football* (French championship soccer), which kicks off at the **Parc des Princes**. The stadium is a real techno-

eceding ges: erry-go-und near atelet. **ft**, playing tanque. **ght**, cling is e of the st pular orts in ance.

logical feat in the use of concrete, holding 48,000 seats, all protected from the elements and all with good visibility.

Perhaps the most illustrious event over the past 10 years has been the international tennis matches at **Roland Garros**. For two weeks at the end of May, 356 of the best players in the world make their appearances here, cheered on by 350,000 fans. The entire Parisian jetset comes out in force: actors, artists, designers and journalists are the main attractions along with McEnroe, Lendl and Noah. Seats that run from 100 to 300 francs can climb to 100 times higher in the hands of scalpers for the semifinals and finals.

The best way to keep up with the Parisian sports calendar is to pick up a copy of the daily sports newspaper *l'Equipe*.

Trade shows its stuff: With over 350 international conventions, Paris is the meeting capital of the world. It is also the number one city in fairs and exhibitions. There are more than 120 a year, 50 or so on an international scale, pertaining to every profession, passion and person, and new ones crop up regularly. These *salons* are held either at the **Parc des Expositions** at the Porte de Versailles on the southeastern rim of Paris, at the **Centre National des Industries et des Technologies** (C.N.I.T.) at La Défense, or at the **Parc des Expositions** in Villepinte, just north of the city. Certain specialized fairs are reserved for professionals only, but the larger international ones are open to the public: the *Salon de l'Auto* (car show) in October, the *Salon du Livre* (Book Fair) in March, the *Salon de l'Informatique-SICOB* (Computer Expo) in April, and especially the *Foire de Paris* in May—the biggest trade fair in the world, uniting thousands of exhibitors in the fields of housing, tourism and leisure. All kinds of better mousetraps are on view here—happy hunting!

The Olympic tradition: It was at the Sorbonne in 1894 that Pierre de Coubertin, a thickly mustachioed,

wealthy aristocrat, launched the idea of the modern Olympic Games, 15 centuries after the ancient Greek games. Contemporary Olympic Games took place in Athens in 1896, then twice in Paris in 1900 and 1924. Inspired by the British educational model, Pierre de Coubertin became the greatest French promoter and popularizer of sports among all classes of society. While at the beginning of the century only a handful of rich young men fenced and rode horseback in exclusive clubs, today Paris boasts over 1,000 sports associations and hundreds of centers open to everyone. Having long championed mental acrobatics over physical fitness, the French have finally begun working out on playing fields, in gymnasiums, as well as in aerobic, dance and exercise classes. Practically any sport can be indulged in here, be it boomerang throwing in the bois de Boulogne, pelota, baseball or polo.

In the swim: With the emergence of fine weather, sunbathers cover the banks of the Seine, catching short lunch-hour rays. If Parisians swam readily in the river at the turn of the century, rare is the intrepid individual today, willing to dive from a bridge in the middle of summer for a stroke or two, only to be fished out onto a police boat. Park wardens also have their hands full keeping children out of the fountains, although it's not for lack of swimming pools.

There are over 40 pools open to everyone in all corners of town. The pool at the **Forum des Halles** is one of the most modern and attractive with its enormous bay windows overlooking a tropical garden. Open until 10 p.m. Tuesdays and Fridays, aquatic gym classes are offered here.

Founded in 1796 and rebuilt several times since, the **Deligny Swimming Pool** is the oldest in France and, perhaps, the last floating pool in the world. In spite of its status as a historical monument, Deligny remains very much in vogue, where topless sunbath-

rse games ring nder s—at the âteau de cennes.

ers of both sexes prepare their tans before hitting the beaches at St.-Tropez. It can even be rented for parties or moonlight swims.

The 1930s style **Pontoise Pool**, also very old, has a squash court and a gymnasium. A nudist club operates here Monday and Thursday evenings. In the 16th *arrondissement* the outdoor pool **Molitor** has often served as a runway for fashion shows. A large sliding board, suana, gym, dance classes and solariums make this *piscine* one of the most pleasant.

Racquets and clubs: No special registration, membership or reservation is necessary to play tennis on any of the 140 municipal tennis courts. Just show up with a racket at one of them and hope that it is free. Prices range from 20 to 30 francs per player per hour. A special phone information service, *Allo Sport* (42.76.54.54) lists all the courts and their locations.

Squash has become more and more popular over the past 10 years, with squash clubs popping up everywhere. Four of the best are the **Club Quartier Latin** at the Piscine Pontoise, the **Front de Seine**, the **Squash Stadium**—the biggest in Paris with 14 courts—and **Squash Montparnasse** located under the Montparnasse Tower.

Golf lovers must head out to the five public courses in the Essone and Yvelines suburbs to satisfy their passion. Private clubs like **Chantilly**, **Morfontaine** and **St.-Nom-la-Breteche** (home to the tournament of the same name) are for members only, though a few clubs open to the public occasionally (minimum green fee: 250 francs). Inside Paris, golfers have to make do with training centers, including the rooftop **Club de l'Etoile**, **City Golf**, with its impressive "natural" decor, and the **Ken Club**, with an 18-hole video golf simulator.

Locomotion: The two large parks, Vincennes and bois de Boulogne, are the main centers for horseback riding. In Vincennes, you will find: **Bayard**

Leisure games under the spreading chestnut trees.

Equitation, and the **Centre Équestre le la Cartouchérie.** Boulogne is home to the **SEP Touring Club** and the **Société Équestre de l'Etrier**. The last center is quite chic and run by a former French champion.

There are two ice rinks for figure skating in town, one near the hilly *Buttes Chaumont Park*, **Patinoire des Buttes Chaumont**, and the other in the Montparnasse neighborhood, **Patinoire de la Gaité-Montparnasse**. For those who prefer roller skating, coast on over to the **Main Jaune** at the Porte de Champerret, which doubles as a discotheque. (Free for women on Wednesdays from 2 p.m. to 4 p.m. and open all night on Friday.)

A votre santé: After having spent long years paying tribute to the cult of rich food and heavy winedrinking, the French as a whole, and Parisians, in particular, have begun to take an interest in their bodies and health. Confronted daily by advertisements of tanned, dreamworld bodies, people are becoming embarrassed about their extra kilos.

War has been declared on fat, sugar and stress. To re-establish their equilibrium, young executives are invading physical fitness centers. These veritable shape-up factories have mushroomed over the past several years, flourishing on promises of youthful shape and vigor. Saunas, jacuzzis, weight-lifting, aerobics and dance are the weapons of this new crusade.

The **Gymnase Club** has a dozen establishments which are equipped for 49 different activities from stretching to yoga, to aquatic exercising, to bodybuilding. **Garden Gym**, with seven locations, is another mass health center with quality service; the branch at Nation (8 rue Lassen) has a supervised playground for children. **Vitatop** has three locales, one of which is on the 22nd floor of the Sofitel Hôtel (8 rue Louis Armand), where one can even learn to windsurf in the pool. **Les Jardins de la Forme** is famous for its weight-lifting room. At the **Club Nicolo** body fluids lost through working out can be replaced by one of the 30 brands of mineral water on sale.

Fitness centers which are more artistically inclined include the well-known **Espace Vit'Halles**, which offers a large selection of jazz, Afro-Brazilian and modern dance classes as well as aquatic exercising, jacuzzi and Turkish bath facilities. The **Centre de Danse du Marais** has ballet, jazz, African, modern and tap dance classes for every level. It is one of the top dance centers in Paris, tucked away in a centuries-old courtyard along with the Studio—a Tex-Mex restaurant where resident Americans gather over margaritas and nachos.

Patterned after the Roman baths, the chic and elegant **Thermes du Royal Monceau** is a haven for relaxation and gentle shaping up. Oil massages, bubbling algae baths and isolation tanks reign here. There is also a swimming pool, Turkish bath, sauna, jacuzzi and baths set at different temperatures to pamper you. Brunch is served on Sunday mornings at poolside.

Child's play: Children, like their parents, need recreation, too. In every domain, be it art, movies or sports, Parisians have bent over backwards to satisfy this demanding clientele. Many museums, including the **Louvre**, **Orsay**, the **Petit Palais** and the **Musée de la Marine**, provide free brochures specially adapted to stimulate the child's interest in a tour of the exhibits: each child becomes an archeologist or explorer looking for the great pyramid's secret. Museums such as Orsay or the **Centre Pompidou** organize workshops for the tots on Wednesdays and Saturdays. The **Musée en Herbe** in the Jardin d'Acclimatation (bois de Boulogne) was specifically designed for children, with temporary displays on the Gauls, elephants and so on. The waxworks museum **Grévin** (one on boulevard Montmartre and one in the Forum des Halles) has classic kid appeal. The **Cité des Sciences et de l'Industrie de la Villette** offers them a chance to make discoveries and learn about science and technology through exhibits and tangible experiments. The **Géode's** hemispheric movie screen, the world's largest, is an impressive visual experience, even for adults!

Children under 10 have their own **Marionette Theaters** at the Champ de Mars, the Luxembourg Garden, the Parc Montsouris and the Jardin du Ranelagh. Traditional Wednesday, weekend and holiday afternoon entertainment, these puppets are simply marvelous, richly costumed, and often tempt parents into taking a seat. There are several specialized cinemas like the **Napoléon** and the **St.-Lambert** that show children's movies (always in French) on Wednesdays, Saturdays and Sundays.

A number of amusement parks have opened in the suburbs, most recently **Mirapolis** in Cergy-Pontoise with acres and acres of games, rides and fantasy houses taken from French legends and fairy tales. Inside Paris, the **Jardin d'Acclimatation** in the bois de Boulogne has, besides the Musée en Herbe, playgrounds, a robot village, a giant dollhouse, a wading pool, a mini-motorcycle course, a zoo and a circus.

Three permanent circuses are the **Cirque Baroque**, just outside the métro station Sully-Morland in the Marais, the **Cirque Diana Moreno Bormann** at the square du Docteur Caimette, and the **Cirque de Paris** in the close suburbs, avenue de la Commune-de-Paris in Nanterre.

The **Jardin des Plantes** has a scruffy sort of zoo and a vivarium full of creepy reptiles, snakes and spiders. The **Musée d'Histoire Naturelle**, in the same park, has recently been refurbished and is now more popular than ever with the younger set and their grandparents. There is also a tropical hothouse and a maze to wander through.

Undoubtedly the city's best zoo is the **Parc Zoologique de Paris** in the bois

Children's Hour at Picasso Museum.

de Vincennes (M° Porte Dorée). Most of the animals are not in cages, but separated from the public by moats. They seem well-cared-for and playful, and the park itself is roomy and well-stocked with souvenir and snack stands. In the nearby **Musée des Arts Africains**, fishy friends may be viewed in a large aquarium.

Parks and gardens: Parks and gardens are wide open spaces, full of attractions for children. Many have playgrounds, roller skating, swings, seesaws and carousels. You might reward a youngster who patiently visited the Marmottan Museum with a ride on the old-fashioned carousel or the just-plain-old donkey in the **Ranelagh Park**. The **Jardin des Halles** is a child's dream come true, with a labyrinth, a ping-pong ball sea, a volcano, a mysterious island and a tropical forest. Kids can't resist playing pirates on the model boat at the **Jardin de l'Arsenal**, just off the place de la Bastille.

The **Parc Floral** is a favorite with the tots who never stop moving: pedal cars, merry-go-rounds, all sorts of set-ups for crawling, running, balancing, shimmying, climbing, bouncing and sliding down. The more sedate, older generation will enjoy the big café and more intimate restaurant (tearoom-style dancing on the weekends), as well as the landscape, highlighted with spectacular flora. Flower shows are held here, including the famous Orchid Show in February.

The parks and gardens of Paris are the emeralds of her crown. Everyone will enjoy the beautiful settings, the happy atmosphere and the many activities available. You'll also want to try some typical park *cuisine*: hot waffles with chocolate sauce and whipped cream, roasted chestnuts, ice cream and crépes.

Today visitors to Paris who want to see more than monuments, musuems or shops, and who want to get to know the people can do so by enjoying one of these activities—a real Parisian experience. Isn't that what you came for?

king
ends.

DV C OEVR DE L'HOMME DE TOVTES LES VO

LA NATVRE JAILLIT LA DIVINE SYMPHONIE

PARIS THEATER

Theater lovers have every reason for wanting to make a special trip to Paris. Although London has long enjoyed the title of the "Theater capital of the world", Paris deserves another distinction: that of being the capital of international theater. From the arrival and great success of the Italian street players in the 17th century, to the reign of Diaghilev's *Ballet Russe* in the 1920s, the fabric of French theater can be seen as a great tapestry of international color.

The city has long welcomed artists in every field: painters, sculptors, musicians, writers—and perhaps the theater, being an amalgam of these other disciplines, best illustrates that "melting pot" tradition. The result, today, is a tremendous variety of options: spectators have the rare opportunity to see South American or Indian seasons, Japanese dance workshops or Russian companies performing in their native language. Even the Comédie Française, bastion of French theater tradition, regularly invites foreign directors.

The Comédie Française: In the heart of Paris, tucked between the Louvre, the Palais-Royal and the avenue de l'Opéra, the **Comédie Française** with its discreet façade and elegant, if somewhat secret, garden behind, is worth a daytime tour and an evening visit. The company, given its Royal Charter over three centuries ago by Louis XIV, had many 'homes' before settling into its present premises. More than a theater, this impressive building is virtually a crafts museum. Wig makers, musicians, cabinet makers, cobblers, milliners and even a blacksmith figure are among the artisans employed here.

Those interested in seeing the company's work will, in an average week, have three productions to choose from—either classical or (often) modern repertoires. (Jean Genet's *The Balcony* was staged here shortly before the his death.) Late summer visitors should remember that the Comédie Française, like so many other Paris theaters, shuts its doors from the first of August to mid-September.

The atmosphere is a curious blend of modern technology and archaic tradition, a cross between the Vatican and the Lincoln Center. Marble busts and magnificent portraits of the present company's predecessors fix one's gaze at every nook and cranny. The vast stage, whose proscenium arch is a study in baroque detail, is equipped with the most recent technological devices.

Backstage, in the actor's *salon* known as the *Jardin d'Hiver* or Winter Garden, actors having their wigs recurled or a change of boots laced up sit on the edge of the Louis XVI *chaise-longue* watching the color house video for their entrance cues. The keen and curious theater buff will be pleased to know that a guided tour of the building provides a glimpse of all this, and more (for example, Molière's famous couch, where he breathed his last onstage during a performance of *Le Malade Imaginaire*).

The Odéon: The Comédie Française holds other seasons at the **Odéon** on the left bank. This impressive theater, twice destroyed by fire, has witnessed many uprisings, both within and without its walls—from the French Revolution to the student's occupation of the building in 1968—and often enough the audience itself has been fraught with hand-to-hand fighting provoked by controversial productions.

The theater has changed its name again and again, according to the political régime in power. It became the Théâtre de France in 1959, and was only recently renamed the **Théâtre de l' Europe.** More than just an occasion of rebaptising, the renaming underscores its importance as the European base for international theater seasons which are presided over by the Italian director, Giorgio Strehler.

Preceding pages: the dome of th Champs-Elysées Theater, painted by M. Denis (circa 191 "From ma heart and the voices of nature springs the divine symphony. Right, Théâtre de Champs-Elysées.

The main house is a magnificent example of the Italian style, with steeply rising balconies which virtually surround the stage. It seats 1,000 and a small space upstairs, named after the late director, Roger Blin (Samuel Beckett's first champion), seats 80. This space, generally known as the **Petit Odéon**, is an excellent forum for new plays, and allows the Comédie Française to pursue its present aim of encouraging contemporary French playwrights.

Just in front of the theater, on the corner of the place de l'Odéon and the rue de l'Odéon, a bookshop—**Le-Coupe Papier**—offers theater and film buffs a great variety of publications on these subjects. You can find just about anything in this shop, be it Louise Brooks's autobiography, a survey of Japanese theater or the screenplay of *A Bout de Souffle*.

Chaillot—the T.N.P.: Both the Odéon and the Comédie Française are two of several state-subsidized theaters in Paris. The other prominent state-subsidized theater is the **Théâtre National Populaire**, of a completely different style. The company which was founded in 1920, has its home in the **Trocadéro Palace**.

The palace is a little intimidating, and has more the feel of a modern day historical monument than a theater. Inside the building, the overpowering perspectives of vast ceilings, immense marble stairways and innumerable foyers give one the impression of being lost in the depths of a pyramid. Crowds milling about for tickets are dwarfed by the gigantic proportions of the building's pre-war architectural style.

The palace could have been a cold and institutional place except for the generosity and incentive of its directors—from Jean Vilar (1951-1963) to today's Antoine Vitez—who succeeded in bringing the potential mausoleum into life.

Brave and often controversial work takes place in the immense theater,

Théâtre De La Ville.

while children's shows, poetry readings and exhibitions animate the foyer. Bookstalls offer a host of publications—not only plays, but also novels, poetry and documentary texts. The main house seats 1,150, and the **Salle Gemier**, accessible from the gardens facing the Seine, seats 450. This theater, like the Petit Odéon, presents mainly modern pieces.

The Paris Opéra: Another monumental Paris landmark is, of course, the **Opéra**. Built between 1861 and 1874 by Charles Garnier, its massive area (118,000 sq. feet or 11,000 sq. meters) makes it the largest theater in the world. However, much of the space is given over to the stage, backstage area and the foyer, so that only 2,200 spectators can be counted in a full house. The Opéra is, in itself, a veritable museum. Among the artists who contributed to its great beauty are Carpeaux, Falgière, Paul Baudry and Louis Boulanger. The ceiling, installed in 1964, was the work of Marc Chagall.

The building houses the **Paris Ballet Company** and a small musuem, a considerable library and numerous rehearsal rooms. Taking a guided tour here is like visiting Ali Baba's famous cavern.

Newest on the lyric scene, and new home to the **National Opera Company**, is the **Opéra de la Bastille**, a shiny palace in a popular neighborhood. Plagued by controversy from its conception and heir to political demons, the Opéra opened its doors in 1990 with a rarely performed work by Berlioz, *Les Troyens*. The ultra-sophisticated machinery has still got a few bugs: on opening night a large bit of the scenery fell down, startling one purportedly dead character back to life

The Boulevard tradition: Several privately funded theaters are tucked into the streets and cul-de-sacs between the Palais-Royal and the Opéra: the **Athenée**, **Arts Hebertot**, **Comédie Caumartin**, **Edouard VII**, **Mathurins** and **Mogador**—to name a few. Although these establishments are private theaters, they have a different profile to what is known as ***boulevard*** theater. "Boulevard" describes the kind of entertainment found in the rather plush theaters on the *grands boulevards* of the *rive droite*—the **Bouffes Parisiens**, the **Théâtre des Varietés**, for example—whose predominant ambition is profit, i.e., packed houses. Light, farcical pieces with a touch of vulgarity and a star-studded cast are the usual fare in these establishments.

The origin of the term, "boulevard" lies in the advent of street theater and circus entertainment, very popular on the *grands boulevards* in the 18th century. A picture of what theatrical competition was like on these boulevards in the mid-19th century is found in the film *Les Enfants du Paradis.*

One of the boulevard theaters reputed for something quite different from the usual commercial productions it now advertises is **Théâtre Antoine**. In the 1890s André Antoine took over the theater on the boulevard de Strasbourg, near the Gare de l'Est. Here, he put into practice his revolutionary concept of realism in theater, a shocking contrast to the fairyland illusions which were then in vogue.

For 10 years, the Théâtre Antoine led the world in what was becoming a new trend in international drama, influencing writers, directors and actors. On this stage, at the turn of the century, real beef-sides dripping with real blood hung from real butchers' hooks, while the themes of the plays were real life dramas of a social nature.

Street theater still thrives in Paris, especially in the warmer seasons around tourist sites like the Pompidou Center, Les Halles and St.-Germain-des-Près. During summer, street performers unfold their bag of tricks at all hours, to whatever passers-by they succeed in distracting. Fire eaters, clowns, mimes, magicians, singers and North African percussionists are but a few of the skills on offer.

The theater in the forest: Adventurous theater goers should visit the **Cartoucherie** in the bois de Vincennes. This rehabilitated, old munitions factory is a thriving theater complex in the middle of a wooded park. Five theaters—the **Théâtre du Soleil**, **l'Aquarium**, **la Tempête**, **l' Epée de Bois** and **Chaudron**—flourish here, with excellent attendance figures, despite the inconvenience the bucolic location presents to busy Parisians. More than a theater center, the Cartoucherie has a riding school and stables, as well as a primary school, both of which bestride the entrance.

The internationally famous Théâtre du Soleil has converted massive factory sheds into a hive of artistic enterprise: scene-builders, cloth-dyers, printers and actors hammer plays into shape. Rehearsals for each of this collectively run company's productions take about one year, followed by an equally long, if not longer, run to packed houses. The spectator is rewarded for his efforts in attending the theater by a high standard of food and drink in the theater foyer, at relatively low prices. The café-bar and bookstalls are manned by the actors, who make no bones about their on or offstage duties to the audience.

Chatêlet: In the center of Paris, two major theaters, the Théâtre Musical de Paris and the Théâtre de la Ville, stand facing each other across the fountains at the place de Châtelet. The **Théâtre Musical du Paris**, built in 1862, is the biggest theater in Paris, with room for 2,400 spectators. As its name suggests, its program consists of musical or dance pieces, ranging from the Peking Opera to the New York production of *West Side Story*.

The **Théâtre de la Ville**, a publicly funded theater, is—like its neighbor—one of the most frequented houses in Paris. The program here is also varied, covering theater, modern dance and music events. This theater was run by Sarah Bernhardt from 1899 until her death. Bernhardt ruled it with a firm hand, playing the lead in legendary productions such as *Cyrano de Bergerac*, *The Samaritan* and *Lady of the Camelias*. The theater, originally named after her, remained The Sarah Bernhardt for 70 years, until 1968, when it was entirely modernized and rebaptised the Théâtre de la Ville. *La* Bernhardt's dressing room, just upstairs off the grand foyer, remains intact—complete with her fans, costumes and opulent *chaise-longue*.

The Bouffes-du-Nord: A present day theatrical legend is the **Théâtre des Bouffes-du-Nord**. Opened in 1876, it was ravaged by fire at the beginning of the century, although the essential forms of the proscenium arch and its moulded walls were left intact. Concealed behind housefronts on the boulevard de la Chapelle, the theater was, quite simply, forgotten. For decades it was used as a stonemason and builders' warehouse. When Peter Brook stumbled on it in his search for a base for the **International Center for Theater Research**, he could hardly believe his luck. The theater was cleaned up and fitted out with the strictly necessary: floorboards, banks of seats etc., while the distinctive structural features were left as they were. The result is a warm and magical space, with perfect acoustics and a shape which draws audience and performers together. Coupled with a setting of spartan simplicity, the center stimulates the imagination of actors, directors, designers and audiences alike.

Peter Brook's company have created many pieces here which have since traveled the world. Their work, perhaps better than any other, illustrates the cross-cultural nature of Parisian theater. It is somehow inconceivable that this company could be based elsewhere than in Paris. Where else would you find a company made up of African, Japanese, Indian, West Indian, Greek, American, Persian, British, Arabic, Polish and German actors—but in the capital of international theater?

Fire-eater.

BAR · BRASSERIE 1900

PARIS BY NIGHT

Like many capital cities, Paris offers a wide range of exciting entertainment. The city itself is so beautiful (and beautifully lit) that the choice of merely wandering through certain neighborhoods can be extremely satisfying—weather, of course, permitting.

One of the best sunset sites is from the newly reopened foot-bridge, the Pont des Arts. The more animated areas for strolling include the place St-Michel, and St.-Germain-des-Prés where there are bars and the price of a drink covers musical entertainment. The Beaubourg area (the Georges Pompidou Center), is always filled with people who have come to watch the "street" entertainment: jugglers, dancers, sword-swallowers, musicians and puppeteers. Or if you have a movie in mind and want to enjoy the more fashionable cafés, the Champs-Elysées and Montparnasse are the best bet.

Paris boasts of being the film capital of the world and this may very well be true; film certainly is big business. First-run, big-budget films are fun to see in the plush, expensive theaters on and around the Champs-Elysées. But the two **very best** theater houses (for atmosphere) are **Le Grand Rex** (a definite must) at 1 boulevard Poissonnière in the second *arrondissement*, and **La Pagode**, (brought over to Paris brick by brick by an orientophile architect in 1896) at 57 bis, rue de Babylone in the seventh *arrondissement*. The more artsy films—classics, *avant-garde* and political films and little known or forgotten works—are usually shown on the side streets of the left bank.

Unfortunately in this city one pays to play. It's quite expensive doing the things everyone wants to do in Paris. The opera, theater, concerts, clubs and *grand spectacles* demand steep entry fees, but ticket agencies handle discounted tickets and publish, monthly, lists of plays, concerts and festivals for which these tickets may be obtained. One such agency is a student organization called **COPAR**, at 39 avenue Georges Bernanos in the fifth *arrondissement* (tel: 43.25.12.43). Another useful agency is **Alpha FNAC: Spectacles** at 136 rue de Rennes in the sixth *arrondissement* (tel: 45.44.39.12) and located strategically elsewhere throughout the city. These organizations have special discount cards enabling up to 40 percent discount on classical music and theater tickets.

Paris is no more dangerous than any other large city, and if you stay around the more animated areas there are usually enough policemen to ward off trouble. Nevertheless, keep a firm hold on your bag and tuck away that wallet. Remember, too, that the métro stops around 12:45 a.m. but cabs are usually no problem unless it's raining. If you're lucky enough to have a car, or know someone who does (or if you have unlimited funds and can afford a taxi)

ceding ges: ntpar- sse at ht. **Left**, nset ngs new to Paris d the ned Arc de omphe on Champs- sées. **ht**, rists oy the eets of ris.

drive up and down both sides of the **quais**—it's a spectacular drive! The Eiffel Tower has recently been relit and it's more beautiful than ever. It really is difficult to list and describe everything available to do and see in Paris. The selected information here should make your choices easier. And to all...a good night!

Jazz clubs: Jazz lovers rejoice! Rumor has it that Paris is, once again, in the throes of the long awaited jazz revival. Be it bop, free jazz and fusion, or New Orleans, Dixieland and swing, the Parisians are determined to re-establish Paris as the jazz capital of the world. Here is a look at the very best of new and old jazz clubs in the city.

New Morning, 7-9 rue des Petites Ecuries, 10th *arrondissement*; (tel: 45.23.51.41). Open from 9 p.m. to 2 a.m. The music gets going around an hour or so after the club opens, but arrive early to ensure a good seat. Sounds are not limited to jazz and programs include bop, fusion, Latin, folk and blues. Anybody who is anybody in the business has played the New Morning including Dizzy Gillespie, Richie Havens, Taj Mahal, Celia Cruz, Wayne Shorter, Stan Getz, Stanley Jordan, and Prince who jammed with his father, John Nelson. Fortunately the club is quite large—it seats 400 but handles 600 when necessary. The décor is pretty sad however, the acoustics are great!

Le Bilboquet, 13 rue St.-Benoit, 6th *arrondissement* (tel: 45.48.81.84). Open from 7:30 p.m. to 3 a.m., jazz after 10:45 p.m. It is a stylish, chic, and good place to hear good jazz. It's above the Club St.-Germain-des-Prés, and draws a rather stylish group, including French filmstars. An added plus, Le Bilboquet serves great food but beware! The 120 seats are quickly filled.

Bar Lionel Hampton, in the Hôtel Méridien, 81 boulevard Gouvion-St.-Cyr, 17th *arrondissement* (tel: 47.58.12.30) this bar is open daily, with jazz after 10 p.m. Situated on the main floor of the hotel, the room holds sev-

Dining out, a favorite nighttime activity in Paris.

eral hundred easily. Regular appearances by the likes of Cab Calloway and Memphis Slim help to make the Méridien a jazz spot with top-notch music. Still another way to enjoy your jazz—with brunch at the hotel every Sunday.

Caveau de la Huchette, 5 rue de la Huchette, 5th *arrondissement* (tel: 43.26.65.05). Open from 9:30 p.m. to 2:30 a.m. daily except Fridays from 9:30 p.m. to 3 a.m. and Saturdays and holidays from 9:30 p.m. to 4 a.m. Caveau de la Huchette is best described as everything everyone has ever imagined an old jazz club to be. With very few changes it retains the same look it had in the 1500s when it was a secret meeting place for religious groups. Once considered the center of Paris jazz life, now the jazz here is mostly New Orleans played by European bands. Although no longer the hot spot of yesterday, it is definitely a place to see.

ving
food
il 2 a.m.

Le Petit Journal, 71 boulevard St.-Michel, 5th *arrondissement* (tel: 43.26.28.59). Open from 8:30 p.m. to 2 a.m., except Sundays.

Le Petit Journal Montparnasse, 13 rue du Commandant-Mouchotte, 14th *arrondissement* (tel: 43.21.56.70). Open from 8:30 p.m. to 2 a.m., except Sundays. The Le Petits bear the same name but play two different beats. Le Petit Journal is strictly Dixieland and the atmosphere is good time fun with hand clapping and singing. Le Petit Journal Montparnasse, on the other hand, caters more to modern musicians which include performances by Herbie Hancock, Art Blakey, Dexter Gordon and the legendary Stéphane Grappelli. Both places serve dinner and the *pot-au-feu* is highly recommended.

Le Petit Opportun, 15 rue des Lavandières-St.-Opportune, lst *arrondissement* (tel: 42.36.01.36). Open from 11 p.m. to 3 a.m. This club is the cream of the crop, so arrive early as there are only 60 seats. The program changes every week, maintaining a wide repertoire from bop on. If you get

hungry, try the one and only thing on the menu—a delicious club sandwich.

Magnetic Terrace, 12 rue de la Cossonerie, lst *arrondissement* (tel: 42.36.26.44). Open from 11 a.m. to 2 a.m. Brand new and already regarded as a "serious music club," it should not be missed. A recently converted Catholic church, the décor is brilliant! On the ground floor is a remarkably good restaurant, and downstairs, the stunning, multi-arched, white stone cellar. The Terrace's good music gets better and better as word gets around.

Discos and rock clubs: Parisians tend to dress up for a night on the town, so keep that in mind before setting out. Many of the clubs are private, which means they have the final say on who gets "in." So don't panic when you can't find the doorknob. Instead, act cool, casual and important because somebody is watching through a peephole deciding whether or not the person seeking entry is cool, casual and important enough. If you're lucky to pass through, get ready to spend. Most clubs are expensive and prices start at 75 francs and go up to 100 or 200 francs for admission and drinks. Some clubs have restaurants and live music. The food is rarely great, but it's the atmosphere and who's who in the club that count. It's difficult to say which are the more "happening" places, as the "in" clubs change drastically from year to year. But those listed are certainly some of the most popular.

ft, evening
ise by
re Dame.
ow, high
hion
gns.

La Locomotive, 90 boulevard de Clichy, 18th *arrondissement* (tel: 42.57.37.37). Open from 11 p.m. to 5:30 a.m. Cover charge is moderate on weekdays, more on weekends. It has three levels, live music every night, a video room, two separate discos and two bars with each room in a different 'flavor'. It is a great place and more fun when you go with small group.

Le Palace, 8 rue du Faubourg-Montmartre, 9th *arrondissement* (tel: 42.46.10.87). Open from 11 p.m. to dawn. Prices are average but higher after midnight and on weekends. Le Palace also has three levels, occasional live music, a projection room, two dance-floors and two bars. One of the most famous clubs in Paris, its Hollywood theme makes for fabulous décor. A different soirée is discovered almost nightly. Some evenings are more private than others but with patience, entry is usually possible. Restaurant le Privilège is located below the club and reservations can be made by calling 45.23.44.62. The restaurant features a fabulous décor, famous personalities and models. After 3 a.m. the restaurant becomes the more private Kit Kat Club.

Les Bains Douches, 7 rue de Bourg l'Abée, 3rd *arrondissement* (tel: 48.87.01.80). Open daily from midnight to 5 a.m. except on Mondays. This club is very expensive and very exclusive. A good way to get in is to dine at the restaurant first. Reservations are made with the same telephone number; and dinner is served from 9 p.m. Turn-of-the-century façade conceals what used to be municipal showers. With good music, two bars and occasional live music, the place attracts an incredible number of American models. It's very "hip" and very "fashionable" here. Consider wearing leather.

Le Balajo, 9 rue de Lappe, 11th *arrondissement* (tel: 47.00.07.87). Open from 11 p.m. to 5 a.m. Le Balajo is inexpensive, yet authentic and very popular. It's one of the rare clubs that open on Mondays. Dance to rumba, java, salsa, rhythm and blues, and rock and roll from the 50s, 60s and 70s.

La Nouvelle Eve, 25 rue Fontaine, 9th *arrondissement* (tel: 48.74.69.25). Open from 1 a.m. to 5 a.m. There is lots of red velvet in this very expensive joint. Weekends are best if you want to mingle with a more French crowd, otherwise don't bother bringing the French dictionary. All types, with a tendency to dress "retro," mix here.

La Scala, 188 bis, rue de Rivoli, lst *arrondissement* (tel: 42.61.64.00). Open from 10:30 p.m. to 6 a.m. It's an inexpensive (free-for-women) place except on Fridays. Three balconies, five bars, a giant video screen, three dance floors and a crazy décor. A rather young crowd patronize La Scala, and while not the most exciting night club, it's worth seeing.

Le Garage, 41 rue Washington, 8th *arrondissement* (tel: 45.63.21.27). Open from 11 p.m. to 6 a.m. This club is fairly expensive but cover charge includes a drink. It's frequented by limousines and sports cars, so once again, think about reserving ahead for dinner. Restaurant La Tonnelle can be reached at the same number. Le Garage offers a light show to various music sounds, and no one seems to mind if the technical timing is at times imperfect.

5th Avenue, 2 avenue Foch, 16th *arrondissement* (tel: 45.00.00.13). Open from 11 p.m. to 6 a.m. An expensive joint with two bars and three dance-floors. The place is frequented by professional dancers doing their stint in the Cabaret. Be in the mood for the tango and bossa nova. If you stick around

Champs-Elysées at night.

until the morning hours, a free buffet is served.

Bars: Bars are becoming more and more popular in Paris, especially with the recent emergence of the American bar. For the visitor and resident, they offer an atmosphere much sought after—warm and relaxed good fun. There are many to choose from, and with the possibility of piano bars and bar-restaurants, an entire evening can be enjoyed at one address.

La Closerie Des Lilas, 171 boulevard du Montparnasse, 6th *arrondissement* (tel: 43.54.21.68). Open from 10 a.m. to 2 a.m. A favorite place to meet before or after dinner, this piano bar is very fashionable as well as extremely beautiful with a large selection of excellent drinks.

Pub St.-Germain-des-Prés, 17 rue de l' Ancienne Comédie, 6th *arrondissement* (tel: 43.29.38.70). Open 24 hours daily. One of the largest pubs in Europe with seven rooms, it offers a vast selection of spirits, 450 types of bottled beer and 24 on tap. Downstairs is more fun. While you have drinks and ice cream you can listen to the nostalgic musical program.

Café Pacifico, 50 boulevard du Montparnasse, 6th *arrondissement* (tel: 45.48.63.87). Open Tuesdays to Sundays from noon to 2 a.m., Mondays from 3 p.m. to 2 a.m. An extremely successful bar-restaurant, the café is usually filled with lots of Americans and the younger French set. Happy hour is made happier with drinks at half-price between 6 p.m. and 7 p.m.

La Rhumerie, 166 boulevard St.-Germain, 6th *arrondissement* (tel: 43.54.28.94). Open daily from 11 a.m. to 3 a.m. La Rhumerie is so popular it's usually hard to find a seat. Enjoy a superb daiquiris with the St.-Germain evening scene floating before you.

Harry's New York Bar, 5 rue Daunou, 2nd *arrondissement* (tel: 42.61.71.14). Open from 11 a.m. to 4 a.m. Usually crowded and hot upstairs, relief can be found downstairs where a

**ists
play
ir works
lace Du
tre.**

new air conditioning system has been mercifully installed. Lots of yuppies congregate here, listening to really good piano by house regulars.

Hotel Plaza-Athénée, 25 avenue Montaigne, 8th *arrondissement* (tel: 47.23.78.33). Open from 11 p.m. The classical English bar, this is a jacket-and-tie kind of place. Try the house special "cocktail rose baccarat"—a raspberry-champagne delight.

Le Jules-Verne, Tour Eiffel, 7th *arrondissement* (tel: 45.55.61.44). Open from 7:30 p.m. to 11 p.m. Experience Paris at your feet from the second level of the Eiffel Tower. Le Jules-Verne is truly exceptional—class, elegant; everything here is perfect. Of course, it's expensive! Just consider it a rare treat that will be long remembered. (Remember to make reservations.)

For men only: Le Sept, 7 rue Ste.-Anne, 1st *arrondissement* (tel: 42.96.25.82). Open 11 p.m. to 5 a.m., disco after midnight, closed on Tuesdays. Le Sept is very well-known, and popular. Be prepared for a crowd.

The Broad, 3-5 rue de la Ferronnerie, 1st *arrondissement* (tel: 42.36.59.73). Open from 11 p.m. to 5 a.m., closed on Mondays. The extraordinary disco packs them in.

For women: Katmandu, 21 rue du Vieux-Colombier, 6th *arrondissement* (tel: 45.48.12.96). Open from 11 p.m. to 5 a.m. This is a chic bar that admits men in addition to the female clientele.

Elle et Lui, 31 rue Vavin, 6th *arrondissement* (tel: 43.26.66.33). Open Sept. to July from 10:30 p.m. to 3:30 a.m. Occasional shows.

Glitter galore: Among the package-tour set, Paris is famous for the Vegas-styled *spectacles*; with lots of brass, bounce and skin. Mostly catering to instamatic camera-toting tourists that arrive by busloads, admission fees are steep. A word of advice; skip the dinner-shows as the food is usually cafeteria standard and outrageously expensive. The best bet is to call ahead, asking different showtimes available, prices

Floor show at the Paradis Latin.

and programs for the current "season."

Folies Bergére, 32 rue Richer, 9th *arrondissement* (tel: 42.46.77.11).

Moulin Rouge, place Blanche, 9th *arrondissement* (tel: 46.06.00.19).

Crazy Horse, 12 avenue George V, 8th *arrondissement* (tel: 47.23.32.32).

Lido, 116 Champs-Elysées, 8th *arrondissement* (tel: 45.63.11.61).

Alcazar, 62 rue Mazarine, 6th *arrondissement* (tel: 43.29.02.20).

Concert and music halls: The French, and particularly Parisians, simply adore music. All types. Fortunately, Paris has a large selection of concert and music halls to choose from. Be it a concert at the **Palais Omnisports de Paris-Bercy** (seating capacity 12,000) or something more intimate at Le Rex Club (seating capacity 550), buy tickets in advance as sell-outs are quite frequent.

L'Olympia, 28 boulevard des Capucines, 9th *arrondissement* (tel: 47.42.25.49). Seating capacity 2,250. Mention the Olympia, and everyone always says: "It's the only true music hall in Paris." It's comfortable, and the acoustics are excellent. This classic hall has attracted the *creme-de-la-creme*, such as Piaf, Brel, Liza Minnelli, the Beatles and Samy Davis Jr.

Le Grand Rex, 1 boulevard Poissonnière, 2nd *arrondissement* (tel: 42.36.83.93). Seating capacity 2,800. Le Grand Rex is a dream come true, not only for its maximal comfort, perfect visibility and superior acoustics, but also for it's unique décor. Once seated, look carefully around...and up, enchanted. The biggest names in jazz and rock have performed here, but the good news is that Le Grand Rex is also a cinema giving everyone a double reason to enjoy this address.

Le Rex Club, 5 boulevard Poissonnière, 2nd *arrondissement* (tel: 42.36.83.98). Seating capacity 550. It's a little on the somber side, but the atmosphere remains warm—probably due to the "hot" rock bands that play here. The sound system isn't always

hestre
Paris.

top-notch, but it remains a good place to have a drink and hear good music.,

Le Zenith, 211 avenue Jean-Jaurés, 19th *arrondissement* (tel: 42.08.60.00). Seating capacity 3,700 to 6,300. Very modern, very functional with no problems whatsoever with visibility and acoustics. However, getting there isn't very convenient and the seats aren't numbered—meaning, get there at least an hour before the concert is scheduled to begin.

Palais des Sports, 1 place de la Porte-de-Versailles, 15th *arrondissement* (tel: 48.28.40.48). Seating capacity 4,500. Although no longer the biggest "space" in Paris for entertainment, it has remained since opening in the early 1960s an ideal place to enjoy the bigger *spectacles*. Acoustics—once a problem—are now excellent and visibility is good.

Unfortunately, it's not very comfortable. Entertainment programs vary from *Holiday On Ice*, to the *Moscow Circus*. You can, however, see current music superstars, Jean-Jacques Goldman and Jeanne Mas.

Palais Omnisports de Paris-Bercy, 2 boulevard de Bercy, 12th *arrondissement* (tel: 43.41.72.04). Seating capacity 12,000. As well as being an international sports center, this gigantic space is the site reserved for those *spectacles* and musical programs that draw in the masses. International superstars such as Prince, Stevie Wonder, The Cure, Liza Minnelli, Bob Dylan and Johnny Hallyday manage to pack full houses with little effort.

Bataclan, 5 boulevard Voltaire, 11th *arrondissement* (tel: 47.00.30.12). Seating capacity 1,300. Constructed at the end of the last century, the Bataclan was remodeled around 1950. The outside of the hall remains more or less in its original form—Chinese pagoda-style, very popular at the turn of the century. Inside is a totally different story: vast murals depicting an atmosphere very gay and very French help to make this address one of the more fun

The Conciergeri

places to hear a concert or see a show. It's definitely a place to discover!

Folies Pigalle, 11 place Pigalle, 9th *arrondissement* (tel: 48.78.25.56). Seating capacity 300. Small and cozy, this is an old striptease club turned music hall. The décor (very 1950s) is delightful, with many golden Venuses and lots of beveled glass. New owners are determined to make the place a hot spot with promises of good music (rock and variety) nightly.

La Cigale, 120 boulevard Rochechouart, 18th *arrondissement* (tel: 42.23.38.00). Seating capicity 1,500. This ancient cinema house is becoming more and more popular for shows and concerts. The owners have recently added a comfortable bar which offers mostly rock—with the French groups **les Rita Mitsouko** and **les Visiteurs**—good fun.

Pleyel, 252 rue du Faubourg-St.-Honoré, 8th *arrondissement* (tel: 45.63.88.73). Seating capacity: Grande Salle—2,300; Salle Chopin Pleyel—400. The Pleyel has celebrated it's 60th birthday and is still going strong with a fabulous program of concerts, recitals, expositions and workshops including music, song and dance. It is also where the **Orchestre de Paris** gives two or three concerts weekly (on Wednesdays and Thursdays). Despite recent renovation, the acoustics remain a bit "dry"—satisfactory for symphonic sounds but less than desirable for instrumental soloists. The smaller Salle Chopin Pleyel is essentially used for chamber music. Both *salles* are very comfortable, however, and offer a wide variety of top quality performances.

de
mphe.

Théâtre des Champs-Elysées, 15 avenue Montaigne, 8th *arrondissement* (tel: 47.20.36.37). Seating capacity 1,900. Looking brand new and beautiful (very recent renovation) their program includes multiple spectacles and concerts. The acoustics are remarkable and visitors are rarely disappointed by whatever's "on."

Other nightlife: A ride on the **Bateaux-Mouches** (day or night) can be fun. At night, spotlights attached to the side of the boat light up the buildings and landmarks not already illuminated. The boat tours are usually given in three languages—German, English and of course, French. Prices are generally the same from any of the many available starting points, and the trip is one of the best deals tourists get here. Boats leave 8:30 a.m. to 10 p.m. every half hour with each trip lasting an hour. There are breakfast and dinner cruises at 200 to 400 francs per person and proper attire is required. (For information call 42.25.96.10.)

Of course, you will want to explore "*Paris By Night*"; the expression is used so often it's almost a cliché for adventure under city lights.

A drive or stroll along the riverbanks or a ride aboard a *bateau mouche* should find a place in everyone's night-time agenda. Then, let your own personal style guide you as you choose a nocturnal destination.

Feuilleté
Praline Royal
LES GALETTES
DE PONT-AVEN
TRAOU
MAD
de PONT-AVEN
Delacre
Tradition
Delacre
Cigarettes Russes
& Tuiles
galettes
bretonnes
tout au beurre

A WORD ON DINING

The revered French *gastronome* Brillat Savarin summed up the experience of fine dining as, simply, bliss. Though many things in France have changed since his *Physiologie du goût* was published in 1826, enthusiasm for food has remained as strong as ever.

Traditions have vanished and fads have come and gone but French cooking has always been marked by its use of a rich variety of the freshest ingredients carefully prepared, and its punctilious rituals of service and protocol. Serious eaters will have no trouble satisfying their longings for these qualities during their stay in Paris, but fast food lovers can have their steak and eat it too, French style.

On a busy schedule: Breakfast fans had best content themselves with the standard *café au lait-croissant*. It's tasty though not copious, and when lunchtime rolls around, you'll be ready for the main meal of the day.

The bottom line of prepared food in Paris (excluding hamburger spin-offs) is the Greek street-sandwich, especially popular in the Latin Quarter, and not recommended for stomachs over 25. Some bakeries sell a milder version, on sliced bread, with more wholesome fillings. In a *traiteur* or *charcuterie* shop, a wide selection of enticing goodies may tempt you to picnic or eat on the run: cold meat, fish and vegetable salads, cold cuts, eggs in aspic, sausage in pastry and slices of *quiche* are just a few of the treats you'll find.

In restaurants, lunch is usually served between 12:30 p.m. and 2 p.m., and dinner after 7:30 p.m. You can get around these hours by eating in a *café-brasserie*, which offers sandwiches made with crusty *baguettes* and hot dishes like *steak-frites*, hot dogs and *croque monsieur* (toasted ham and cheese). They are open at all hours—but don't expect miracles.

In the middle of a busy day, it's easy enough to look around the neighborhood for one of the innumerable cafés, bistros, brasseries or restaurants that offer one or several menus at a fixed price. These may range from 60 to 175 francs per person, and may or may not include three courses, wine and service. One of the most popular and well-known restaurants in this category is **Chartier** (rue Faubourg Montmartre, near the Opéra)—very French, very busy and very moderately priced. The gay 1890s decor includes hundreds of little drawers set in the walls. They were previously used to hold regular guests' weekly napkins.

Of course, quality varies a lot. Let your nose guide you, or have a look at what other patrons are eating. If a smallish place has too many items on the menu, it's a good guess they've been prepared elsewhere and delivered by refrigerated truck, heaven knows how long ago. Stick with a *plat du jour* (daily special), grilled meat or roast chicken.

The best brasseries: Working conditions have somewhat gnawed away at the French custom of the two-hour lunch, followed by a lighter meal or supper later in the evening. But many of the finer class of brasseries, like **Bofinger** (near the Bastille, with an appealing *art nouveau* decor), **Flo** (hidden away in a busy downtown neighborhood in the 10th district, with turn-of-the-century ambience), or **Lipp** (at St.-Germain-des-Prés, famed hangout of the literary and political crowds) still cater to midday guests with hearty appetites and time of their own. Traditional French fare (including fine seafood and Alsatian specialties) is served with deference and care, at around 200 francs per person, with wine. Other brasseries in this class are the **Coupole**, **Julien** and **Terminus Nord**. Brasseries are a typically Parisian eating experience not to be missed, both for the cuisine and the *atmosphère*.

From the delicious to the sublime: Technically, a brasserie is a place

eceding ges: rusing the ny varied oices of ench isine. **ft**, bakery lights.

which serves drinks and cold or quickly prepared dishes, whereas a restaurant is simply "a place where meals are served in exchange for money." Though many restaurants in Paris meet little more than this criterion, some far exceed the basic requirement.

La novelle cuisine has made its mark, and it is rare to eat more than four courses at one sitting these days, but a complete meal still has a number of elements, which follow each other in an imperial order. First comes the *entrée*, or starter; then a meat, poultry or fish dish accompanied by a vegetable; a salad, cheese, fruit and dessert (fabulous pastries, pies, cakes, ices, meringues, creams and sweets—impossible to sample them all—then coffee and to top off the meal a *digestif* liqueur is served after all that.

French cheese is justly praised around the world for its quality and variety—there are over 400 types. Often, a waiter brings the cheeseboard to the table and diners make their own selection. Don't hesitate to sample several right away, for according to French gastronomic custom, the cheese board is never passed twice.

Paris has several fine restaurants with a reputation built on a year-round availability of fresh oysters, seafood and fish (with a few mainstay dishes available as well, like *coq au vin*, veal in creamy mushroom sauce, and the reliable *bifteck*—if you like it well-done, be sure to say so). Try **Charlot Roi des Coquillages** (place Clichy) or the **Pied de Cochon** (rue Coquillere, near Les Halles). *Passion* magazine calls the latter, with round-the-clock service, "a monument to Paris nightlife." Seafood lovers won't resist once they've seen the fresh, iced, *fruits de mer* enticingly displayed along the sidewalk terrace, bringing a breath of sea air to the city.

Some Parisian restaurants have become historical as well as gourmet landmarks. The **Procope** (near Odéon) reports that Benjamin Franklin ate

Celebrated Chef Paul Bocuse.

there, while the **Closerie des Lilas** was Ernest Hemmingway's preferred spot. **Laperouse** (quai des Grands-Augustins), open since 1768, has an authentic Louis XVI decor, and offers intimate dining rooms for two.

At the upper end of the scale are restaurants like **Maxim's**, **La Tour d'Argent**, **Taillevent** and **Lasserre**. Here, the food is prepared with a passion and science unknown elsewhere in the world, served with perfect discretion, and as the definition says, exchanged for (a great deal of) money.

Dining in one of these restaurants is certainly an unforgettable experience for visitors. The price of the exquisite attention, fancy cutlery, and perfect wine, however, may be more than some budgets can handle. There are many fine restaurants in the moderate price range where the chef's specialties are devine and the wines are well-chosen and affordable.

Orient express: Parisians themselves enjoy trying the hundreds of foreign restaurants in their city. Chinese and Vietnamese food are widely available and inexpensive; Tunisian, Moroccan or Algerian *cous-cous* restaurants are also popular. Italian and American or British restaurants are mostly in the moderate price range, along with a number of Indian, Russian and Latin varieties—you name it! Any weekly entertainment magazine will carry a list of restaurants with average prices and phone numbers. Do call ahead if you've selected a restaurant you want to try, to make sure they're open (especially on Sunday and Monday) and to get a reservation if you don't like waiting.

If you have the good fortune to be invited into a Parisian home for dinner, plan to arrive around 8 p.m. and dress well as a compliment to your host. It is customary to offer flowers or sweets.

Whether your style is a jug of wine and a loaf of bread or exquisite creations served with full ceremony, Paris offers the world's finest dining. Only don't forget to leave room for dessert!

sh
food
ounds.
lowing
ges:
net's
den in
erny;
artres
thedral.

DAY TRIPS

Any visitor to Paris will want to make an excursion out of town. Even the shortest trip should include a visit beyond the city limits. During a quick half day in Versailles, or a weekend in the Loire Valley, learn French history; see the countryside unfold gracefully and quietly, leaving the wild and wicked metropolis behind.

A subway ride to **Sevres** leaves you with only a bridge to cross over to the left bank, where a wooded park along the Seine has been home to the **Porcelaine de Sevres** ceramics workshops for over 200 years. **Le Musée de la Céramique** is set at the foot of a hill that rises another 7 miles (11.5 km) to the **Terrace de Meudon**. The Château and terrace were built in the 17th century, and part of the surrounding forest is now occupied by National Observatory instruments and offices. On a clear and cloudless day, sunlight dapples through the bright leaves and settles like gold dust on the city of Paris below in the distance.

Saint Denis Cathedral is less than 3 miles (4 km) outside of Paris, and the *métro* takes you right there. Recent urban sprawl has crept in around it, but the Cathedral is revered as an early masterpiece of Gothic architecture, it is also a favored final resting place of France's kings and queens. The renaissance and medieval sculptures which mark their tombs are some of the finest in France.

An RER line will bring you to **Saint-Germain-en-Laye**, for centuries a royal retreat and now a wealthy bourgeois surburb. The Château, which still has a lovely Gothic chapel, was largely reconstructed under François I (his royal salamander and "F" can be seen in the courtyard) and again in the 19th century. Inside, you won't find any period furnishings or portraits, but rather a museum devoted to prehistoric

and medieval times. The Gallo-Roman collection and the lifesized replica of the Lascaux cave drawings are favorite exhibits. The terrace gardens overlooking the Seine were designed by Le Nôtre, and later inspired impressionist painter Alfred Sisley.

Let them eat cake: Historians debate whether or not Marie Antoinette actually gave that advice to the starving population, clamoring for bread. But any visitor to **Versailles** will certainly be struck by the notion that so much splendor, now freely admired by millions, was once the exclusive domain of a monarch and his court. Louis XIV ordered the transformation of the simple Château into a glittering jewel; the magnificent gardens were laid out and decorated with statuary.

In the form of a *fleur-de-lys* (symbol of royalty), the **Grand Canal** stretches out from the foot of the terrace steps, dividing the wooded park in two. Seen from the far end of the canal, the palace appears to float on the breeze, bouyed up by the fluffy mass of trees on either side, as the bright windows and gilded ornaments wink and glimmer in the sunlight. Be warned before you set out, however, that the canal first appears foreshortened by a trick of perspective, and it is nearly 3 miles (5 km) down and back!

The two sides of the park, with the fantastic chariot and horses rearing out of the waters of **Apollo's Pool** between them, are studded with delightful groves, goldfish ponds, blooming flowerbeds, bushes, exotic, ancient trees and velvet green lawns. There are so many fountains, it's impossible to keep them going all the time, but the first and third Sundays of the month, June through September, a glorious show begins at 4:30 in the afternoon.

Inside, from the king's apartments (his bedroom set in the exact center of the symmetrical palace) to the long **Galerie des Glaces**, whose mirrors reflect the French windows open to the terrace and park, it is an unequaled display of wealth and privilege. And when the palace was too busy, or the constant problem of backed-up sewage made it too smelly, Louis could head off to one of the **Trianons** (either Grand or Petit), while Marie Antoinette was content playing milkmaid at the **Hameau**, a make-believe farm.

On the banks of the Eure: Seen from the distance, the two spires of **Chartres Cathedral** soar above the surrounding fields in majestic homage. They rose up over 30 years at the turn of the 12th-13th centuries, and have since remained, drawing pilgrims and travelers from around the world. The famous **Rose Windows** fill with light and pattern the cathedral with changing colors. Traces of an ancient maze mark the floor, said to be an echo of pre-christian religious practices. Penitents and pilgrims followed its paths on their knees to reach the altar.

Below, is a 9th-11th century crypt (guided tours only); and above, the view over the rich plain is exhilarating.

ceding ges: ambord vel in night. ft, the ndeur of Palace of rsailles.

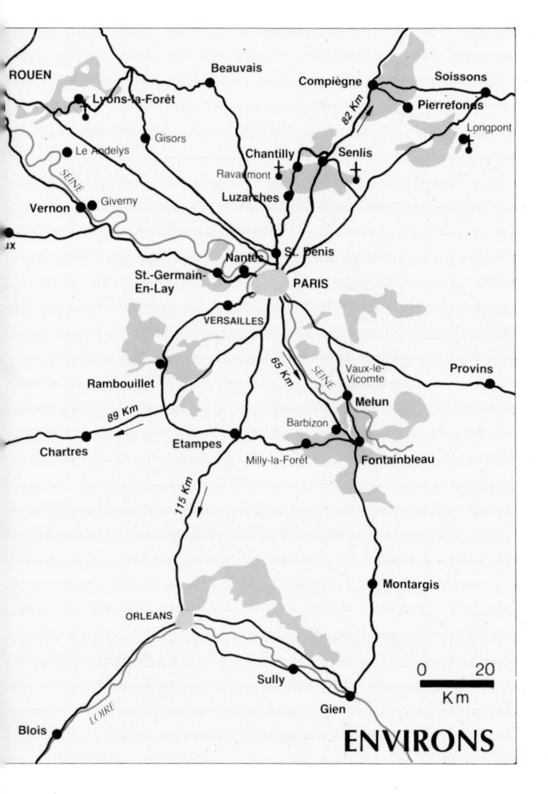

The town itself provides a precious glimpse of French life "in the provinces." As you wind through the city's oldest quarters, you can easily forget that Paris is only an hour's train ride away. It isn't hard to find a bakery you will never forget or a cheese shop with more varieties than you can imagine.

Along the river banks, a path passes by typical countryside *lavoirs*, where you can almost hear the laughter of the laundresses splashing linen in the water. Continue on the promenade along the quaint streets, past the **Église St.-Pierre**, to the remains of the old city wall, which for centuries protected the aristocracy of Blois and Champagne.

Royal options: There are other sumptuous palaces to visit on an excursion from Paris. **Chantilly** nestles in a grove in the forest of the same name. Wild ducks settle in the moat around the fairytale castle, with white walls mounting to a slate-blue roof. Inside, the Conde Museum's collection of Boticelli, Raphael, Giotto and Holbein paintings will amaze you.

Near Melun, **Vaux-le-Vicomte** was the inspiration for Versailles, built by Louis XIV's Royal Treasurer, Nicolas Fouquet. A devoted patron of the arts, Fouquet built an impeccable house and garden *à la française,* but his own good taste defeated him. Jealous advisors whispered to the King that Fouquet had paid for the dream with treasury funds. The hapless dilettante was imprisoned at Vincennes and Louis set out to build something even more splendid, using the same architect and designers.

The Château, its grounds and furnishings make for an interesting visit. One room traces the histories of its various owners, others are decorated in period style, with coffered, painted ceilings and Gobelins tapestries for decoration. The kitchen is equipped with a battery of shiny brass pots and pans, and different objects used for preparing cheeses, preserving meats, and keeping the flies away! For a real treat, take the candlelight tour, given

King of the forest.

every Saturday evening, June through September, and watch the castle glow with vanished glory.

Forestlands: All around Paris, thick forests help maintain the temperate, humid climate, releasing their morning mists into the country air. To the northeast, the town of **Compiégne** sits between the Oise River and the **Forest**, one of the largest in France. The **Hôtel de Ville** in the center of town boasts the oldest bell in France in its clock tower, where little figures known as *picantins* strike the hour. The ruins of the **Saint Corneille Abbey** are in the historic zone, where the pedestrian streets make restaurant-shopping a pleasure.

There are a number of things to see in the Forest. On foot, head for **Les Beaux Monts** for a view over the Château and the Oise, under a canopy of stately trees. SNCF buses service the **Armistice Clearing**, where you can visit the railroad car used for the signing of the 1918 Armistice between France and Germany. A compact, unique museum is devoted to World War I: hundreds of photos of life in the trenches and on the different fronts are set up on flip cards and can be viewed through stereoscopes. This fascinating collection makes an eloquent statement on a tragic and terrible conflict.

In a car, head for the village of **Vieux Moulin** and the **Étangs de St.-Pierre**, the favorite fishing hole of Napoléon's wife, the Empress Eugenie. The couple also had an unusual hunting palace nearby, the **Château de Pierrefonds**. Entirely reconstructed in the 19th century, in idealized medieval style by Violet-le-Duc, it is truly an architectural oddity.

The **Fontainebleau Forest**, once a royal hunting ground, is now used by rock climbers in training and mushroom hunters at work. The Château dominates the town, with its sprawling, eclectic buildings. Every king from the 12th century onwards seems to have added his own touch to the palace: François I was responsible for the best

ntainbleau a crisp rning.

of it, and Napoléon I had a throne room built for himself.

Visitors who want to see something off the ordinary tourist itinerary should head for the **Forêt de Lyons**. The centennial beech trees are thin and tall, letting the sunlight through, making a tour a special pleasure. There are fine views over bucolic villages with the typical look of Normandy about them and pretty half-timber façades set off by potted geraniums in the windows.

A poet, a painter: Another out-of-the-way spot is **Milly-La-Forêt**, not far from Fontainebleau. The massive covered **Marketplace** has been standing since 1479, and is the village's centerpiece.

Just outside lies the **Chapelle Saint Blaise**, the only remains of a 12th-century leprosarium, redecorated by the artist Jean Cocteau in 1958. Medicinal herbs and flowers have been grown traditionally in this area, and you won't want to leave without a packet of *Menthe de Milly* bonbons.

Along the Seine River west of Paris, **Giverny**, home of painter Claude Monet, is set on a hillside. His gardens are living works of art in themselves, from which he clearly drew inspiration. The bright contrasts of green foliage and luminous flowers, the Japanese bridge, the waterlilies, the willow and the pond—many of his favorite subjects are still growing. His house is also an explosion of colors. The dining room is shocking yellow, priceless china plates line the walls. Japanese prints from his large collection are displayed all over.

All of the noble forests of the Ile-de-France and surrounding regions are well worth the tour. SNCF trains are generally quite convenient and on arrival at the station, you will find a number of services, including maps and information on tourist sights, hotels, restaurants and taxis. In Compiègne and Fontainebleau, tour buses are frequently scheduled for trips into town or through the countryside. From June through September, the SNCF runs a bike rental service. This is the best way to visit Monet's house or the Lyons Forest.

If you rent a car, take to the back roads and your wanderings will certainly lead you to quaint old *auberges* where you can enjoy a hearty evening meal by the fire or lunch on a terrace overlooking a river. Some out-of-the-way villages have lovely shops and restaurants, and you can easily find out about the surrounding local attractions—natural sites, old abbeys, or archeological activities.

A long weekend: Take a weekend away from the city, and you may feel like you extended your trip by a week. Time expands in the rolling countryside along the Loire River. **Gien** is only about 100 miles (160 km) from Paris, due south of Fontainebleau, but worlds apart in temperament. This pretty little town is the gateway to the **Loire Valley Châteaux**. The bridge, castle, cloisters and church date from the 15th century. The town is also the home of the

t,
:teau's
pel and
ıb. Right,
ıging
ne the
ad.

Faïencerie de Gien ceramics works. The outlet shop has great bargains on end-of-stock items, handpainted in the typical colors and patterns that have brought them such renown.

The château, successfully restored in the regional style of patterned brickwork, now houses a hunting museum. In the summer, the lively streets are festooned with pennants and flags and the market is busy. On the hills bordering the Loire River, a few vineyards still remain to produce the local Côtes de Gien wines, red, rosé and white. These little-known wines, though less sumptuous than their cousins from Pouilly-sur-Loire and Sancerre, are especially good with the regional cuisine, and quite reasonably priced.

Just downstream, **Sully-sur-Loire Castle** seems to drift along with the ducks and swans around it. It has two distinct parts: an early 14th-century defensive fortress, and a 17th-century pleasure palace added on by Sully, finance minister to Henry IV. In the older section, a high, keel-shaped timber roof made of huge chestnut tree trunks is 600 years old. In the newer wing, beams are hidden by delicately painted coffered ceilings.

Nearby, **Orléans** is a busy little city with many interesting monuments and museums. Among them, the **Cathedral** and the **Maison de Jeanne d'Arc**. It was here, where the Loire leaves its northward course to flow southwest, that young Joan, the nation's most revered saint, drove the English from France. "I like the English," she is reported to have said, "in England."

Off the beaten track: The industrial city of **Rouen** was once the capital of Normandy, and despite the damage it suffered during World War I, it still has a number of Gothic churches and picturesque houses, as well as several fine museums. There Joan was burned at the stake by a tribunal of clerics in cahoots with the English. They accused her of being a witch and relapsed heretic, although her real "crimes" were courage and patriotism.

Provins lies on the opposite side of Paris, and it is the opposite of Rouen in many other ways as well. Forgotten by industry, spared by the wars, this medieval village seems to be under a spell. In ancient times it was a Roman outpost perched above the Voulzie River. In the 12th and 13th centuries, it was the powerful seat of the counts of Champagne, the third largest city in France, and an important center of trade.

That Paris is a special place is news to no one. For centuries, visitors have been drawn to the buzzing metropolis—a busy hive of artistic, scholarly, industrial and political activity. In the same way, the artists, scholars, and ordinary people who live there have always been drawn to the outlying countryside. There you will find what's missing from Paris and make your trip complete and unforgettable: the hush of the forest, the rich perfume of fields and gardens, the slow pace of life in the country, peace and inspiration.

Left, Louis XIV at Versailles. Right, Chartres rooftops. Following page: Ile St.-Louis.

TRAVEL TIPS

GETTING THERE

BY AIR

There are two international airports just outside Paris. Roissy-Charles-de-Gaulle 15 miles (23 km) north and Orly 9 miles (14 km) south. Major airlines from most capitals fly to Paris, the hub of domestic flights as well. All the usual services can be found at either airport: restaurants, cafés, public restrooms, exchange counters, rent-a-car, duty-free shops, newspaper stands, telephones, post offices and tourist information counters. After disembarkation passengers must show their passports and visas, pick up their luggage, and then go through Customs.

BY SEA

From Victoria Station in London there is a train boat/train service to Paris, day and night. Hovercrafts run from Dover and Pegwell Bay to Calais and Boulogne. Cars can be taken on all hovercraft and most ferries.

BY RAIL

Paris can be reached by train from all over continental Europe. There are six railway stations and each one is on at least two *métro* or RER lines. The name of the *métro* stop is the same as the station. There are baggage check counters *(consigne)* and coin-operated lockers *(consigne automatique)* at every station.

BY ROAD

The fastest highways to Paris are the *autoroutes,* toll roads run by private companies. There are service stations every 15 miles (25 km) or so, with gas, food, coffee and restrooms, generally open 24 hours a day. At the border, there are no special formalities for cars entering France for less than six months, but you will have to show proof of insurance. It's best to avoid confusion by presenting an international green card (ask your insurance agent) or by buying one at the border (good for eight, 15 or 30 days). For more information about driving in France, consult the transportation section.

FROM ROISSY TO PARIS

Roissy rail: Take the free shuttle bus *(navette)* from Aérogare 1, arrival level gate *(porte)* 30, Aérogare 2A gate A5, or Aérogare 2B gate B6 to the Roissy train station *(gare)*. Take the RER to M° Gare du Nord or M° Châtelet. The RER runs every 15 minutes from 5 a.m. to 11:50 p.m. (Note: the abbreviation "M°" stands for "*métro* stop").

RATP Bus 350 (to Gare du Nord, Gare de l'Est) or bus 351 (to Nation) from Aérogare 2A gate A5, Aérogare 2B gate B6, or Aérogare 1 *boutiquaire* (shops) level. They run every 15 minutes from 6 a.m. to 11:30 p.m.

Air France bus (to M° Porte Maillot) from Aérogare 2A gate A5, Aérogare 2B gate B6 or Aérogare 1 arrival level gate 34. This bus runs every 12 minutes from 6 a.m. to 11 p.m.

Taxi: This is by far the most expensive, but unquestionably the easiest solution, especially for first timers or those laden with bags or children. The price of the ride will be clearly indicated on the meter, although a supplement is usually charged for each big piece of luggage. It is customary, although not required, to tip the driver (5 to 10 francs) who can also provide a receipt *(un recu* or *une fiche)*. French cabbies are honest and the cabs comfortable.

FROM ORLY TO PARIS

RER: Take the shuttle from gate H (Orly Sud) or from arrival level gate F (Orly Ouest) to the Orly train station. The RER stops at Austerlitz, Pont St.-Michel and the Quai d'Orsay. It runs every 15 minutes, from 5:30 a.m. to 11:15 p.m.

Orlybus (to place Denfert-Rochereau) from Orly Sud gate F or Orly Ouest arrival level gate D. This bus runs every 15 minutes, from 6 a.m. to 11:30 p.m.

Air France bus (to Invalides and Gare Montparnasse) from Orly Sud gate J or Orly

Ouest arrival level gate E. It runs every 12 minutes from 6 a.m. to 11 p.m.

Taxi: More expensive, but definitely easier. The comments about cabs from Roissy also apply here.

TRAVEL ESSENTIALS

VISAS & PASSPORTS

Changes in regulations have created some confusion in recent years. EEC and American nationals are exempt from visa requirements (actually, the visa is delivered on arrival at the airport, a simple stamp), and all other nationals must apply for a visa before travelling. To do so, contact your travel agent or the nearest French Consulate or Embassy. EEC nationals may not be required to show a passport to enter the country, but it is highly advisable to carry one as the most acceptable form of identification.

MONEY MATTERS

The basic French monetary unit is the French Franc, divided into 100 centimes. Coins come in 5, 10, 20, 50 centime and 1, 2, 5, 10 franc pieces. Bills come in 20, 50, 100, 200 and 500 franc notes. The exchange rate between the dollar and the franc can vary, so be sure to check your local bank for the latest figures. Traveling with a lot of cash is never a good idea, traveler's checks (in dollars or in FF) are the best solution. Certain credit cards are accepted, especially VISA *(carte bleue or CB)*. Some places accept American Express, Carte Blanc, Diner's Club or Eurocard/Mastercharge. Always ask first if you intend to charge your purchases.

Most banks have an exchange counter *(change)*, which is open from 9 a.m. to 4 p.m. (some close for lunch). Airports, open daily from 6 a.m. to 11:30 p.m. The *bureaux de change* at train stations are open every day of the week:

Nord, 6:30 a.m.-10 p.m.
Austerlitz, 7 a.m.-9 p.m.
Montparnasse, 9 a.m.-8 p.m. (Sun., 10 a.m.-8 p.m.)
Lyon, 7 a.m.-10 p.m.
Est, 7 a.m.-9 p.m.
St.-Lazare, 7 a.m.-9 p.m.

On the Champs-Elysées the bank at number 154 (M° Charles-de-Gaulle-Etoile) is open Mon. to Fri. from 9 a.m. to 5 p.m., Sat. and Sun. from 10:30 a.m. to 6 p.m. Main post offices (but not smaller branches) will also change cash and American Express traveler's checks. Remember to bring your passport when cashing traveler's checks.

HEALTH

There are no special health warnings for visitors to Paris.

WHAT TO WEAR

Parisians like to dress well. French women wear make-up, jewelry and high-heels to the supermarket! Men almost never wear plaid and tend to dress conservatively. No one wears shorts. Sneakers and jeans, cleaned and pressed, are mainly for students. The most important consideration for the tourist, however, is comfort. Comfortable walking shoes (or lack of them) can make or break a vacation, so bring a pair of sturdy sneakers and save the heels for evenings. In winter, warm coats are a must, while in summer light jackets and sweaters will do. Spring and fall are tricky, pack a couple of sweaters and a raincoat.

CUSTOMS

In general, personal goods (including bicycles, sporting equipment and cars) are admitted duty-free and without formality as long as it is obvious that they are for personal use and not for sale (these items must be re-exported). Certain goods are strictly prohibited such as narcotics, copyright infringements, fakes and counterfeits, certain illegal alcohols and some animal products including delicatessen from Africa, Andorra or Spain. A maximum of three dogs or cats may be imported only if they are over three months of age and have an anti-rabies certificate. Gold bars, ingots or coins need au-

Various commodities	Passengers from ECC countries	Other countries
Tobacco		
Cigarettes [units]	300	*200
or cigarillos [units]	150	*100
or cigar [units]	75	*50
or smoking tobacco [grams]	400	*250
*Note this amount is double if you live outside of Europe.		
Alcohol		
Wine	5 liters	2 liters
and either		
—drinks over 38.8° Proof [22° Gay Lussac]	1.5 liters	1 liter
—or drinks 38.8° proof or under	3 liters	2 liters
Perfume	75 g	50 g
Eau de Toilette	3.8 liters	¼ liter
Coffee	1000 g	500 g
or coffee extracts	400 g	200 g
Tea	200 g	100 g

thorization from the Banque de France, but less than a pound (500 grams) of gold jewelry need not be declared. Any other gold items must be declared. Restrictions are imposed on guns and ammunition, medicines, syringes, mineral water and radio transceivers. You may not leave France with more than 12,000 FF, but you can take out the same sum or more in foreign currency if you fill in the Customs Form on arrival declaring that you possess over 12,000 FF.

The table above shows duty-free allowances that are determined by the European Economic Community, these are subject to change at short notice. Passengers under 17 are not allowed to import duty-free tobacco or alcohol.

GETTING ACQUAINTED

GOVERNMENT & ECONOMY

Paris is the capital of the democratic republic of France, and one-tenth of the nation's population lives in and around the city. It is not only the political capital, but the intellectual and economic capital as well. The process of *centralisation* began under Napoléon I, who unified national administrations, codified law, standardized language, and brought the city together under the roof of Paris. The city is still a main port, and a major industrial and commercial center. Today's politicians have proclaimed a policy of *décentralisation*, meant to restore some autonomy to France's regions and preserve their cultural heritage and linguistic characteristics, but what Napoléon wrought is not so easily set asunder.

Since 1977, Paris has an elected Mayor, who works from the *Hôtel de Ville*. He is seconded by the members of the Town Council and the Mayors of each of the 20 districts (*Conseil Municipal* and the *Maires d'Arrondissements*), all elected. In fact, each *arrondissement* has its own Town Hall *(Mairie)* and carries on the business of registering births, deaths, and various legal documents, performing marriages (in France, the civil ceremony is required and the religious ceremony optional), and, of course, hearing complaints. The most important political parties are: the *Parti Communiste Français* (PCF), and the *Parti Socialiste* (PS) on the left; the *Rassemblement pour la République* (RPR) and *the Union pour la Démoncratie Française* (UDF) on the right.

Paris is France's largest consumer market, and the focal point of all of the country's communications systems. Most local industries (the automobile industry is the largest) are in the suburbs, and many major companies have moved their headquarters outside of town to accommodate their needs for space. The service sector is developing rapidly, especially in the West, creating a transportation problem in the capital, whose labor force lives mostly in the East.

TIME ZONES

France is one hour ahead of Greenwich Mean Time, 6 hours ahead of Eastern Standard (New York) Time. The French put their clocks forward in the spring and back in the fall at about the same time as the U.S. and Britain. Time schedules use the 24-hour system, so that 1 p.m. is 13:00, 2 p.m. is 14:00 and so on.

CLIMATE

Temperate weather means average winter temperatures of 39°F (4°C); in summer the thermometer occasionally hits 86°F (30°C); spring and fall are mild with an average temperature of 52°F (11°C). June, September and October may be the ideal months for visiting, pleasant and usually sunny, but less crowded than the warmer months of July and August.

CULTURE & CUSTOMS

Tipping: By law, the waiter's tip *(le service)* is included in the bill, but it is customary to leave a little something extra, particularly for good service (from a few centimes for a coffee to 10 francs for dinner). Taxi drivers are also tipped (15 percent), as are bell-hops, porters and, surprisingly, ushers at theaters and cinemas (1 to 5 francs).

Greeting: It is considered a sign of good breeding to say hello *(bonjour, Messieursdames)* when entering and good-bye *(au revoir, Messieursdames)* when leaving a shop, restaurant or café. And smile.

Lines: Standing in what passes for a line in Paris is not often an orderly experience. Parisians don't often pay attention to who-was-there-first, so don't be shy, "when in Rome..."

WEIGHTS & MEASURES

The French use the metric system for all measurements, so this chart might prove useful:

1 kilogram = 2.2 lbs
1 oz = 28 grams
1 liter = a little over a quart
1 km = 0.62 miles
1 mile = 1.6 km
1 meter = a little over a yard
1 cm = 0.39 inches
1 inch = 2.5 cm
0° Celsius = 32° Farenheit
100° Celsius = 212° Farenheit

To convert Farenheit into Celsius, subtract 32, multiply by 5, and divide by 9. To convert Celsius into Farenheit, multiply by 9, divide by 5, and add 32.

For size conversion of clothings and shoes for men, ladies and children, refer to the conversion table on page 218.

ELECTRICITY

As a general rule, the electric current in use is 220 volts AC. If you intend to bring any electrical appliances, such as a razor, don't forget to pack the appropriate transformer. Otherwise, your appliances will be ruined if they are not correctly adapted.

BUSINESS HOURS

The one cardinal rule to remember is that small shops, particularly food stores, are closed for lunch, roughly between 1 p.m. and 4 p.m., each having chosen its own fantastically conceived hour (or two or three). If a holiday falls on Mon., Tues., Thur. or Fri., these same stores are likely to make a long weekend of it, the banks first and foremost. Grocery stores are usually closed on Sun. afternoon and all day Monday. Most museums close on Tuesday. All the major department stores are open from Mon. to Sat., 9:30 a.m. to 6:30 p.m.

HOLIDAYS

New Year's Day *(Jour de l'An)*—January 1st
Easter *(Pâgues)*—the first Sunday after the first full moon in Spring
Easter Monday *(lundi de Pâques)*—the day after Easter
May Day *(Féte du Travail)*—May 1st
Memorial Day (Victoire 1945)—May 8th
Ascension Day (Ascension)—40th day after Easter
Pentecost *(Pentecôte)*—the Monday following the seventh Sunday after Easter
Bastille Day *(Fête Nationale)* —July 14th
Assumption *(Assomption)* —August 15th
All Saints Day *(Toussaint)*—November 1st
Armistice Day *(Armistice 1918)*—November 11th
Christmas *(Noël)*—December 25th

Many small shops and restaurants close for the entire month of August when thousands of Parisians take their summer vacations. Over the past years there has been an attempt to stagger holidays, but most people still take their leave in August and still go to the Côte d'Azur.

			WOMEN				
Dresses, coats and suits							
American/English	36	38	40	42	44		
French	42	44	46	48	50		
Shirts and sweaters							
American	32	34	36	38	40	42	44
English	34	36	38	40	42	44	46
French	40	42	44	46	48	50	52
Shoes							
American	5	5½	6½	7½	8½	9	9½
English	3½	4	5	6	7	7½	8½
French	36	37	38	39	40	41	42
			CHILDREN				
American	1	4	6	8	10	13	15
English	1	2	5	7	9	10	12
French	1	2	5	7	9	10	12
			MEN				
Suits and coats							
American/English	36	38	40	42	44	46	48
French	46	48	50	52	54	56	58
Shirts							
American/English		15	15½	15¾	16	16½	17
French	38	39	40	41	42	43	44
Sweaters	S		M		L		XL
American/English	34		36-38		40-42		44
French	44		46-48		50-52		54
Shoes							
American/English	7½	8	8½	9½	10	11	
French	40	41	42	43	44	45	

FESTIVALS

The **Festival du Marais**, dance, music and theater, goes on throughout June and July, making up for the annual closure of many theaters and concert halls.

On June 21, the **Féte de la Musique** provides free concerts all over the city from dawn to dawn on the longest day of the year.

Bastille Day on July 14, is the occasion for a military parade on the Champs-Elysées in the morning, fireworks at dusk, and all-night Firemen's Balls, held in neighborhood fire stations and well worth a polka.

October is wine month, with the arrival of *Beaujolais nouveau*, and the annual **Montmartre Wine Harvest**. Check posters for dates.

RELIGIOUS SERVICES

France is predominantly Catholic and the many churches and Notre Dame Cathedral are open to the public and post Mass schedules. For a complete list of all denominational churches, temples and synagogues around town, pick up a copy of the small book, "*Plan des rues de Paris*", divided into districts, and on sale in *Tabac* stores and kiosks. Non-denominational services are held in English in the American Church on the quai d'Orsay near the Pont d'Alma bridge.

COMMUNICATIONS

MEDIA

Newspapers and magazines are sold at *kiosques* and in shops marked *journaux*. One excellent English language daily, the *International Herald Tribune* is actually published in Paris and is sold almost everywhere (the *IHT* runs the Sunday *New York Times* crossword puzzle on Saturday). *Passion* is a monthly magazine, also in English, and a good source of cultural happenings in the capital. Another small magazine, *Pariscope,* on the stands every Wednesday, gives complete listings of museums, art galleries, concerts, ballets, operas, rock concerts, television programs, theater, nightlife, movies (*V.O.* if it's subtitled, *V.F.* if it's dubbed into French), and many other items of interest. Don't go out without it.

If you'd like to glance at some of the French dailies, you might pick up the prestigious *Le Monde,* a world famous intellectual left-of-center paper. Also on the left of the political spectrum is *Le Matin,* the socialist paper; *l'Humanité,* a French Communist Party publication; and *Libération,* Jean-Paul Sartre's brainchild. On the other side of the fence there's *France Soir,* with marked leanings towards sensationalism and *Le Figaro,* an Establishment bulwark. There are no Sunday papers. Political and news magazines include *l'Express* and *Le Point*. Those interested in fashion can leaf through *Vogue, Vogue Hommes,* or *l'Oficiel de la Mode. Paris Match* resembles *Life* magazine.

RADIO

There has been a veritable explosion of Em stations in France, a far cry from the solitary three or four on the airwaves before 1981. Just turn the dial or tune into one of the following: *Radio Classique* (101.1 MHz) classical music with no interruptions 24 hours a day; *Europe* 1 (104.7 MHz) talk shows and games; *FIP* (90.4 MHz) an insolent blend of all types of music, jazz from 7:30 p.m. to 9 p.m.; *Radio Montmartre* (102.7 MHz) French music from the days of black and white movies; NRJ (100.3 MHz) top of the charts; *RFM* (103.9 MHz) relaxed rock 'n roll with news flashes.

You can also listen to the *Voice of America* in English, 6000 or 6040 kHz, or *Radio Canada*, 9760 or 6140 kHz (early morning), 15,325 or17,820 kHz (late afternoon), 6000, 7285 or 11,960 kHz (late evening).

TELEVISION

There are now six channels in France, with a seventh on the way. In general, there are French and American series on during the day and films—political or variety shows in the evening. Everything is in

French, of course, except for the occasional late night subtitled movie.

POSTAL SERVICES

The French post office is run by the PTT *Poste et Télécommunications,* and although delivery may be prompt and efficient, customer services are not; unless you arrive at an odd time in an out of the way bureau, be prepared to wait. Fortunately there are many *bureaux de postes* around town—each marked by a stylized blue airplane on a yellow sign—where you can consult the phone book *(bottin),* buy telephone cards, send or receive money orders *(mandats),* call anywhere in the world, and of course, mail a letter (look for the counter marked *affranchissement, timbres,* or *poste aérienne).* Most branches are open Mon. to Fri., 8 a.m. to 7 p.m., and Sat., 8 a.m. to noon. All general delivery, if not otherwise specified, is sent to the main post office at 52 rue du Louvre, 75001 (42.33.71.60) M° Louvre, which is open 24 hours a day for the telephone and telegraph and until 7 p.m. for other services.

You can also drop your letters into the yellow mail boxes, often located at *tabacs,* tobacco stores, where they sell stamps as well. To send a telegram in English, dial 42.33.21.11.09.

TELEPHONE

The telephone service is getting better and better every year in France, and if you want to make a call, functioning phone booths are not as rare a commodity as in the past. There are two kinds of phone booths in Paris from which you can make local and international calls: coin-operated (rare and usually out of order) and card-operated. *Télécartes* are practical, easy to use, and can be bought at any post office or at the airports. To use your card follow the instructions as they appear on the screen: *Décrochez,* pick up the receiver, *Introduire votre carte,* insert card; *Patientez,* hold on; *Numérotez,* dial; *Raccrochez,* hang up; *Reprenez votre carte,* don't forget your card.

You can also call from all post offices, where they have both coin- and card-operated phones. Or if you wish to call long distance, tell the man or woman at the counter marked *téléphone* and pay afterwards. Cafés and *tabacs* often have public phones, located next to the *toilettes,* which require coins or *jetons,* tokens you buy at the bar.

For information *(renseignements)* in French dial 12, or in other languages 42.33.44.11. The international information number is 19.33.33. Collect calls, *PVC,* are long and complicated (you cannot call collect within France, anyway). Dial 10, give the operator the name and number of your correspondent and your name and number as well. Then hang up and wait. The process can take hours and hours, especially during the holiday season. Direct dialing can be faster. To place a direct call to the United States or Canada dial 19, wait for the dial tone, then dial 1 plus the area code and then the number.

Public telex services are also available at some post offices. Check the front pages of a telephone directory for information on telex, telefax and telegram services.

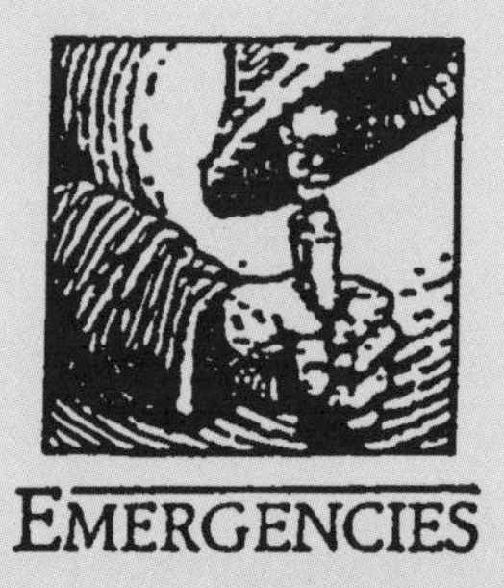

EMERGENCIES

SECURITY & CRIME

Paris is relatively safe, but it does present the same problems as other big cities. The worst most tourists may be faced with is pickpockets (especially in the subway), and this can easily be avoided by carrying your money safely. Areas which are obviously prostitution centers (rue St.-Denis) are best avoided late at night.

LOSS

If you are victim of a theft, be it your personal documents, cash, personal property or traveler's checks, you must first go to the *Commissariat de Police* (Police Station) nearest where the theft occurred, and as soon as possible. This is necessary before taking steps with the travel check service or your embassy or consulate. If you carry credit cards, note the hotline for lost or stolen cards before you travel. Here are a few: American Express (47.77.72.00); Diners Club (47.62.75.75); Carte Bleu/Visa (42.77.11.90).

MEDICAL SERVICES

A doctor will pay a house call in an emergency if you dial one of the following **SOS Medecins** numbers 43.37.77.77 or 47.07.77.77 and explain your situation in French. You can reach English-speaking health services at the American Hospital (47.47.53.00) or the British Hospital (47.58.13.12). There is a **British and American Pharmacy** at 1 rue Auber across from the Opéra, open Mon. through Sat., 8:30 a.m. to 8 p.m. Another, the **Pharmacie Anglo-Americaine**, is located near the Louvre, at 6 rue Castiglione, open Mon. through Sat. 9 a.m. to 7:30 p.m. If you have a personal crisis or don't know where to turn for help, you can call the SOS-Help Hotline in English at 47.23.80.80, recently operating from 3 p.m. to 11 p.m. (subject to change).

PHARMACIES

Pharmacies can easily be spotted in Paris thanks to their green crosses prominently posted out front. Vitamins, hypo-allergenic make-up, tampons and medicines can be found here. Just tell the pharmacist what you want, or what hurts, and he or she will find the solution. Basic French for some common complaints:

I would like some medicine for...	*Je voudrais un médicament contre...*
headache	*le mal de tête*
stomach-ache	*le mal de ventre*
sore throat	*e mal de gorge*
cold	*le rhume*
flu	*la grippe*
menstrual pains	*les règles douloureuses*

Pharmacies are usually open from 9 a.m. to noon and from 2 p.m. to 7 p.m. At night, every pharmacy will have the address hanging in the doorway or window of the nearest one that's open. French law requires that a certain number of drugstores remain open, or be on call, at all times. One that is open 24 hours a day everyday is Pharmacy Dhéry, 84 ave. des Champs-Elysées, 75008 (45.62.02.41) M° Franklin D. Roosevelt.

HOSPITALS & DOCTORS

American Hospital
63 blvd. Victor-Hugo
92200 Neuilly M° Sablons
47.57.24.10

British Hospital
48 rue de Villiers
92300 Levallois-Perret M° Anatole-France
47.57.24.10

The American and Canadian Embassies in Paris can provide you with a list of American and Canadian doctors. The American Hospital also has this information.

For health emergencies, call *les pompiers* first and aforemost by dialing 18. Firemen are trained to move fast and efficiently and have great dedication to their work. Other emergency numbers are *Police-secours* 17 and *SAMU* 43.78.26.26 or 45.67.50.50. In less urgent cases you can also call *SOS Medecins* for a house visit at any time of the day or night (47.07.77.77). An English crisis center functions between 3 p.m. and 11 p.m., *SOS Help* (47.23.80.80).

GETTING AROUND

DOMESTIC AIR TRAVEL

The French domestic airline is **Air Inter**, a division of Air France. Air Inter runs over 50 flight routes inside France with no destination more than 90 minutes from Paris. Air Inter offers three different price categories: red (full fare), white (up to 30 percent off) and blue (up to 60 percent off). To take advantage of these reductions, North American residents must procure a "France Pass" card, obtained in their home country. Discounts apply to specific destinations, hours and type of traveler (children between the ages of two and 12, students up to 27, people under 25, senior citizens, couples and groups). Tickets may be purchased at the airports, tourist information offices or at one of the many Air France or Air Inter agencies in Paris: including Air Inter, 12 rue de Castiglione 75001 M° Tuileries, and the Esplanade des Invalides 75007 M° Invalides. Both offices are open Mon. through Sat., 9:30 a.m. to 6 p.m. For general information and schedules call 45.39.25.25, or toll-free in the United States 1-800-AF-PARIS.

RAIL TRANSPORT

The railway is run by the *Société Nationale des Chemins de Fer* (SNCF) which offers two types of service in Paris:

Banlieue (suburbs)—the suburbs, including Versailles, are all within the five-zone network. If you don't have a five-zone orange or yellow card, you will have to buy a *billet* (ticket) if you take the train out of the second zone. You can pick one up at the *guichet* (counter). Make sure to stamp it in one of the orange validation machines *(composteur)* located on the *quais* (platforms).

Grandes lignes (long distance)—traveling by train is a French tradition. The comprehensive rail system plus wide range of services offered by the SNCF reflects this custom. You can go almost anywhere by rail, under a multitude of conditions. Perhaps you'd prefer the patrician treatment of a comfortable, carpeted, discreetly beige compartment with glass doors on a first-class-only train. Take the **Trans-Europe Express** and sink back into comfort.

Or maybe you'd like a colorful touch of old Europe in a crowded compartment, packed with locals eating their *saucisson*, talking about the weather, or petting their neighbor's dog. Wander out to the corridors where young lovers fulfill their secret rites or daydreamers pensively puff their *gitanes*. Stop off at the *toilettes*, but check if there's paper before committing yourself. Pop into the *bar* for a sandwich (and wish you'd brought your own) or into the *voiture restaurant* for a sit-down dinner (not all trains have this service).

In a hurry? Rush to reserve a seat on the **TGV** *(train à grande vitesse)*, the fastest in the west. Now here's a dilemma. You want to go to Nice on the train but you don't want to miss a day, and of course, you need your car. Relax. Take the over-night *couchette* (second class, six beds to a compartment; first class, four beds) or a *wagon-lit* (second class, two or three beds to a room; first class, one or two beds to a room) and drop the car off at its own wagon. On second thought, maybe you'd rather leave the car at the station. Suppose you feel like riding a bike? Rent one! at one of the 280 participating stations.

Though not always required, it is advisable to reserve a seat if you plan to travel by train. There are special fares for young people, couples, families, senior citizens, and on certain routes. North Americans should ask their travel agents about the **Eurailpass**. For further information contact the **French National Railroads**, 610 Fifth Ave., New York, NY 10020 (212-582-2516), or in Canada, 1500 Stanley St., Suite 436, Montréal H3A 1R3 (514-288-2516). In Paris for information call 45.82.50.50, and for reservations call 45.65.60.60, or go to one of the tourist offices, train stations or airports (Orly, gate H; Roissy, terminal 1 gate 26, terminal 2 gate B6).

METRO & RER

Run by the *Régie Autonome des Transports Parisiens* (RATP), the Paris *métro* and express RER are a cheap and simple way of getting around the city. There are *métro* stations in virtually every neighborhood where you can buy tickets and pick up a free public transportation map. Individual tickets are good for one trip, transfers included, at any time of the day for any distance within zones one and two (Paris and the immediate suburbs). If you intend to take the *métro* more than once don't bother buying one ticket at a time. There are many other possibilities, one of which is bound to suit your particular situation:

Un carnet, s'il vous plait—purchasing 10 tickets at once ends up being cheaper and saves time.

Paris-Sésame—a special first-class ticket good for two, four or seven days, on all public transportation. This *billet* is sold at the main tourist office, in 80 different *métro* stations, at all the train stations and airports.

Une carte jaune, deux zones, s'll vous plaît—a yellow card gives you unlimited travel within the zones you specify from one Monday morning to the next. All you need is a photomat picture of yourself (see the *carte orange* section below for more details). You can buy this fabulous ticket at any *métro*, RER or train station.

Une carte orange, deux zones, s'il vous plaît —an excellent example of French transit pioneering, the orange card allows unlimited travel on any public transportation system for an entire month. To obtain a *carte orange* or a *carte jaune* go to the *guichet* (ticket counter) at any *métro*, RER or train station with a photomat picture of yourself. Give your picture to the vendor and ask for the appropriate card, including the number of zones (minimum two zones for all of Paris and the immediate suburbs, maximum five zones for the greater Paris area). He will take your photo, stick it on an orange card, stamp it, and give it back to you with an orange or yellow *coupon* and a special plastic case to put them in. Sign the card, copy its number on the ticket, slide them into their plastic holder and *voilà!* You are set for the month (or week)!

To use the *métro* or RER, consult the map posted in any station to find your departure and arrival stops. If they are on different lines, you will need to transfer. Lines are referred to by their terminal points and by number. For example, the number one line, which stops at the Louvre and Champs-Elysées, is called Château de Vincennes/ Pont de Neuilly, because these two stations are the last stops on either end of the line. Take the *direction* you are headed towards. For example, if you take line one, you head towards Pont de Neuilly, or in the opposite direction, Château de Vincennes. Stops and transfer stations are listed above each door in every car.

To transfer to another line, follow the orange *correspondence* signs. To exit, follow the blue *sortie* signs. A map of the surrounding neighborhood *(plan de quartier)* can be found in all the stations.

The first *métro* leaves its terminus at 5:30 a.m. and the last at 12:30 a.m. After passing the turnstiles, keep your (unfolded, un-

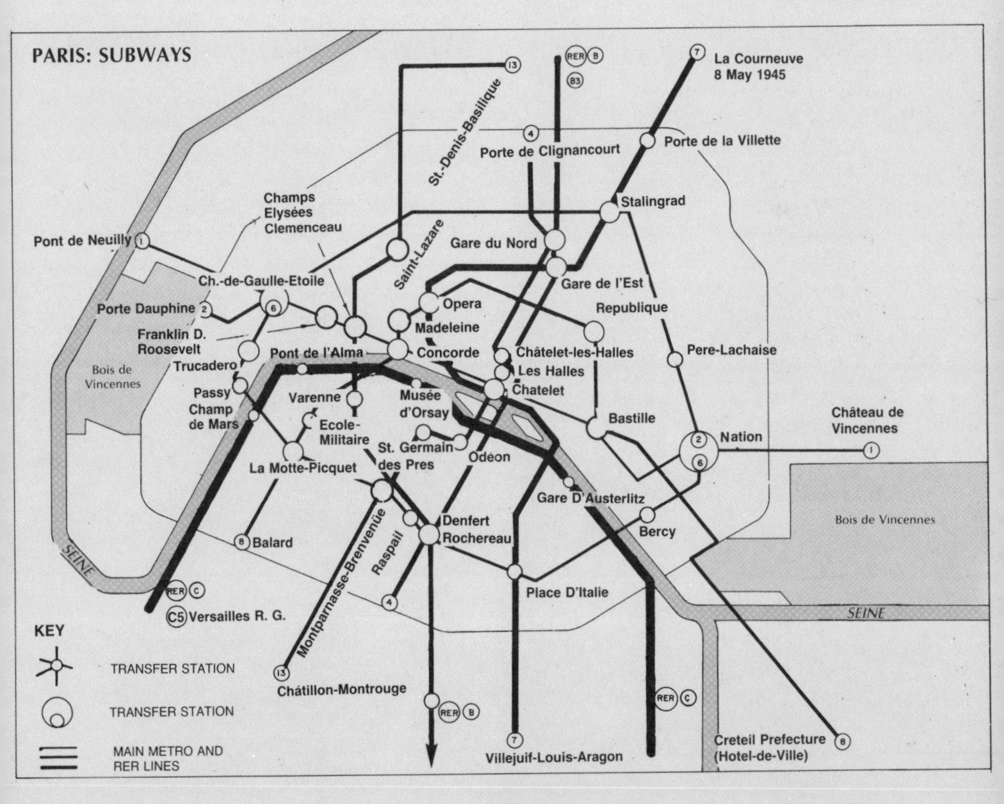

spindled, unmutilated) ticket until you leave. There may be other turnstiles along the way, or ticket inspectors. The first and second class system functions between 9 a.m. and 5 p.m. The first class cars are in the middle and differ from the others by a "1" painted on the side. For further information contact the

Bureau de Tourisme RATP
53 quai des Grands Augustins, 75006
(43.46.14.14) M° St-Michel
Open daily from 6 a.m. to 9 p.m.,

Services Touristiques de la RATP
place de la Madeleine, 75008
(42.65.31.18) M° Madeleine
Open every day from 7:30 a.m. to 7 p.m.

BUSES

Taking the bus is a good way to get where you're going and see the city at the same time. The buses are run by the same company as the *métro*, so you can use the same tickets. If you don't already have one, the drivers sell them (they even have change!). Board at the front, punch your ticket (or two, ask how many are necessary) in the validation machine, or if you have an orange or yellow card or *Paris-Sésame*, flash it at the driver. DON'T PUNCH IT!

Buses don't automatically stop at every station, so if you wish to get off, push one of the *arrêt* buttons. When you do this, or if it has already been done, a red *arrêt demandé* sign will light up at the front. Each bus has a map of its route posted at the front and back, and also at every stop. Most buses run from 6:30 a.m. to 8:30 p.m. Some continue until 12:15 a.m. There is a special night service that leaves Châtelet at 1:30, 2:30, 3:30, 4:30 and 5:30 in the morning, branching out in 10 different directions.

TAXIS

Taxis are not as cheap as the *métro* or bus, but at times, particularly after 1 a.m. when the *métro* has stopped running, they do the trick. There are three different kinds of fare:

A: From 6:30 a.m. to 10 p.m.
B: From 10 p.m. to 6:30 a.m. and during the day from the airports.
C: From the airports from 10 p.m. to 6:30 a.m.

The tariff in use is indicated by a light on top of the taxi.

You can hail a cab from a stand *(arrêt taxis)* or from any sidewalk that is not within 50 meters of a stand. You can also call for one by dialing 42.00.67.89, 47.39.33.33 or 42.03.99.99. Other radio-cab numbers are listed in the phone book, in *Pariscope* (see section on publications), or available at your hotel reception desk.

BICYCLES

Riding a bike in Paris is inevitably a harum-scarum experience. The cyclist is low man on the locomotion ladder, following mopeds, pedestrians and even dogs. If you will wish, however, to live dangerously you can rent a bicycle at **Paris Vél**, 2 rue de Fer-â-Moulin 75005 (43.37.52.22) M° Censier-Daubenton, open Mon. to Sat., 10 a.m. to 12:30 p.m. and 2 p.m. to 7 p.m., or **Bicy-club de France**, 8 place de la Porte de Champerret 75017 (47.66.55.92) M° Porte de Champerret, open Mon. to Sat., 9:30 a.m. to 1:30 p.m. Mopeds are no longer available due to insurance problems.

PRIVATE TRANSPORT

Parisian drivers are a breed apart and road courtesy is not exactly their distinguishing feature. Unless your nerves are rock solid, you don't even want to try navigating in this morass of competing fiends. Undaunted? Like a tough challenge? Get a city map with one way streets and public parking lots indicated. Most car rental companies require the driver to be at least 21 years old, possess a driver's licence for at least one year, a passport and one major credit card (VISA or American Express). The price of the car includes third party insurance, but it is advisable to pay the extra for full coverage. You can rent a car at both the airports or at one of the following agencies. Naturally it's difficult to find cars in the summer, so reserve in advance.

CAR RENTALS

Avis (minimum age 23)
184 rue Faubourg St-Martin, 75010
46.07.82.45
M° Château-Landon,

Mon. to Fri., 7 a.m. to 8 p.m.; Sat., 7:30 a.m. to 7:30 p.m.

Budget
71 blvd. Couvion St.-Cyr, 75017
45.72.11.13 or toll-free 05.01.00.01
M° Porte Maillot,
Mon. to Fri., 8 a.m. to 9 p.m.; Sat., 8:30 a.m. to 12:30 p.m. and 1:30 p.m. to 5:30 p.m.

Europcar
48 rue de Berri, 75008
45.63.04.27
M° George V,
Mon. to Sat., 8 a.m. to 7 p.m.

Hertz (minimum age 20)
27 rue St.-Ferdinand, 75017
45.74.97.39, or for reservations 47.88.51.51
M° Argentine,
Mon. to Sun., 6:30 a.m. to 10 p.m.

For chauffeur-driven cars, contact:
A.B.C. Limousine
(Associated Business Car)
48 rue Sarrette, 75014
45.45.53.30
M° Alésia

Carey Limousine,
25 rue d'Astorg, 75008
42.65.54.20
M° St.-Augustin

DRIVING ADVISORIES

The French highway code is based on the International Road Sign system, so if you are going to drive, make sure you are familiar with it. A booklet showing all the commonly used signs is available through local AAA clubs. One difficult but essential rule to keep in mind is *priorité à droite*, yielding to cars coming from the right. Many intersections do not have stop signs and remembering to yield to the right can become a matter of life or death. At circles, arriving cars yield to those already engaged. The speed limit is 130 kph on the *autoroutes* (toll highways), 110 kph on two-lane divided highways, 90 kph on roads outside towns and cities, 80 kph on the *périphérique* (Paris beltway) and 60 kph (or less) in town. Honking is strictly forbidden, except in emergencies. Parisians flash their high beams instead. You must wear a seatbelt in the front seats, and children are required to sit in the back. The maximum alcohol level accepted for the driver is 0.8 grams.

Petrol is almost three times the price in the United States, but this is often counterbalanced by the significantly better petrol mileage of European cars. There are petrol stations at the city's *portes* (exit points), in some underground lots, and at various well-hidden spots. The **Automobile Club**, 8 place de la Concorde, 75008 (42.66.43.00) M° Concorde, has a list of stations, including those open 24 hours a day.

Parking in Paris can be very frustrating if you don't head directly for a public lot. On the street, parking places are presided over by the eternal meter, or by the *horodateur*, a French innovation, that gives you a printed slip for your money which you display prominently on the dashboard. Don't park in no parking zones, even if everyone else does. They tow cars in Paris and it's not fun getting them back.

WHERE TO STAY

HOTELS

There are hundreds of hotels in Paris, ranging from the jet-setter's gadget-filled, ultra-luxury palace to the poor student's eight-story walk-up with dubious communal bathrooms down the hall. The Ministry of Tourism has set up a system of *étoiles*, or stars, to help prospective lodgers determine how much comfort they can expect.

The one-star category offers rooms with a bed, a few pieces of furniture and for 80 percent of the rooms, shared bathrooms. Many of these hotels are located in the Marais or the Latin Quarter, and can be pleasant if well-run and kept clean. As they are generally operated by families, there is often a curfew, after which time the front door is locked.

A two-star hotel is required to equip 40 percent of its rooms with private bathrooms (shower or tub), provide breakfast for everyone and telephones. Eighty percent of the rooms in a three-star hotel must have full private baths, plus in all cases, telephones, televisions and breakfast, including breakfast in bed.

In four-star hotels the reception staff is required to speak several languages. All rooms are equipped with full private baths, telephones and televisions. Breakfast may be taken in the dining room or in bed, and restaurant service must be made available mornings and evenings. Four-star deluxe hotels have all the conceivable amenities, top quality service and very spacious rooms and bathrooms.

There are hotels that function outside the star system, but they are neither inspected nor guaranteed by the French government. The most interesting areas to stay in are St.-Germain-des-Prés, Champs-Elysées, Opéra, the Latin Quarter, the Marais and the Ile St.-Louis.

Finding a room during the summer season in Paris is like searching for the proverbial needle in a haystack. Some hotels claim they are fully booked two months in advance, so try to reserve as early as possible. When confirming a reservation, ask what type of payment is requested, *accompte* (on account) or *arrhes* (deposit), and get a receipt. If you reserve by phone, state your arrival time, as the hotelier is not required to keep your room after 7 p.m. While a hotel may be obliged to provide breakfast, you don't have to take it and should not be charged for it if you do not.

The following list is not at all exhaustive and the prices indicated may increase over time. For further information contact the French Tourist Office (see Tourist Information section).

175 TO 300 FRANCS

Ducs d'Anjou (38 rooms)
1 rue Ste.-Opportune, 75001
M° Châtelet, 42.36.92.24
Credit cards: VISA. Doubles: 270-320 FF, full bath and breakfast. Small, quiet rooms and excellent location.

Esmeralda (19 rooms)
4 rue St.-Julien le Pauvre, 75002
M° St.-Michel, 43.54.19.20
Near Notre Dame and Shakespeare and Co. Bookstore. 16 rooms have bath or shower, small but pleasant, bustling central location.

Hotel du Grand Turrene (50 rooms)
6 rue de Turenne, 75004
M° St.-Paul, 42.78.43.25
Doubles: 280 FF with breakfast. Respectable, all rooms have shower or bath.

Kensington (26 rooms)
79 ave. de la Bourdonnais, 75007
M° École Militaire, 47.05.74.00
Credit cards: VISA, American Express (AE), Diner's Club (DC). Doubles: 270-320 FF with breakfast. Small, clean and quiet.

Le Lamière (54 rooms)
4 rue Petit, 75019
M° Laumière, 42.06.10.77
Doubles: 124-255 FF with breakfast. Modern, quiet, far from the center of town, but in an authentic *quartier* and cheap.

Nevers-Luxembourg (26 rooms)
3 rue Abbé-de-l'Epée, 75005
M° Luxembourg, 42.26.81.83
Only 8 rooms have bath or shower, modest but cheap.

Palais (19 rooms)
2 quai de la Mégisserie, 75001
M° Cité, 42.36.98.25
Adequate rooms, a few with bath, near the Ste.-Chapelle.

Palais Bourbon (34 rooms)
49 rue Bourgogne, 75007
M° Invalides, 47.05.29.26
26 rooms with bath or shower, modern, has a bar, quiet distinguished neighborhood.

Perreyve (30 rooms)
63 rue Madame, 75006
M° St.-Sulpice, 45.48.35.01
Credit cards: VISA, AE. Doubles: 260-315 FF with breakfast. Comfortable with small but clean bathrooms.

Place des Vosges (16 rooms)
12 rue Birague, 75002
M° Bastille, St.-Paul, 42.72.60.46

Credit cards: VISA, AE, DC, MC. All rooms have bath or shower; small and friendly in the Marais district—reserve in advance!

Vieux Paris (21 rooms)
9 rue Gite-le-Coeur, 75006
M° St.-Michel, 43.54.41.66
Mostly single rooms, 14 with bath or shower, and a few more expensive doubles, near the river.

300 TO 500 FRANCS

Banville (40 rooms)
166 blvd. Berthier, 75017
M° Porte de Champerret, 42.67.70.16
Credit cards: VISA. Doubles: 400 FF with breakfast. Carpet and marble bathrooms.

Bradford (48 rooms)
10 rue St.-Philippe-du-Roulé, 75008
M° St.-Philippe-du-Roulé, 43.59.24.20
Doubles: 440-460 FF with breakfast. Big, light rooms near Champs-Elysées.

Hôtel Moulin Rouge (50 rooms)
39 rue Fontaine, 75009
M° Blanche, 42.81.93.25
Credit cards: VISA, AE, DC. Doubles: 420-560 FF with breakfast. Roomy and charming in a very animated neighborhood.

Regyn's Montmartre (22 rooms)
18 place des Abbesses, 75018
M° Abbesses, 42.54.45.21
Credit cards: VISA, AE, DC. Doubles: 380 FF with breakfast. Direct-dial phones, color TV, simple and calm.

Scandanavia (22 rooms)
27 rue de Tournon, 75006
M° Odéon, 43.29.67.20
Doubles: 370-420 FF with breakfast. Rich and refined, a Left Bank treasure.

St.-Louis (21 rooms)
75 rue St.-Louis-en-l'Ile, 75004
M° Sully-Morland, 46.34.04.80
Doubles: 350-500 FF with breakfast. Lovely hotel in a much-coveted neighborhood.

Timhôtel
This new chain has several branches in town, all fairly small and completely modern (all rooms with bath). Call the central reservation offices at 42.96.28.28. Credit cards: VISA, AE, DC, MC. The locations are as follows:
"Italie", 22 rue Barrault, 75013
"Tolbiac", 35 rue du Tolbiac, 75013
"Montmarte", 11 place Emile Goudeau, 75018
"Le Louvre", 4 rue Croix des Petits Champs, 75001
"La Bourse", 3 rue de la Banque, 75002
"St. Lazare", 113 rue St.-Lazare, 75008.

500 TO 700 FRANCS

Angleterre (29 rooms)
44 rue Jacob, 75006
M° St.-Germain-des-Prés, 42.60.34.74
Credit cards: VISA, AE, DC. Doubles: 600-750 FF with breakfast. High ceilings, great bathrooms in a chic Left Bank *quartier*.

Aramis (42 rooms)
124 rue de Rennes, 75006
M° St.-Placide, 45.48.03.75
Credit cards: VISA, AE, DC. Doubles: 470-600 FF with breakfast. Pretty rooms and well-equipped bathrooms.

Gaillon Opéra (26 rooms)
9 rue Gaillon, 75002
M° Opéra, 47.42.47.74
Credit cards: VISA, AE, DC. Doubles: 550-570 FF with breakfast. Old world character, color TV and minibars.

Résidence Elysées Maubourg (30 rooms)
35 blvd. de Latour-Maubourg, 75007
M° Latour-Maubourg, 45.56.10.78
Credit cards: VISA, AE, DC, Eurocard (EC). Doubles: 450-600 FF with breakfast. Modern, well-equipped, and free sauna available .

Rothray
10 rue Nicolas-Flamel, 75004
M° Châtelet, 48.87.13.37
This is an apartment rental service that provides lovely flats near the Marais, the Place des Victoires or Châtelet. With fully-equipped kitchens, TV and maid service. Prices start at 500 francs.

Victoria Palace (113 rooms)
5 rue Blaise-Desgoffe, 75006
M° St.-Sulpice, 45.44.38.16

Credit cards: VISA, AE, DC, EC. Doubles: 620-720 FF with breakfast. Traditional, quiet, with marble bathrooms.

700 TO 1,000 FRANCS

Baltimore (119 rooms)
88 bis ave. Kléber, 75016
M° Boissière, 45.53.83.33
Credit cards: VISA, AE, DC, EC. Doubles: 800-1,000 FF with breakfast. Sober, comfortable, minibars and videos.

Château Frontenac (103 rooms)
54 rue Pierre-Charro, 75008
M° Franklin D. Roosevelt, 47.23.55.85
Credit cards: VISA, AE, DC, EC. Doubles: 850 FF with breakfast. Modern, stylish, nice bathrooms and intimate.

Deux-Iles (17 rooms)
59 rue St.-Louis-en-l'Ile, 75004
M° Sully-Morland, 43.26.13.35
Lovely 17th century house, the rooms are small but modernized, very gracious sitting room and bar in a quiet neighborhood right in the center of town.

Holiday Inn
69 blvd. Victor, 75015
M° Porte de Versailles, 45.33.74.63 and
10 place de la République, 75010
M° Republique, 42.55.44.34
The first has 90 modern rooms and is located near the Porte de Versailles exhibition center. The second has 333 rooms and many conveniences, including a gym and sauna. Both have a restaurant, bar, air conditioning.

Normandy (138 rooms)
7 rue de l'Echelle, 75001
M° Concorde, 42.60.30.21
Credit cards: VISA, AE, DC, MC. Restaurant and bar. In the heart of downtown.

Pavillon de la Reine (49 rooms)
28 place des Vosges, 75003
M° Chemin Vert, 42.77.96.40
Credit cards: VISA, AE, DC, EC. Doubles: 900-980 FF. Old style, wooden beams, marble bathrooms and a fabulous location.

Résidence du Bois (19 rooms)
16 rue Chalgrin, 75016
M° Charles-de-Gaulle-Etoile, 45.00.50.59
Doubles: 900-1,300 FF. Old world luxury with very modern bathrooms.

Splendid Etoile (57 rooms)
1 bis ave. Carnot, 75017
M° Charles-de-Gaulle-Etoile, 47.66.41.41
Credit cards: VISA, AE, DC, EC. Doubles: 700-900 FF with breakfast. Comfortable, spacious and well-equipped bathrooms.

Terass (108 rooms)
12-14 rue Joseph-de-Maistre, 75018
M° Anvers, 46.06.72.85
Credit cards: VISA, AE, MC, DC. All rooms with bath. Restaurant and bar, in charming Montmartre.

1,000 TO 1,200 FRANCS

Hilton (479 rooms)
18 ave. de Suffren, 75015
M° Bir Hakeim, 42.73.92.00
Credit cards: VISA, AE, DC, EC. Doubles: 1,250-1,750 FF with breakfast. Excellent hotel with all the extras and children (any age) can stay free in their parents' room.

Le Prince des Galles (171 rooms)
33 ave. George V, 75008
M° George V, 47.23.55.11
Toll free in North America, 800-228-9290
Credit cards: VISA, AE, DC, EC. Doubles: 1,700-2,200 FF with breakfast. Elegant and spacious, near the Champs-Elysées.

Raphael (87 rooms)
17 ave. Kléber, 75016
M° Kléber, 45.02.16.00
Credit cards: VISA, AE, DC, EC. Doubles: 900-1,400 FF with breakfast. Intimate, spacious, dark and luxurious.

Relais Christine (51 rooms)
3 rue Christine, 75006
M° St.-Michel, 43.26.71.80
Credit cards: VISA, AE, DC, EC. Doubles: 1,000-1,500 with breakfast. 16th-century cloister, comfortable and roomy.

San Régis (44 rooms)
12 rue Goujon, 75008
M° Alma-Marceau or FDR, 43.59.41.90
Credit cards: VISA, DC. Doubles: 1,300-1,700 FF with breakfast. Discreet, refined, lovely bathrooms and excellent service.

2,000 FRANCS & ABOVE

Crillon (189 rooms)
10 place de la Concorde, 75008
M° Concorde, 42.65.24.24
Credit cards: VISA, AE, DC. Doubles: 2,400-2,800 FF. Classic, classy and authentic French luxury.

George V (292 rooms)
31 ave. George V, 75008
M° George V, 47.23.54.00
Credit cards: VISA, AE, DC, MC. Completely modernized and luxurious, with a popular restaurant and bar frequented by international businessmen.

Le Bristol (200 rooms)
112 rue du Faubourg St.-Honoré, 75008
M° St.-Philippe-du-Roulé, 42.66.91.45
Credit cards: VISA, AE, DC, EC. Doubles: 2,000-2,800 FF (+18.6 percent Value Added Tax, VAT). Splendid bathrooms, enormous beds and sumptuous everything.

Meurice (161 rooms)
228 rue de Rivoli, 75001
M° Concorde, 42.60.38.06
Credit cards: VISA, AE, DC, MC. Midtown luxury in a beautiful setting, all modern conveniences including air conditioning, restaurant, sitting rooms, bar and shops.

Plaza Athénée (218 rooms)
25 ave. Montaigne, 75009
M° Alma-Marceau, 47.23.78.33
Credit cards: VISA, AE, DC, EC. Doubles: 2,100 FF and up (+15 percent service charge). Perfect service and incredibly vast, luxurious, super-equipped rooms.

Résidence Maxim's de Paris
42 ave. Gabriel, 75008
M° Champs-Elysées-Clémenceau, 45.61.96.33
Credit cards: VISA, AE, DC. Pierre Cardin's unparalleled contribution to ultra-luxury hotels. Each exquisite room is designed differently and decorated by the hand of a real artist (prices reflect this).

Ritz (163 rooms)
15 place Vendôme, 75001
M° Opéra, 42.60.38.30
Credit cards: VISA, AE, DC, EC, Doubles: 2,800 FF and up (+15 percent service charge). Beauty, luxury, excellent service and fabulous furnishings. The word "ritzy" was invented to describe it.

Royal Monceau (220 rooms)
35-39 ave. Hoche, 75008
M° Charles-de-Gaulle-Etoile, 45.61.98.00
Toll free in North America, 800-221-2340
Credit cards: VISA, AE, DC, EC. Doubles: 2,200-2,600 FF. Discreet, classy and plush, with all the conveniences.

FOOD DIGEST

WHAT TO EAT

The French are very, very proud of their cooking, and with good reason. One of the most sublime experiences in the world is a perfect dinner in a French restaurant. As eating out is often the goal of a Parisian's entire evening, people take it seriously and dress up.

While lunch is a relatively relaxed affair, dinner is a sacred rite with an immutable succession of acts: *l'aperitif*, the before dinner drink (optional); *l'entrée*, the starter (not optional, even at lunch); *le plat principal*, the main dish; *la salade*, salad greens (optional, but nice); *les fromages*, a selection of cheeses, and/or *le dessert*, the sweet note, *le café*, black of course; and finally, if you're still in a conscious state, *le digestif*, an after dinner drink. If this seems like a lot don't worry, portions are small by American standards. Spare yourself the contempt of everyone within hearing distance and don't order milk, soda, coffee or any alcoholic beverage but wine with your meal. If you'd rather not have wine, try some mineral water (still: Evian or Vittel; bubbly: Badoit or Perrier).

If you don't know what wine to order, ask your waiter, he knows what he's talking about and won't push an expensive bottle on you if you don't want one. In a *grand restaurant* ask for the *sommelier*. Don't be shy about asking what some of the illegible, complicated names are on the menu. Many have been invented by the chef and even the French couple at the next table doesn't know what they are. Most restaurants have a *menu*, a fixed-price menu, and a *carte* from which you order...*à la carte!* Ordering from the menu is significantly cheaper, but often rather limiting. The 15 percent *service*, or tip, is now required by law to appear on your *addition*, or bill, but it is not necessarily included in the prices. Check to see if the *carte* is marked SNC (*service non compris*, tip not included) or SC (*service compris*, tip included). It is customary to leave a little something extra.

While it's imperative to reserve for dinner, lunch is best sought by wandering through the streets (don't wander too long, lunch is only served from noon to 2 p.m.), and consulting the menus posted in the windows. Be prepared for the shock of seeing American fast-food joints on the Champs-Elysées, almost every quarter of Paris has been invaded by them.

If you'd like a relatively inexpensive dinner, there are several *quartiers* that abound in little French, Greek, Chinese and North African restaurants (order a *cous-cous* here): the Latin Quarter (M° St.-Michel), the neighborhood around the rue du Faubourg-Montmartre (M° Montmartre), the rue Grégoire-de-Tours (M° Odéon), the streets around the Marché St.-Germain (M° Mabillon) and the Mouffetard area (M° Censier-Daubenton). As to prices, an easy rule of thumb is, multiply the cost of an average main course by three, and that should give you a fair idea of what you can expect to pay for the whole meal.

There are certain French specialties which you may wish to sample. Starting at the top of your repast, you might try a *kir* (white wine and *crême de cassis*) or a *kir royal* (*crême de cassis* and champagne). For the *entrée*, overcome your repugnance and order *escargots*, they are fabulous, or mussels, fish *terrines* (a vague cousin of *pâté*), *foie gras* (which is not a *pâté*), fish *feuilleté* (flaky fish pastry), raw oysters (the *fines de claires moyennes* size is recommended) or a *crottin de chavignol chaud en salade*, a green salad with a soft warm mound of goat cheese. For the main course try a *magret de canard* (a delicious duck steak), a *confit d'oie* (a southern specialty of goose preserved in its own fat, you've got to be hungry for this rich dish), lamb in any guise or rabbit. If you are not familiar with the over 365 French cheeses you might want to taste a *camebert, brie* (soft cheese), a *boursault* (rich in cream), *chèvre frais* (fresh goat cheese), a *reblochon* (mountain cheese) or just experiment. Dessert ideas include *tarte tatin* (a wonderful upside-down apple pie), *charlotte* (mousse with ladyfingers), or *profiterolles* (vanilla ice cream stuffed into pastry balls with chocolate sauce on top). Some modest wines to sip are *Cahors, Madiran, Gamay* or *Beaujolais*. As to *digestifs* order a *poire Williams, armagnac* or a fruit *eau-de-vie*.

WHERE TO EAT

The following list of restaurants is not anywhere near exhaustive. Consult *Pariscope* or *Passion* for foreign food places. Prices indicated are for one person ordering *à la carte* and include a glass of moderately-priced wine. In many cases, the amount you choose to spend on wine or champagne may increase your bill considerably. Dinner service starts at 7:30 p.m.

UNDER 100 FRANCS

A la Bonne Crêpe
11 rue Grégoire-de-Tours, 75006
M° Odéon, 43.54.60.74.
Closed for Sun. lunch. A darling little *crêperie* where you can start with a savory and end with a sweet *crêpe*, accompanied by a *bolée* or bowl of French *cidre*, bubbly and alcoholic.

Au Trou Normand
9 rue Jean-Pierre Timbaud, 75011
M° Parmentier, 40.05.80.23
Closed on Sun. Near République, popular with students for its low prices, the restaurant is run by a formidable French woman who is a fixture behind the counter, and doesn't take any nonsense (or checks!) from her clients. Typical French food at low prices.

Aux Artistes
63 rue Falguière, 75015
M° Pasteur, 43.22.05.39.
Closed on Sun. Credit cards: VISA. A *menu* only restaurant that serves good steaks. Paintings cover the walls and ceilings, friendly atmosphere (you write the order yourself), but they don't accept reservations.

Le Chartier
7 rue du Faubourg-Montmartre, 75009
M° Montmartre, 47.70.86.29.
No reservations. Open everyday. An immense, venerable Parisian institution. The menu is long, the fare unbelievably honest, and the crowds permanent.

Le Commerce
51 rue de Commerce, 75015
M° La Motte-Picquet, 45.75.03.27.
No reservations. Open everyday. Run by the same people as Chartier, the clientele is mostly French, the atmosphere less hectic and the food good and more than reasonable.

Polidor
41 rue Monsieur-le-Prince, 75006
M° Odéon.
Closed on Sun., Mon. and in August. No reservations. A real art-deco literary restaurant frequented by students, professors and intellectuals for its home-style cooking.

Thoumieux
79 rue St.-Dominique, 75007
M° Invalides, 47.05.49.75
Open every day and serving until 11:30 p.m. Credit Cards: VISA, AE. Traditional recipes from the southwest, like *cassoulet* and varieties of *charcuterie* fill out the big menu. You can eat for as little as 52 francs here, but you'll probably be tempted to go beyond. This busy and attractive place is highly recommended for visitors on any budget, for its authenticity and quality.

100 TO 250 FRANCS

Bofinger
3-7 rue de la Bastille, 75004
M° Bastille, 42.72.87.82.
Open everyday. Credit cards: VISA, AE, DC, EC. A *brasserie* with original and beautiful turn-of-the-century décor, serving *choucroute* and shellfish all year round.

Flo
7 cour des Petits-Ecuries, 75010
M° Château d'Eau, 47.70.13.59.
Closed in August. Credit cards: VISA, AE, DC. A wood, leather and brass turn-of-the-century décor makes this *brasserie* one of the most intimate in Paris. The *formidable choucroute* is what people come for, as well as the *foie gras* and shellfish. If you want to get in, reserve several days in advance, this place is a true hotspot.

Julien
16 rue du Faubourg St.-Denis, 75010
M° Strasbourg-St.-Denis, 47.70.12.06
Open everyday. Credit cards: VISA, AE, DC. This *brasserie* is an authentic art-nouveau edifice and the décor is breathtaking. Excellent *foie gras, cassoulet*, oysters and other temptations are on the *carte*. Unfortunately it can get pretty noisy.

L'Auberge du Village
3 place des Grès, 75020
M° Porte de Montreuil, 43.73.46.39
Closed on Sun. Credit cards: VISA. On a lovely little back street in a forgotten corner of town, this place is like a trip to the country, with its simple, tasteful decor, quaint terrace, and traditional French menu. It's worth wandering over here, especially if you're in the Père-Lachaise Cemetery neighborhood.

La Coupole
102 blvd. du Montparnasse, 75014
M° Vavin, 43.20.14.20.
Closed in August. Credit cards: VISA. An enormous restaurant dating back to 1925 where the elite go to see and be seen, so make sure you're dressed for that kind of scrutiny. The food can be disappointing, but never the shellfish.

Le Bar des Théâtres
6 ave. Montaigne, 75008
M° Franklin D. Roosevelt, 47.23.34.63
Open weekdays. Credit cards: VISA. This is busy, noisy place, without pretensions (rare in the ritzy, Champs-Elysées neighborhood). Don't mind the paper napkins, and keep away if you hate cigrarette smoke. The food is always fresh and well-prepared, the ambience warm.

Le Chien Qui Fume
Two locations:
68 ave. des Ternes, 75017
M° Ternes, 45.74.03.07; and
33 rue du Pont-Neuf, 75001
M° Pont Neuf, 42.36.07.42
Open everyday and serving from noon until 1 a.m. (2 a.m. at the second location); private rooms available for groups from 15 to 80 people. Traditional French dishes and seafood have made these "Smoking Dogs" a standby for hungry Parisians.

Le Muniche
27 rue de Buci, 75006
M° Mabillon, 46.33.62.09
Open everyday. Credit cards: VISA, AE, DE, EC. One of the best *brasseries* in Paris with friendly service and fresh food including wonderful shellfish and *choucroute*. Great neighborhood for an after dinner stroll.

Le Totem
Musée de l'Homme, Palais de Chaillot.
M° Trocadéro, 47.27.15.73
Closed for Sun. dinner and on Tues. This restaurant, which you reach by going through the entrance to the museum, is superbly located over the terrace and fountains leading down to the river and facing the Eiffel Tower. The specialties are grilled meats and tasty salads. In the beautiful setting, the delicious meal becomes a memorable event.

Les Fêtes Gourmandes
17 rue de l'École Polytechnique, 75005
M° Maubert-Mutualité, 43.26.10.40
Closed on Tues. and the first two weeks in January. Credit cards: VISA. A tiny pink restaurant with eight tables. Fresh, inventive, refined and delicious French cooking. The duck, the fish, the rabbit—everything is very tasty indeed.

Procope
13 rue de l'Ancienne Comédien, 75005
M° Odéon, 43.26.99.20.
Closed in July. The old Procope is not what it used to be. Recently, this historical café-restaurant, once frequented by the likes of Voltaire, Napoléon, Balzac, Benjamin Franklin and Victor Hugo, has been bought up and sold out to high-priced nouvelle cuisine ambience, a far cry from the hearty and happy days past. If you loved the place before, don't go back!

Terminus Nord
23 rue de Dunkerque, 75010
M° Anvers, 42.85.05.15
Open daily. Credit cards: VISA, AE, DC. Run by the same proprietor as Julien and Flo, this *brasserie* differs from the others only in its 1925 décor (and in the higher ratio of French natives to tourists).

250 TO 400 FRANCS

Apicius
122 ave. de Villiers, 75017
M° Pereire
Closed on Sat., Sun. and in August. Credit cards: VISA, AE. A darling new restaurant that combines classic cuisine with successful inventiveness. Everything—the salmon, the prawns—is cooked perfectly. And the assorted chocolate dessert plate (cake, mousse, sorbet, cream and sauce)...devilish!

Au Pavillon Puebla
In the Parc des Buttes-Chaumont, 75019
M° Buttes-Chaumont
Closed for Sat. lunch and on Sun. Credit cards: VISA. A large garden restaurant of open spaces with large windows overlooking the Napoléon III greenery, all luxury, taste and comfort. Delicious lamb, fish and many other items on the menu combine to make dinner, and especially lunch, a most refined experience.

Au Pied de Cochon
6 rue Coquillière, 75001
M° Châtelet-Les Halles
Open 24 hours daily throughout the year. Credit cards: VISA, AE, DC. A crazy, delightful, multi-layered *brasserie*, decorated with the most wonderful kitsch imaginable. Good food including the *soupe à l'oignon*, the shellfish and pork sepcialties keep people coming back: A fixture on the Paris after-hours scene, it has remained the same while all the neighborhood has changed fantastically.

Aux Quai des Ormes
72 quai de l'Hótel de Ville, 75004
M° Pont-Marie, 42.74.72.22

Closed on Sat., Sun. and in August. Credit cards: VISA. An excellent restaurant for light-handed cooking with incredibly delicious fish of all sorts, good meats, fine desserts and a location that couldn't be more central.

Bistro de Paris
33 rue de Lille, 75007
M° Solferino, 42.61.16.83
Closed for Sat. lunch and on Sun. Credit cards: VISA. A charming restaurant with excellent and very fresh food, prepared lovingly with both taste and imagination. The fish is wonderful, the desserts tempting and the *plat du jour* surefire.

Charlot
12 place Clichy, 75008
M° place Clichy, 84.74.49.64
Open everyday. Credit cards: VISA, AE, DC. If you're a fish lover, this is the place for you. Completely renovated, Charlot exudes clean freshness, as do its marvelous fish, cooked to perfection.

Chez Philippe
106 rue de la Follie-Méricourt, 75011
M° Oberkampf, 43.57.33.78
Closed on Sat., Sun. and in August. This unassuming restaurant, tucked away in a forgotten corner of Paris, serves some of the most sublime, sinfully fattening food. French regional cooking is their specialty and they make an irresistible *confit d'oie.*

La Closerie des Lilas
171 blvd. du Montparnasse, 75006
M° Port-Royal
Open everyday. Credit cards: VISA, AE, DC. The Closerie has always been a writer's restaurant. Hemingway, Gide, Rimbaud and Verlaine (among others) ate here and this tradition continues today. The dining room is intimate and classic, but people-watchers prefer the busier atmosphere on the outdoor terrace or in the *brasserie* section. It's often crowded, but you can wait for a table at the piano bar.

Lapèrouse
51 quai des Grands-Augustins, 75006
M° St.-Michel, 43.26.68.04
Open everyday. Credit cards: VISA, AE. A truly beautiful building, hundreds of years old, with an intelligently restored 19th-century baroque interior. How can any meal be less than noble in such a rich setting? Lovers may want to reserve (at extra cost) a private dining room for two, with impeccable service.

Le Croquant
28 rue Jean-Maridor, 75015
M° Lourmel, 45.58.50.83
Closed for Sun., Mon. and in August. Credit cards: VISA, AE, DC. A wonderful regional restaurant in a warm comfortable atmosphere, serving such delights as truffles, salmon and perfect *confit*, not to mention the heavenly *tarte tatin.*

Lipp
151 blvd. St.-Germain, 75006
M° St.-Germain-des-Prés, 45.48.53.91
Closed on Mon., eight days for Halloween, 15 days for Christmas, Easter and in July. No reservations. Lipp is one those hallowed, internationally famed sites where only the chosen get in, and even the chosen are divided into the favored (seated downstairs) and the disfavored (seated upstairs). The top politicos in Paris dine here and the food's not bad for a *brasserie.*

Ma Cuisine
18 rue Bayen, 75017
M° Ternes, 45.72.02.19
Closed for Sat. lunch and on Sun. Credit cards: VISA, AE, DC. A *menu* only restaurant with charming modern décor serving some of the best meats in the capital. The price is almost ridiculous considering the wonderful choice of dishes.

400 TO 500 FRANCS

Beauvilliers
52 rue Lamarck, 75018
M° Anvers, 42.54.54.42
Closed on Sun., for Mon. lunch and the first two weeks in September. Credit cards: VISA. An excellent restaurant filled with flowers and papered with 10th-century portraits. Absolutely perfect dishes, light and imaginative with that significantly extra attention to detail and research in conception that marks the gulf between cuisine and cooking.

Bourdonnais
113 ave. de la Bourdonnais, 75007
M° École-Militaire, 47.05.47.96
Closed on Sun. Credit cards: VISA, AE, DC. A young up-and-coming chef, already among the best in town, is responsible for the renaissance of this enticing little restaurant. Excellent fish and poultry, followed by remarkably fine desserts.

Carré des Feuillants
14 rue de Castiglione, 75001
M° Tuileries, 42.86.82.82
Closed on Sat. and Sun. Credit cards: VISA. Dining at the Carré is something of an event. Divided into several rooms that fan out from the entrance, a completely unusual mood is created (the paintings are a little strange). Some unusual concoctions are also created by an extremely innovative chef, who also turns out some of the best southwestern traditional specialties (the meats are divine).

Jules Verne
Tour Eiffel, 75007
M° Trocadéro, École Militaire or Bir-Hakeim, 45.55.61.44
Open everyday. Credit cards: VISA, AE. On top of the Eiffel Tower, the key word is view. Everything is elegantly black, fading discreetly into the background, allowing the marvelous panoramic view of Paris to take its place (especially at night). Fortunately the food doesn't take a back seat, especially the delicious veal and fish. Be sure to reserve well in advance (several weeks) and request a table next to the window when you do.

Le Manoir de Paris
6 rue Pierre-Demours, 75017
M° Wagram, 45.72.25.25
Closed on Sat., Sun. and in July. Credit cards: VISA, AE, DC. Although the dining room itself may be a surprising pot-pourri of styles, the exquisite food served here is certainly not. Ranging from the disarmingly simple to the amazingly complicated, each course is a celebration of kitchen mastery.

500 FRANCS & ABOVE

La Tour d'Argent
15 quai de la Tournelle, 75005
M° Maubert-Mutualité or Sully-Morland, 43.54.23.31.
Closed on Mon. Credit cards: VISA, AE, DC. This lovely restaurant is known the world over for its magnificent view of Notre Dame (careful, there is a second room...) Duck is the specialty here (the birds are even numbered) but the veal, fish and lamb are excellent as well. The service, (what a joy!) is impeccable.

Lasserre
17 ave. Franklin D. Roosevel,t 75008
M° Franklin D. Roosevelt, 43.59.53.43
Closed on Sun., Mon. and in August. The main dining room upstairs at Lasserre is the place to be when they roll back the sky-painted ceiling to make way for the real thing. Everything here is silk, crystal, porcelain and silver. The cuisine, once one of the greatest in France, has suffered from lack of innovation, although efforts are now being made to remedy the situation (stick to the fish, always beautifully prepared). Bring cash, no credit cards are accepted, but foreign currency (U.S. dollars especially) can be converted.

Le Grand Véfour
17 rue de Beaujolais, 75001
M° Palais-Royal, 42.96.56.27
Closed on Sun. and in August. Credit cards: VISA, AE, DC. One of the most, if not the most, beautiful restaurants in the world, having recently restored its ancient luxury trappings. The Grand Véfour is nestled among the arcades of Palais-Royal and haunted by spirits of its former clients: Napoléon Bonaparte, Danton, Victor Hugo and George Sand (to name a few). The fish, duck, *foie gras* and meat are choice, even though prices are a bit heady. Be sure to reserve several weeks in advance, and request a table next to the window.

Lucas-Carton
9 place de la Madeleine, 75008
M° Madeleine, 42.65.22.90
Closed on Sat., Sun., and in August and over Christmas and New Year's. Credit cards: VISA. This is the most expensive restaurant (with Maxim's) in Paris, and naturally the *Belle Epoque* décor, the glittering clientele and the food are nothing less than divine (although quite a bit less than copious).

Maxim's
3 rue Royale, 75008
M° Concorde, 42.65.27.94.
Closed on Sun. Credit cards: VISA, AE, DC. Probably the most beautiful *Belle Epoque* restaurant in the world, Maxim's has a grandiose reputation for its cuisine, which is indeed very good, but not quite up to the prices which are literally astronomical.

Robuchon (originally Jamin)
32 rue de Longchamp, 75016
M° Trocadéro.
Closed on Sat., Sun. and in July. Credit cards: VISA, AE, DC. A small restaurant, perfectly decorated where every table is the best in the house. Is this why people need to reserve eight weeks in advance to dine at Robuchon? Not at all. The answer is Robuchon himself, master of masters, a chef acclaimed by chefs, and an impassioned artist who never stops searching, experimenting and refining his art. Eureka!

Taillevent
15 rue Lamennais, 75008
M° Georges V, 45.63.39.94.
Closed on Sat., Sun.; in February from 14th to 22nd, and in August. An outstanding restaurant lodged comfortably in a 18th-century townhouse, renowned internationally for its unparalleled cuisine, formidable wine cellar and heavenly desserts.

THINGS TO DO

TOUR PACKAGES

Two companies offer double-decker bus tours around the city day or night, complete with English commentary piped in over headphones. This is a good way to get a feel of how Paris is laid out and where the different monuments are.

Bateaux-Mouches
On the Seine at M° Alma-Marceau
42.25.96.10
Lunch, tea and dinner cruises available.

Cityrama
4 places des Pyramides, 75001
M° Pyramides, 42.60.30.14

Les Bateaux Parisiens—Vedetees Tour Eiffel
On the river at M° Bir-Hakeim or Iéna
47.05.09.85
Lunch and dinner cruises available.

Les Vedettes de Paris-Ile-de-France
M° Bir-Hakeim, 47.05.71.29.

Les Vedettes du Pont Neuf
On the river at M° Pont-Neuf
46.33.98.38.

Paris-Vision
214 rue de Rivoli, 75001
M° Tuileries, 42.60.31.25
Boat tours up and down the Seine are also available, some with lunch or dinner.

If you would like the services of a guide interpreter, contact the **Amicale Inter-Guides** (42.68.01.04), the **Guides-interpreters and Speakers Association** (47.82.24.91), the **National Club of Guides and Messengers** (42.80.01.27), **Troismil** (45.63.99.11), or even the national employment agency *(agence Nationale pour* *l'Emploi*, 42.03.13.55. Guide-chaffeurs can be hired, along with the car, at "Meet the French," 9 blvd. des Italiens, 75002 (M° Richelieu-Dreuot, 47.42.66.02).

PARKS

Jardin de l'Acclimatation
Bois de Boulogne

Jardin des Plantes
Quai St. Bernard, 75005

Parc Zoologique de Paris
Bois de Vincennes

DAY TRIPS

Chantilly
There is a regular train service to Chantilly from the Gare du Nord. It's a 30-minute ride and you can rent a bike at the station when you arrive. The castle is open everyday 10:30 a.m. to 5 p.m. (6 p.m. in summer) except Tues.

Chartres
There are regular trains from Montparnasse Station that will get you to Chartres in an hour where there is a bicycle rental service at the station. Two restaurants you might look into are le Henri IV, rue Soleil d'Or (traditional, a bit expensive but quite delicious) and Banquetti, 20 rue St.-Maurice (cheap and hearty).

Compiègne
Hop on the train at the Gare du Nord and one hour later you'll be in Compiègne. The tourist office is located in the Hôtel de Ville where you can also rent a bicycle (or at the station). An excellent restaurant to try also doubles as an inn. The Auberge de la Bonne Idée (Vieux Moulin Village) is fairly expensive but very comfortable (44.42.84.09).

Fontainebleau
Take a train from the Gare de Lyon to Avon (a 50-minute ride), where you can either rent a bike or take a bus to the castle. The *château* is open everyday from 9:30 a.m. to 12:30 p.m. and from 2 p.m. to 6 p.m. (5 p.m. in the winter) except Tues.

Gien
There are six to 10 trains a day to Gien from the Gare de Lyon, both express and local. One hotel suggestion is the Hôtel Jeanne d'Arc, right in the center of town (38.67.11.00).

Giverny
In one hour from the Gare St.-Lazare you can be in Giverny, but you have to get off at Vernon and take a taxi (or rent a bike) to get to Monet's house. There is a restaurant/tea room at the actual house, rather expensive but quite chic. In Verdun you might try the Bar-Restaurant de la Poste, inexpensive and unusually copious.

Lyons-la-Forêt
Take the train to Rouen from the Gare St.-Lazare. At the bus station in Rouen you can catch the (rare) bus on Wed. and Sat. at 10:45 a.m. (arrives at 11:50 a.m.). On other days this bus leaves at 6:30 p.m. (no Sun. service). Two nice hotels are the Auberge du Grand Cerf (32.49.60.44) and the Hôtel de la Licorne (32.49.60.02).

Orléans
You can catch a train for Orléans from the Gare d'Austerlitz every hour, and rent a bike at the station. If you'd like further information on Loire Valley tours, go to the tourist office at the place Albert I. You can also rent a car at Thrifty, 76 Faubourg Madeleine (38.88.22.21).

Provins
To get to Provins take a train at the Gare de l'Est that's heading towards Troyes. Get off at Longueville and transfer to the train going to Provins which runs every 2 hours. The whole trip takes about an hour and a half. You can also take a bus from the porte de Vincennes. The bus company is called Car Bizière (64.25.60.46).

Vaux-le-Vicomte
Catch the train to Melun at the Gare de Lyon. From here you'll have to grab a cab for the last 7 kilometers. The castle is open everyday from April to October, 10 a.m. to 6 p.m., and there is a restaurant on the grounds. The candlelight tours take place every Sat. from June to September, 9 p.m. to 11 p.m.

Versailles
Take the RER line C. The castle is open everyday, 9:45 a.m. to 5:30 p.m., except Mon. The gardens are open from morning to nightfall.

LANGUAGE & COOKING SCHOOLS

If you are interested in some of the long-term activities suggested, be sure to contact the organizations concerned to see if you need a special visa. The language and cooking schools listed here will send you information by mail and may help you plan travel and housing. Other schools and associations are less formal and some even handle "walk-ins". You can also check with the French Consulate for visa application forms.

Académie Du Vin
25, rue Royale—Cité Berryer
46.65.09.82/42.65.92.40

Alliance Française
101, blvd. Raspail
75006 Paris, 45.44.38.28

American Legion—American Club of Paris
49, rue Pierre Charron
75008 Paris, 43.59.24.33

Amicale Culturelle Internationale
27, rue Godot de Mauroy
75009 Paris, 47.42.94.21

Association Pour la Sauvegarde du Patrimoine Archéologique
11, rue Lacarriére
94370 Sucy-en-Brie, 45.90.01.84

Association Pour le Development de L'Animation Culturelle
27, quai de la Tournelle
75005 Paris, 43.26.13.54

Atelier D'Art Floral
Sylvie Expert Besancon
40, quai des Célestins
75004 Paris, 42.71.52.31

Atelier Théâtre D'Aujourd'Hui
37, rue Monge
75005 Paris, 46.33.36.74

Bureau du Cours Municipal D'Adultes
9, rue de la Perle
75003 Paris, 42.77.66.77

Centre de Danse du Marais
41, rue du Temple
75004 Paris, 42.77.58.19

Centre de Documentation et D'Information Rurale
92, rue du Dessous des Berges
75013 Paris, 45.83.01.92

Centre Odéon Franco-Americain
1 place de l'Odéon
75006 Paris, 46.34.16.10

Chantiers Histoire et Architecture Medievales
5-7, rue Guilleminot
75014 Paris, 45.35.15.51

Chantiers Recontres Internationales
6, rue Mesnil
75116 Paris, 45.05.13.14

Ciné Amateur Club Montmartrois
Mr. J. Renault
140, rue de Clignancourt
75018 Paris, 46.06.31.73

Club du Vieux Manoir
10, rue de la Cossonnerie
75001 Paris, 45.08.80.40

Comite National de L'Enseignment Catholique
277, rue St.-Jacques
75005 Paris, 43.29.12.77

Comite de Coordination du Service Volontaire International
1, rue Miollis
75015 Paris, 45.68.27.31/45.68.27.32

CONCORDIA, Association de Chantiers et d'Exchanges Internationaux
B. P. 238, 27, rue du Pont Neuf
75024 Paris, Cédex, 01.42.33.42.10

Contact Intervac Vacation Exchange Club
55, rue Nationale
Tours, France 37000, 45.51.73.67

Council on International Educational Exchange
1, place de l'Odéon
75006 Paris, 46.34.16.10

École du Louvre
34, quai du Louvre
75001 Paris, 42.60.25.50/42.60.39.26

École Internationale de Mimodrame de Paris
Marcel Marceau
17, rue René Boulanger
75010 Paris, 42.09.65.86

École Jacques Lecoq
Le Central, 57, rue du Faubourg St.-Denis
75010 Paris, 47.70.44.78

École Superior de Cuisine Francaise (Ecole Ferrandi)
11, rue Ferrandi 75014
Call: Chambre Syndicale de la Cuisine Francaise, 43.87.73.70

Église Americaine—American Church
65, quai d'Orsay
75007 Paris, 47.05.07.99

Federation Française de Danse, D'Art Chorégraphique et D'Expression Corporelle
12, rue St.-Germain l'Auxerrois
75001 Paris, 42.36.12.61

Global Home Exchange
124, blvd. Auguste Blanqui
75013 Paris, 43.37.85.72

Holiday Exchange
Box 878, Belen,
New Mexico 87002 U.S.A.
(505) 864-8680

Home Exchange International
9, ave. de la Mésange
94100 St. Maur des Fosses
48.72.92.80/42.83.07.41

Institut D'Art Théâtral
Laurent Azimioara
6-8, place Carrée, Porte St.-Eustache Nouveau Forum des Halles
75001 Paris, 43.67.26.78

Institut de Langue et du Culture Française
Institut Catholique
21, rue d'Assas
75006 Paris, 42.22.41.80

Inter Service Home Exchange
c/o Voyages A.T.H.
9, ave. de la Motte Picquet
75007 Paris, 45.51.73.67

Jeunesse et Reconstruction
10, rue de Trévise
75009 Paris, 47.70.15.88

La Varenne
34, rue St.-Dominique
75007 Paris, 47.05.10.16

Le Cordon Bleu
24, rue du Champ de Mars
75007 Paris, 45.55.02.77

Le Petit Atelier
Acting in English for the Camera,
11, rue Jacob
75006 Paris, 46.33.55.08/45.44.14.13

Le Pot Au Feu
14, rue Duphot
75001 Paris, 42.60.00.94

Maison de la Jeunesse et de la Culture de St.-Michel
9, place St.-Michel
75005 Paris, 43.54.16.58

Martine Moisan
6-8, galerie Vivienna
75001 Paris, 42.97.46.65

Ministère de la Culture et de la Communication
Direction du Patrimoine
Sous-Direction de l'Archéologie Service de Documentation
4, rue d'Abourkir
75002 Paris, 42.96.10.40, ext. 20-17

Paris American Academy
Jardin et Pavillion du Val de Grâce,
277, rue St.-Jacques
75005 Paris, 4.-25.08.91/43.25.35.09

Promattt (Syndicat des Professionnels du Travail Temporaire)
6, blvd. des Capucines
75009 Paris, 47.42.14.13

Schola Cantorum
269, rue St.-Jacques
75005 Paris, 43.54.15.39/43.54.56.74

Service de Placement Enseignement Prive
76, rue des St.-Péres
75007 Paris, 42.22.62.50

Théâtre de L'Opprime
Augusto Boal
29, ave. Laumiére
75019 Paris, 42.05.89.31

Théâtre et Anglais
14, rue Lapeyrére
75018 Paris, 42.54.34.04

Unett (Union Nationale des Enterprises de Travail Temporaire)
9, rue Thabor
75001 Paris, 42.97.41.50

Union des Associations Pour la Rehabilitation et L'Entretien des Monuments et du Patrimoine Artistique
1, rue des Guillemites
75004 Paris, 42.71.96.55

Union Nationale des Entreprises du Travail Temporaire
9, rue du Mont Thabor
75001 Paris, 42.97.41.50

Université de Paris (Pierre et Marie Curie)
4, place Jussieu
75005 Paris, 43.36.25.25 ext. 3608
(for sports, ext. 3289)

Université de Paris, Academie de Creteil, Paris VIII,
2, rue de la Liberté
93206, St. Denis, Cédex 1
48.21.63.64/48.29.08.44

Université de Paris Censier, Paris III
13, rue de Santeuil, Bureau 14,
75005 Paris, 45.70.12.90 ext. 313

Université de Paris Pantheon-Sorbonne, Paris I
Education Permanente
14, rue Cujas
75005 Paris, 43.54.67.80/43.29.75.23

Université de Paris Sorbonne, Paris, IV, Cours de Civilisation Francaise de la Sorbonne
Galerie Richelieu, Salle 9,
45, rue des Ecoles
75005 Paris, 43.29.12.13 ext. 3430

Worldwide Home Exchange Club
139-A Sloane Street
London SW1 England, 589-6055

CULTURE PLUS

MUSEUMS

There is a museum for everyone in this culturally rich city. Plan ahead, because museums close alternately on Monday (city museums) and Tuesday (national museums). Most public museums charge half-price or not at all on Sunday. There are also special rates for students, large families, senior citizens, and a new system called C'ARTE, which is a single fee for virtually unlimited access to public museums. Information on reduced rates is available in the major museums and the tourist office. To check current exhibits, go to a newsstand and pick up the *Pariscope* or the *Officiel des Spectacles*, which have complete listings, hours, rates, etc. Regulations vary on the use of cameras, but in general flash is forbidden and tripods can be used only in certain areas.

Affiche et Publicité
(Posters and Advertising)
18, rue de Paradis
M° Château d'Eau, 42.46.13.09
From 12 p.m. to 6 p.m. Closed on Tues.

Archives Nationales (National Archives)
87, rue Veille du Temple
M° Filles de Calvaire, 42.77.11.30
Daily, 12 p.m. to 6 p.m.

Armee, Hotel Des Invalides
(Army, Napoleon's Tomb, etc.)
Esplanade des Invalides
M° Invalides, 45.55.92.30
Daily, 10 a.m. to 5 p.m.

Arts Decoratifs
107-109, rue de Rivoli
M° Palais-Royal, 45.55.92.30
From 12:30 p.m. to 6 p.m. Closed on Mon. and Tues.

Carnavalet (History of Paris)
23, rue de Sévigné
M° St.-Paul, 42.72.21.13
From 10 a.m. to 6:40 p.m. Closed on Mon.

Centre National D'Art Et Culture Georges Pompidou.
Rue Rambuteau and rue St.-Merri
M° Rambuteau, Chatelet, Les Halles, 42.77.12.33
Daily from noon to 10 p.m., weekends from 10 a.m. Closed on Tues.

Cernushi (Oriental Art)
7, ave. Velasquez
M° Villiers, 45.63.50.75
From 10 a.m. to 5:40 p.m. Closed on Mon.

Cinema—Henri Langlois
Place du Trocadéro
M° Trocadéro, 45.53.21.86
Scheduled guided visits only. Call or check *Pariscope*. Closed on Tues.

Cité Des Sciences Et De L'Industrie
(La Villette)
Parc de la Villette
M° Porte de la Villette, 40.05.72.72
Tues., Thur., Fri., 10 a.m. to 6 p.m.; Wed., 12 p.m. to 9 p.m., Sat., Sun., holidays, 12 p.m. to 8 p.m. Closed on Mon.

Cluny (Medieval Art and History)
6, place Paul Painlevé
M° St.-Michel, 43.26.62.00
From 9:45 a.m. to noon and 2 p.m. to 5 p.m. Closed on Tues.

Guimet (Asian Art)
6, place de l'Iéna
M° Iéna, 47.23.61.65
From 9:45 a.m. to noon and 1:30 p.m. to 5 p.m. Closed on Tues.

L'Homme (Ethnology)
Place du Trocadéro
M° Trocadéro, 45.53.70.60
From 9:45 a.m. to 5:15 p.m. Closed on Tues. and holidays.

Louvre
Rue de Rivoli
M° Palais Royal or Louvre, 42.60.39.26
From 9:45 a.m. to 6:30 p.m. Closed on Tues. Free on Sun. Guided tours in English are available.

Maison De Balzac (Balzac's House)
47, rue Raynouard
M° Passy, 42.24.56.38
From 10 a.m. to 5:40 p.m. Closed on Mon.

Marmottan (Monet and Impressionism)
2, rue Louis-Boilly
M° La Muette, 42.24.07.02
From 10 a.m. to 5:30 p.m. Closed on Mon.

Monuments Français
Place du Trocadéro
M° Trocadéro, 47.27.35.74
From 10 a.m. to 12:15 p.m. and 2 p.m. to 5:15 p.m. Closed on Tues.

Orsay (Late 19th- and 20th-century art)
1, rue de Bellechasse
M° Solferino, 45.49.48.14
Recorded info: 45.49.11.11
From 10 a.m. to 6 p.m., Thur. to 9:15 p.m. Tickets sold until 45 min. before closing time. Closed on Mon.

Picasso (Hôtel Salé)
5, rue de Thorigny
M° Chemin-Vert or St.-Paul, 42.71.25.21
From 9:15 a.m. to 5:15 p.m., Wed. to 10 p.m. Closed on Tues.

Rodin (Hôtel Biron)
77, rue de Varenne
M° Varenne, 47.05.01.34
From 10 a.m. to 5 p.m. Closed on Tues.

Zadkine (Sculpture)
100, bis rue d'Assas
M° Notre-Dame-des-Champs, 43.26.91.90
From 10 a.m. to 5:40 p.m. Closed on Mon. Free on Sun.

SHOPPING

SHOPPING AREAS

There is no end of shopping to do in Paris. Here is a special selection of shops, which includes places where you'll find the most uniquely Parisian products in town. Though French wines, perfumes and fashions are now available (at similar prices) all over the world, there are still new treats to be discovered! Collectors, souvenir-hunters, fashion plates, gourmets, can all meet their heart's desire at the addresses listed below.

For late night cravings and emergencies, 24 hours a day, one of the biggest supermarkets in the heart of Paris—everything from fresh produce, coffees, books and clothes—is called *As-Eco* and you'll find it near the Pompidou Center on rue Beaubourg.

A l'Image du Grenier sur l'eau
45, rue des Francs-Bourgeois, 75004
M° St.-Paul, 42.71.02.31
Mon. to Fri., 9:30 a.m. to 6:30 p.m., Sat., 2 p.m. to 6 p.m. Closed on Sun.

A L'Olivier
77, rue St.-Louis-en-l'Ile, 75004
M° Pont Marie, 43.29.58.32
Tues. to Sat., 10 a.m. to 7 p.m. Closed on Sun. and Mon.

Alain Vian
8, rue Grégoire-de-Tours, 75006
M° Mabillon/Odéon, 34.54.02.69
Mon. to Fri., 9:30 a.m. to 12 p.m., 2 p.m. to 7 p.m. Closed on Sat., Sun. and in August.

Artisanat Monastique
68, bis ave. Denfert Rochereau 75014
M° Denfert, 43.35.15.76
Closed on Sun.

Au Beau Noir
6, rue de l'Echaude, 75006
M° Mabillon, 43.25.70.72
Mon., 2:30 p.m. to 6:30 p.m., Tues. to Sat., 10:30 a.m. to 1 p.m. and 2 p.m. to 6:30 p.m. Closed on Sun. and in August.

Au Bon Marche
38, rue de Sèvres, 75007
M° Sèrvres-Babylone, 42.60.33.45
Mon. to Sat., 9:30 a.m. to 6:30 p.m. Closed on Sun.

Au Nain Blue
408, rue St.-Honoré, 75008
M° Concorde, 42.60.39.01
An incredible luxury children's toy store.

Au Pain De Sucre
12, rue Jean-du-Bellay, 75004
M° Pont Marie, 46.33.26.07
Tues. to Sat. 10 a.m. to 6 p.m. Closed on Sun., Mon. and in August.

Boutique Chic et Choc
In the *métro* station Les Halles.
A great little shop that sells notebooks, jogging outfits, towels, wallets, pens, keychains, umbrellas, etc., all bearing the mark of the chicest *métro* ticket in the world.

Cacharel Menswear
5, place des Victoires, 75001
M° Pyramides/Bourse, 42.33.29.88
(The Ladies' Boutique is next door at 49, ave. Etienne Marcel). Mon. to Sat., 10:15 a.m. to 7 p.m. Closed on Sun.

Cartier
7, place Vendôme, 75001
M° Invalides, 42.61.55.55; and
12, ave. Montaigne, 75008
M° Alma-Marceau, 47.20.06.73

Chanel
42, ave. Montaigne, 75008
M° Alma-Marceau, 47.23.74.12
From 9:30 a.m. to 6:30 p.m. Closed on Sun.

Chateau Rentals
Bureau of Historic Monuments (*Caisse Natioinale des Monuments Historiques et des Sites*)
62, rue St.-Antoine, 75004
42.74.22.22.
Open daily, rents out 40 châteaux around France for your parties or conventions.

Chez Androuet
41, rue d'Amsterdam, 75008
48.74.26.90
Cheese Shop: Mon. to Sat., 9:50 a.m. to 7 p.m. Closed on Sun. Restaurant: Mon. to Sat., noon to 12:30 a.m. Closed on Mon.

Christian Dior
30, ave. Montaigne, 75008
M° Franklin D. Roosevelt, 47.20.6.82
Tues. to Sat., 9:30 a.m. to 6:30 p.m., Mon., 10 a.m. to 1 p.m. and 2:30 p.m. to 6:30 p.m. Closed on Sun.

Comme Des Femmes
31, rue St. Placide, 75006
M° St.-Placide, 45.48.97.33
From 10 a.m. to 7 p.m. Closed on Sun.

Cour du Commerce Saint André
59-61, rue St.-André des Arts, 75006
M° Odéon

Credit Municipal De Paris
55, rue des Francs-Bourgeois, 75004
M° St.-Paul, 42.71.25.43

Dietetique Regime
45, rue St.-Paul, 75004
M° St.-Paul 48.87.08.82
From 9:30 a.m. to 1:15 p.m. and 2:30 p.m. to 7 p.m. Closed on Sun. and Mon.

Diptyque
34, blvd. St.-Germain, 75006
M° Maubert Mutualité, 40.33.88.90
Mon. to Sat., 10 a.m. to 7 p.m. Closed on Sun.

Fauchon
26 and 28, place de la Madeleine, 75008
M° Madeleine, 47.42.60.11
Tues. to Sat., 9:40 a.m. to 7 p.m. (Delicatessen open on Mon. too). Closed on Sun.

Flirt
19, rue Vignon, 75008
M° Madeleine, 47.42.85.31

FNAC
136, rue de Rennes, 75006,
M° Rennes, 45.44.39.12;
Forum des Halles: Niveau—3
M° Chlâtelet-Les Halles, 40.26.81.18;
Wagram: 26, ave. Wagram, 75008, 47.66.52.50
Tues. to Sat., 10 a.m to 7:30 p.m.

Galeries Lafayette
40, blvd. Haussmann, 75009
M° Havre-Caumartin, 42.82.34.56
Mon. to Sat., 9:30 a.m. to 6:30 p.m. Closed on Sun.

Gerard
8, ave. Montaigne, 75008
M° Alma-Marceau, 47.23.70.00

Gucci
27, rue du Faubourg St.-Honoré, 75008
M° Madeleine, 42.96.83.27
Mon. to Sat., 9:30 a.m. to 6:30 p.m. Closed on Sun.

Halle Bys'
60, rue de Richelieu, 75002
M° Bourse, 42.96.65.42.
Mon. to Sat., 10 a.m. to 6:30 p..m. Closed on Sun.

Hermès
24, rue du Faubourg St.-Honoré, 75008
M° Concorde, 42.65.21.60
Mon. to Sat., 10 a.m. to 6:30 p.m. July and August, Mon. to Sat., 2:15 p.m. to 6:30 p.m. Closed on Sun.

HG Thomas
36, blvd. St.-Germain, 75006
M° Maubert-Mutualité, 46.33.57.50
Tues. to Sat., 10:30 a.m. to 8 p.m. Closed on Sun. and Mon.

Hotel Drouot
9, rue Drouot, 75009
M° Richelieu-Drouot, 42.46.17.11
Mon. to Sat., 11 a.m. to 6 p.m. Closed on Sun.

Issey Miyake
201, blvd. St.-Germain, 75006
M° Rue du Bac, 45.48.10.44
Mon. to Sat. 10 a.m. to 7 p.m. Closed on Sun.

Jardin De Flore
24, place des Vosges, 75004
M° St.-Paul/Bastille, 42.77.61.90
Tues. to Sat., 2 p.m. to 6:30 p.m. Closed on Sun. and Mon.

Jean Baptiste Besse
48, rue de la Montagne Ste.-Geneviève, 75005
M° Maubert-Mutualité, 43.25.35.80
Tues. to Sat., 10:30 a.m. to 2 p.m. and 4:30 p.m. to 8:30 p.m.; Sun., 11 a.m. to 1:30 p.m.

Jean Phillippe Pages
67, rue Rambuteau, 75004
M° Rambuteau, 42.72.05.27
Tues. to Sat., 11:30 a.m. to 8 p.m. Closed on Sun. and Mon.

Kenzo
3, place des Victoires, 75001
M° Pyramides/Bourse, 42.36.81.41

La Danse
14, rue de Beaune, 75006
M° Rue du Bac, 42.61.24.42
Mon. to Sat., 9:30 a.m. to 12 p.m. and 2 p.m. to 6:30 p.m. Closed on Sun.

La Hune
170, blvd. St.-Germain, 75006
M° St.-Germain-des-Près, 45.48.35.85
Mon., 2 p.m. to midnight; Tues. to Fri., 10 a.m. to midnight; Sat., 10 a.m. to 7:30 p.m.

La Maison Du Miel
24, rue Vignon, 75008
M° Madeleine, 47.42.26.70
Mon. to Sat., 9:30 a.m. to 7 p.m. Closed on Sun.

La Samaritaine
19, rue de la Monnaie, 75001
M° Pont Neuf, 45.08.33.33
Mon., Wed., Thur. and Sat., 9:30 a.m. to 7 p.m.; Tues. and Fri., 9:30 a.m. to 8:30 p.m. Closed on Sun. (Café: Mon. to Sat., 11:30 a.m. to 6:30 p.m.; Wed. until 10 p.m.)

Lalique
11, rue Royale 75008
M° Concorde, 42.65.33.70
The most beautiful crystal you can buy.

Lanvin
18, rue du Faubourg St.-Honoré, 75008
M° Concorde, 42.65.14.40
Mon. to Fri., 9:30 a.m. to 12 p.m. and 2 p.m. to 6:30 p.m.; Sat., 10 a.m. to 6 p.m. Closed on Sun.

Le Cabinet De Curiosite
23, rue de Beaune, 75006
M° Rue du Bac, 42.61.09.57
Mon. to Sat., 2 p.m. to 7 p.m. Closed on Sun. and in August.

Le Printemps
64, blvd. Haussmann, 75009
M° Havre-Caumartin, 42.82.50.00
Mon. to Sat., 9:35 a.m. to 6:30 p.m. Closed on Sun.

Le Sphinx
104, rue du Faubourg St.-Honoré, 75008
M° St.-Philippe du Roulé, 42.65.90.96
Mon. to Sat., 10:30 a.m. to 7 p.m. Closed on Sun.

Le Village Africain
2, rue de l'Arbalète, 75005
M° Censier-Daubenton
Mon. to Sat., 9 a.m to 12:30 p.m. and 4 p.m. to 7:30 p.m. Closed on Sun.

Les Comptoirs De La Tour D'Argent
2, rue Cardinal Lemoine, 75005
M° Maubert Mutualité or Cardinal Lemoine, 46.33.45.58
Tues. to Sun., noon to 12:30 a.m. Closed on Mon.

Louis Vuitton
54, ave. Montaigne, 75008
M° Alma Marceau, 45.62.47.00;
78 bis, ave. Marceau 75008
47.20.47.00

Louvre Des Antiquaires
2, place du Palais-Royal, 75001
M° Palais-Royal, 42.97.27.00

Madame Pierre Fain
34, rue St.-Louis-en-l'Ile, 75001
M° Pont Marie, 43.26.44.72

Magic Beauty
51, rue de Rivoli, 75001
M° Châtelet, 42.36.06.35
Tues. to Sat., 10 a.m. to 8 p.m.; Mon., 12 p.m. to 8 p.m.

Manuel Canovas Boutique
5, place de Fürstenberg, 75006
M° St.-Germain-des-Prés, 43.26.89.31
Mon. to Sat., 10 a.m. to 7 p.m. Closed on Sun.

Marithe Et François Girbaud
38, rue Etienne Marcel, 75002
M° Les Halles/Etienne Marcel, 42.33.54.69

Mythes Et Legendes
18, place des Vosges, 75004
M° St.-Paul/Bastille
Tues. to Sat., 10 a.m. to 12:30 p.m. and 2 p.m. to 7 p.m. Closed on Sun. and Mon.

Nina Ricci
39, ave. Montaigne, 75008
M° Franklin D. Roosevelt, 47.23.78.88
Mon. to Fri., 10 a.m. to 6 p.m.; Sat., 10 a.m. to 1 p.m. Closed on Sun.

Pain d'Epices
29, passage Jouffroy, 75009
M° Montmartre, 57.70.82.65
An enchanting *mélange* of miniature children's items.

Papeterie Moderne
12, rue de la Ferronnerie, 75001
M° Les Halles
Mon. to Sat., 7:30 a.m. to 12 p.m. and 1 p.m. to 7 p.m. Closed on Sun.

Pierre Cardin
82, rue du Faubourg St.-Honoré, 75008
M° St.-Philippe du Roulé, 42.65.26.88
Factory outlet at: 11, blvd. de Sébastopol, 75001, 4th floor. M° Chatelet, 42.61.74.73
Mon. to Sat., 9:15 a.m. to 1 p.m. and 2 p.m. to 6 p.m. Closed on Sun.

Quai De Montebello Booksellers
M° St.-Michel
Generally: Tues. to Sat., 11 a.m. to 7:30 p.m.

Rene Gerard Saint Ouen
111, blvd. Haussmann, 75008
M°Miromesnil, 42.65.06.25
Mon. to Sat., 8 a.m. to 7 p.m. Closed on Sun.

Réunion des Musées Nationaux
10, rue de l'Abbaye, 75006
M° St.-Germain-des-Prés, 43.29.21.45
Mon. to Fri., 9 a.m. to 12:30 p.m. and 2 p.m. to 5 p.m. Closed on Sat., Sun. Museum items can also be purchased at the Forum des Halles, at 89 ave. Victor Hugo and at the main store of the Galeries Lafayette on blvd. Haussmann.

Smart (*Société des Métiers d'Art*)
22, rue des Francs-Bourgeois, 75004
M° St.-Paul, 42.77.41.24
Tues. to Fri., 10 a.m to 12:30 p.m. and 2 p.m. to 7 p.m.; Sat., 10:30 a.m. to 12:30 p.m. and 2:30 to 6 p.m. Closed on Mon. morning and Sun.

Tokio Kumagai
52, rue Croix des Petits-Champs, 75001
M° Pyramides/Palais Royal, 42.33.47.46

Ungaro
2, ave. Montaigne, 75008
M° Alma-Marceau, 47.23.61.94

Valentino
19, ave. Montaigne, 75008
M° Alma-Marceau, 47.23.64.61;
Victoire, 10-12, place des Victoires, 75001
M° Pyramides/Bourse, 45.08.53.29

Vittoria
26, rue Vignon, 75008
47.42.66.34

Yveline
4, rue de Fürstenberg, 75006
M° St.-Germain-des-Prés, 43.26.56.91
Tues. to Sat., 11 a.m. to 6:30 p.m. Closed on Sun., Mon. and in August.

MARKETS

Even if you're not a big shopper, do make time for a visit to a typical Parisian market. Those listed below are among the nicest, but you can also ask your hotelkeeper where the nearest one is, and start your day perfectly by paying an early morning visit. Bring your camera along—the colorful displays and lively vendors will inspire you.

Flower And Bird Market
Center of the Ile de la Cité,
Place Louis Lépine,
M° Cité

Mouffetard Market
Begins at rue de l'Epée-de-Bois in the 5th, M° Monge, not far from the Latin Quarter. Tues. to Sat., 9 a.m. to 1 p.m. and 4 p.m. to 7 p.m.; Sun., 9 a.m. to 1 p.m. Closed on Mon.

Buci Market
At the intersection of rue de Buci and rue de Seine in the 6th, M° Monge.
Tues. to Sat., 9 a.m. to 1 p.m. and 4 p.m. to 7 p.m.; Sun., 9 a.m. to 1 p.m. Closed on Mon.

Marché St.-Pierre
2, rue Charles Nodier
75018, M° Anvers, 46.06.92.25

March´ D'Alligre
Place d'Aligre, 75012
Daily, 9 a.m. to 1 p.m. Closed on Mon.

Puces De St.-Ouen
Porte de Clignancourt,
St.-Ouen, M° Porte de Clignancourt,
Sat., Sun. and Mon., 5 a.m. to 6 p.m.

Puces De Montreuil
Ave. de la porte de Montreuil, 75020
M° Porte de Montreuil
Sat., Sun. and Mon., 7 a.m. to 7:30 p.m.

ENGLISH BOOKSTORES

Albion
13, rue Charles V
42.72.50.71

Attica
34, rue des Ecoles
43.26.09.53

Brentano's
37, ave. de l'Opéra
42.61.52.50

Galignani
224, rue de Rivoli
42.60.76.07

Interculture
141, blvd. St.-Germain
43.29.38.20

Le Nouveau Quartier Latin
78, blvd. St.-Michel
43.26.42.70

Shakespeare and Company
37, rue de la Bûcherie
(no telephone)

W.H. Smith & Son
248, rue de Rivoli
42.60.37.97

Trilby's
18, rue Franklin
45.20.40.49

Village Voice
6, rue Princesse
46.33.36.47

BEAUTY & HAIR TREATMENT

With so many last minute preparations for your trip to Paris you may have completely forgotten to get your hair trimmed (*rafraîchir*) or you've seen such marvelous styles in Paris you'd like to try a new cut (*coupe*). Perhaps the way you set your hair, *mis-en-plis*, doesn't please you any more, or you want to *colorer* your blond hair or *décolorer* your dark hair. A *rincage* (rinse) to bring out highlights and cover gray or a *balayage* (streaking) might suit your mood. You've got a marvelously romantic evening coming up—dinner, opera, the whole works—and you've been pounding the pavements sightseeing for days now, looking more and more tired. Let someone else perk up your hair with a *shampooing* and *brushing* (blow dry), tidy up your nails with a *manicure*, and bring out the vitality in your face with a *soin de visage*.

Almost any *salon de coiffure* can give you a good trim, color rinse and manicure. Your neighborhood *institut de beauté* can wax your legs (*épilation*, or any other part of your body, give you a facial, while others offer *messages* or *bronzage*, tanning sessions).

The following list contains some of the more well-known *salons* if you want the royal treatment (for royal prices). Otherwise keep your eyes open and pop into the nearest one to make a reservation (a must).

Alexandre de Paris
3, ave. Matignon, 75008
M° Franklin D. Roosevelt , 42.25.57.90

Carita
11, rue du Faubourg St.-Honoré, 75008
M° Concorde , 42.65.79.00

Jacques Dessange
37, ave. Franklin D. Roosevelt, 75008
M° Franklin D. Roosevelt, 43.59.33.97

Mod's Hair
7, rue de Ponthieu, 75008
M° Franklin D. Roosevelt, 43.59.06.50

Salon de Coiffure Bruno
15, rue St.-Pères, 75006
M° Sèvres-Babylone, 42.61.45.15

V.A.T.

Value Added Tax is tacked on to just about everything sold in France, and is considered "invisible" as it's always included in the sales price. Theoretically VAT is refunded to tourists, but recovering it is a long and complicated battle. First snag—the price: each item you attempt to recover VAT on must have cost a minimum of 1,200 francs (non-EEC members) or 2,400 francs (EEC members). Second snag—the exceptions: there is no refund on food, wine, tobacco or any items shipped back. You must carry them to be eligible. Third snag—the procedure: at the time of your purchase ask for a *bordereau pour détaxe*, a triplicate form on which the items must appear along with your signature. Make sure your have your passport with you as proof of your tourist status. At this point get an envelope, put the store's address on it and stamp it before you forget. On the day of your departure, go to the airport or train station hours in advance and BEFORE YOU DO ANYTHING, line up outside the Customs office marked *détaxe*, with your documents, purchased goods and envelope (that you did not forget to stamp). Show all this to the officer. Careful! Only the person who signed the *bordereau* may do this. The Customs officer will stamp your three sheets, put one of the pink ones in your envelope send it back to the store, and the store will mail you a check (in francs). If you arrive at the airport during banking hours, you may be able to get your refund on the spot. Clarify with the Customs officer.

Some stores make it easy for their clients and give the refund immediately. However if you don't mail back the validated *bordereau*, these shops will be forced to stop providing this invaluable service.

One strategy to avoid losing money on bank fees is to charge the goods using two credit slips, one for the pre-tax price and the other with the VAT. Ask the store to hold the VAT slip until they receive the stamped *bordereau* and then tear it up. *Bon Courage!*

EXPORT

United States: When returning to the United States be prepared to declare *everything* you have bought or received as a gift. US Customs officer do not joke around, so don't try to fool them. Any amount of money may be imported into the States, but if the amount exceeds $10,000, it must be declared on form CF 4790. Duty free exemptions apply to a maximum of $400 worth of goods for personal use, including one liter of alcoholic beverages (You must be at least 21), 100 cigars and 200 cigarettes. Liquor cannot be mailed to the USA. Some prohibited articles are certain fruits, vegetables, plants, animals, meat, poultry, products made from endangered species (e.g. ivory and certain furs), absinthe, liquor-filled candy, fireworks, lottery tickets and drugs. There are restrictions on the importation of firearms. You need a special licence to import goods made in North Korea, Vietnam, Cambodia and Cuba (like cigars, which are sold everywhere in Paris).

Canada: As with the United States, you must declare *everything* you have bought or received as a gift. Canadian Customs officials are more relaxed than Americans, but if they have the slightest suspicion, for any reason whatsoever, that you are cheating or carrying drugs, you are in for a long, hard haul of searching and questioning. No liquor may be imported into Canada, except for the amount allowed as duty-free exemptions, 1.1 liter of alcoholic beverages or 8 liters of beer (you must be 18). Other exemptions are 50 cigars, 900 grams of tobacco, 200 cigarettes (you must be 16) and gifts of up to $25 each (gifts for other people, that is, don't push this too far...) Prohibited articles include meat (fresh or canned, so forget the *foie gras*), plants, drugs, products made from endangered species (e.g. ivory and certain furs), and there are restrictions on the importation of arms and ammunition.

SPORTS

PARTICIPANT

Allo Sport (phone information service)
42.76.54.54

BASEBALL

Baseball Club de France
29, rue de la Quintaine 75008

EQUITATION

Bayard Equitation
Ave. du Polygone, Bois de Vincennes,
Centre Equestre de la Cartoucherie,
Rue du Champs-de-Man-oeuvre, Bois de Vincennes

SEP Touring Club
Route de Neuilly at La Muette, Bois de Boulogne

Société Equestre de l'Etrier
Route de Madrid, Bois de Boulogne

GOLF

City Golf
115, rue du Bac, 75007

Club de l'Etoile
10, ave. de la Grande-Armée, 75017

Ken Club
100, ave. du President Kennedy

GYMS & FITNESS CENTERS

Centre de Danse du Marais
41, rue du Temple, 75004

Espace Vit'Halles
48, rue Rambuteau

Garden Gym
8, rue Lasser 75012

Gymnase Club
10, rue Victoire, 75012,
8, rue Frémicourt, 75015,
11, rue Chanez, 75016

Jardin de la Forme
47, rue des Francs-Bourgeois, 75004

Vitatop
Sofitel Hotel
8, rue Louis Armand, 75015

PELOTA

Fronton de Paris Club
2, quai St.-Exupèry, 75016

POLO

Polo de Bagatelle
Bois de Boulogne

SQUASH

Front de Seine
21, rue Gaston-de-Caill-evet, 75015

Squash Montparnasse
37, ave. du Maine, 75014

Squash Stadium
66, ave. d'Ivry, 75013

SWIMMING POOLS

Deligny
Quai d'Orsay, 75007

Piscine des Halles
Inside the Forum commercial center 75004

Pontoise (Pool and Squash Club)
14, rue Pontois, 75005

Special Information

DOING BUSINESS

Paris is definitely the business capital of France, and a major European center for service sector activities. Despite a certain reputation for Latin laziness, Parisians, in private and public industry, generally work very hard. They may seem less frank than British or Americans, even downright evasive at times. Women are only slowly finding their place in the business world, where the heavy drinking, heavy smoking crowd still dominates, and deals are made over a cognac after a heavy meal.

Aside from these generalities, if you plan to do business in France, brush up on your language skills or hire an interpreter, in most cases it will be necessary and welcome. Parisians tend to be rather formal, but don't take a certain distance for disrespect. There are often many administrative formalities to go through before you can carry out your intensions, so be prepared to be patient, and don't automatically blame your partners for slow action—they may be victims of the system themselves!

CHILDREN

Weekly magazines like the *Official* and *Pariscope* give details on plays, movies, marionettes and circuses. They also list baby-sitting services. In better hotels, the *concierge* can arrange for child care. *Passion Magazine* also often carries advertisements for English-speaking sitters.

BABY SITTING SERVICES

Allo! Maman Poule
47.47.78.78

Babysitting Service
47.37.51.24

Grandmères Occasionelles
46.33.28.45

Kid's Services
42.96.04.16

CHILDREN'S THEATER

Napoléon
4, ave. de la Grande-Armée, 75017

Saint Lambert
6, rue Pécle, 75015

GAYS

Homosexuality has long been tolerated in Paris, especially among artists and intellectuals. There are a few bars and clubs favored by gay men or women, and several legendary transvestite performances. Pick up a copy of *Gai Pied* for information and messages. Lesbians won't find many organized activities.

DISABLED

Some progress has been made recently as far as improving access to transportation, monuments and museums for handicapped travelers, although it is far from a breeze for people with physical disabilities to visit the city. An invaluable source of information is the government booklet, *Touristes Quand Même*, in French but including an English glossary. The book covers travel in all of France and is available from the French National Tourist Office, the Paris Tourist Office, or the *Comité National Français de Liason pour la Readaptation des handicapés*, 38 blvd. Raspail, Paris 75007.

STUDENTS

Student travelers should have an international student card (check with your school or university, or contact the Council on International Education Exchange, 205 East 42nd Street, New York, N.Y. 10017. In Canada, the Association of Student Councils, 187 College St., Toronto, Ont. M5T 1P7. Students are eligible for many discounts in movie theaters, museums, rail transport and air fare. Just across from the Georges Pompidou Center, the Accueil des

Jeunes en France (119 rue St.-Martin, 75003) can help direct students to lodging or hostels, and provides pertinent information and support for student travelers.

LANGUAGE

A great many Parisians speak English, and even like speaking it. However, no one likes to be hit in the face with a barrage of foreign words without any warning. Accordingly, the French will respond much more willingly if you approach them in their native tongue, even if the conversation ends up in English. Do make the effort and you'll be surprised how easy it will become.

BASIC PHRASES

Hello	*Bonjour*
Good bye	*Au revoir*
Good evening	*Bon soir*
Good night	*Bon nuit*
Thank you	*Merci*
You're welcome	*Je vous en prie*
Where is the...	*Ou est...*
...embassy	*...l'ambassade*
...train station	*...la gare*
...bank	*...la banque*
...phone booth	*...la cabine téléphonique*
...police station	*...le commissariat de police*
Where are the...	*Ou sont less...*
...restrooms	*...toilettes*
...seats	*...places*
...dressing rooms	*...cabines d'essayages*
I would like...	*Je voudrais...*
...a pack of...	*...un paquet de...*
...a lighter	*...un briquet*
...some matches	*...des allumettes*
...a loaf of bread	*..une baguette*
...a cup of coffee	*...un café*
...the check	*...l'addition*
...some aspirin	*...de l'aspirine*
...to reserve	*...réserver*
...to buy	*...acheter*
...to try on	*...essayer*
How much/many...?	*Combien...?*
I don't understand	*Je ne comprend pas*
Do you speak English?	*Parlezvous anglais?*
What time is it?	*Quelle heure est-il?*
What time do...	*A quelle heure...*
...you open/close?	*...ouvrez/ferméz vous?*

DAY & NIGHT

morning	*le matin*
afternoon	*l'après-midi*
evening	*le soir*
noon	*midi*
midnight	*minuit*
hour	*heure*
week	*semaine*
month	*mois*
year	*an, année*
Monday	*lundi*
Tuesday	*mardi*
Wednesday	*mercredi*
Thursday	*jeudi*
Friday	*vendredi*
Saturday	*samedi*
Sunday	*dimanche*
yesterday	*hier*
today	*aujourd'hui*
tomorrow	*demain*

ANSWERS & DESCRIPTIONS

yes	*oui*
no	*non*
maybe	*peut-être*
a little	*un peu*
a lot	*beaucoup*
big	*grand*
small	*petit*
cheap	*pas cher*
expensive	*cher*
old	*vieux*
new	*neuf, nouveau*
cold	*froid*
hot	*chaud*
late	*tard*
early	*tôt*
near	*près de*
far	*loin*
beige	*beige*
black	*noir*

blue	*bleu*
brown	*marron*
gray	*gris*
green	*vert*
orange	*orange*
pink	*rose*
purple	*mauve, violet*
red	*rouge*
white	*blanc*
yellow	*jaune*

NUMBERS

one	*un, une*
two	*deux*
three	*trois*
four	*quatre*
five	*cinq*
six	*six*
seven	*sept*
eight	*huit*
nine	*neuf*
ten	*dix*
eleven	*onze*
twelve	*douze*
thirteen	*treize*
fourteen	*quatorze*
fifteen	*quinze*
sixteen	*seize*
seventeen	*dix-sept*
eighteen	*dix-huit*
nineteen	*dix-neuf*
twenty	*vingt*
thirty	*trente*
forty	*quarante*
fifty	*cinquante*
sixty	*soixante*
seventy	*soixante-dix*
eighty	*quatre-vingts*
a hundred	*cent*
a thousand	*mille*

CLOTHES

a coat	*un manteau*
a dress	*une robe*
gloves	*des gants*
a hat	*un chapeau*
jewelry	*des bijoux*
a scarf	*un foulard, une écharpe*
a jacket	*une veste*
a shirt	*une chemise*
shoes	*des chaussures*
socks	*des chaussettes*
a sweater	*un pull*
a tie	*une cravate*
an umbrella	*un parapluie*
underwear	*des sous-vétements*

TOILETRIES

aftershave	*aftershave*
brush	*une brosse*
comb	*un peigne*
make-up	*maquillage*
razor blades	*des lames de rasoir*
soap	*un savon*
toilet paper	*du papier hygiénique*
toothbrush	*une brosse à dents*
toothpaste	*pâte de la dentifrice*
a towel	*une serviette*

INDOORS & OUTDOORS

a chair	*une chaise*
a door	*une porte*
a table	*une table*
a window	*une fenêtre*
basement	*le sous-sol*
ground floor	*rez-de-chaussée*
second floor	*premier étage*
elevator	*l'ascenseur*
escalator	*l'escalator*
stairs	*l'escalier*
building	*le bâtiment*
street	*la rue*
corner	*le coin*
red light	*le feu rouge*
straight ahead	*tout droit*
left	*gauche*
right	*droite*
next to	*à côté de*
facing	*en face de*
entrance	*l'entrée*
exit	*la sortie*
emergency exit	*la sortie de secours*
no outlet	*sans issue*
forbidden	*interdit*
no smoking	*défense de fumer*

PARTS OF THE BODY

arm	*le bras*
back	*le dos*
ear	*l'oreille*
eye, eyes	*l'oeil, les yeux*
finger	*le doigt*
foot	*le pied*
hair	*les cheveux*

hand *la main*
head *la tête*
heart *le coeur*
leg *la jambe*
kidney *le reins*
mouth *la bouche*
nail *l'ongle*
nose *le nez*
stomach *le ventre*
toe *l'orteil*
tooth *la dent*
tongue *la langue*

A FEW VERBS

I can *Je peux*
I go (to go) *Je vais (aller)*
I see (to see) *Je vois (voir)*
I know (to know) *Je sais (savoir)*
I hear (to hear) *J'entends (entendre)*
I take (to take) *Je prend (prendre)*
I give (to give) *Je donne (donner)*
I have (to have) *J'ai (avoir)*
I do (to do) *Je fais (faire)*
I make (to make) *Je fais (faire)*
I like (to like) *J'aime bien (aimer bien)*
I love (to love) *J'aime (aimer)*
I walk (to walk) *Je marche (marcher)*
I buy (to buy) *J'achète*
I order (to order) *Je commande (commander)*

PEOPLE

I, me *Je, moi*
You *vous*
he, him *il, lui*
she, her *elle, elle*
we, us *nous, nous*
they, them *ils (elles), ils elles*
man *un homme*
woman *un femme*
child *un, une enfant*
Mister *Monsieur*
Mrs. *Madame*
Miss *Mademoiselle*

SHOPS

grocery store *alimentation*
jewelry store *une bijouterie*
butcher's *une boucherie*
bakery *une boulangerie*
hairdresser's *salon de coiffure*
green grocer *cours des halles*
delicatessen *charcuterie*
housekeeping *droguerie*
bookstore *librairie*
store *magasin*
stationary shop *une papeterie*
pastry shop *une pâtisserie*
dry cleaner's *un pressing*

FISH & SHELLFISH

(Poissons, Coquillages et Fruits de Mer)

sea bass *bar*
pike *brochet*
scallop *coquille St.-Jacques*
shrimp *crevette*
crayfish *écrevisse*
herring *hareng*
lobster *homard*
oyster *huitre*
prawn *langoustine*
mackerel *maquereau*
mussel *moule*
cod *morue*
skate *raie*
red snapper *rouget*
salmon *saumon*
tuna *thon*

MEAT & POULTRY

(Viandes et Volailies)

lamb *agneau*
chitterling sausage *andouillette*
well-done *bien cuit*
beef *boeuf*
blood sausage *boudin*
quail *caille*
duck *canard*
duckling *caneton*
brains *cervelle*
rooster *coq*
liver *foie*
frog *grenouille*
ham *jambon*
tongue *langue*
rabbit *lapin*
hare *lièvre*
mutton *mouton*
goose *oie*
guinea hen *pintade*
pork *porc, cochon*
hen *poule*
chicken *poulet*
thymus (gland) *ris*

kidney	*rognon*
sausage	*saucisse*
rare	*saignant*
medium rare	*à point*

VEGETABLES

(Legumes)

garlic	*ail*
artichoke	*artichaut*
asparagus	*asperge*
eggplant	*aubergine*
beet	*bettrave*
carrot	*carotte*
celery root	*céleri*
mushroom	*champignon*
cabbage	*chou*
sauerkraut	*choucroute*
cauliflower	*choufleur*
watercress	*cresson*
zucchini	*courgette*
spinach	*épinards*
bean	*haricot*
green bean	*haricot vert*
turnip	*navet*
noodles	*pâtes*
leek	*poireau*
bell pepper	*poivron*
potato	*pomme de terre*
rice	*riz*
lettuce	*salade*

DESSERTS

apricot	*abricot*
almond	*amande*
pineapple	*ananas*
blackcurrent	*cassis*
mousse and ladyfingers	*charlotte*
lemon	*citron*
lime	*citron vert*
light custard sauce	*crême anglaise*
whipped cream	*crême chantilly*
strawberry	*fraise*
raspberry	*framboise*
fresh fruit	*fruits frais*
cake	*gateau*
ice cream	*glace*
vanilla ice cream, pastry, chocolate sauce	*profiterolles*
floating islands	*iles flotantes*
chestnut	*marron*
blackberry	*mûre*
blueberry	*myrtille*
hazelnut	*noisette*
walnut	*noix*
grapefruit	*pamplemousse*
marzipan	*pâte d'amande*
pear	*poire*
apple	*pomme*
pie	*tarte*

TABLE TALK

(Autour de la Table)

butter	*beurre*
cheese	*fromage*
mustard	*moutarde*
egg	*oeuf*
bread	*pain*
pepper	*poivre*
soup	*potage*
salt	*sel*
breakfast	*petit déjeuner*
lunch	*déjeuner*
dinner	*dîner*
the check	*l'addition*
a plate	*une assiette*
a bottle	*une bouteille*
a pitcher	*une carafe*
an ashtray	*un cendrier*
a knife	*un couteau*
a spoon	*une cuillère*
a fork	*une fourchette*
a receipt	*un reçu*
the waiter	*le serveur*
the waitress	*la serveuse*
a napkin	*une serviette*
Oh, waiter!	*s'il vous plâit!*
a cup	*une tasse*
a glass	*un verre*
the cloak room	*le vestiaire*

BEVERAGES

(Boissoms)

a beer	*une bière*
soft drinks	*boissons gazeuses*
a cup of coffee	*un café*
coffee and milk	*un café-crême*
hot chocolate	*un chocolat chaud*
squeezed lemon, water and sugar	*un citron pressé*
decaffinated	*un déca*
a beer on tap	*un demi*
water	*de l'eau*
ice cubes	*des glaçons*
orange juice	*un jus d'orange*

milk	*du lait*
a cup of tea	*un thé*
herbal tea	*une tisane*
white wine	*du vin blanc*
red wine	*du vin rouge*
rosé	*du vin rosé*

FURTHER READING

Each person who visits Paris seems to have his or her own dream of the city. For some, it's the mythical twenties, or the painters revolutionizing art in Montmartre. Others have fallen in love with Surrealist poetry, Dada weirdness, or Impressionism, to name just a few of the movements that were brought to life here. From the Gothic beauty of Notre Dame to the daring originality of the Pompidou Center, everyone has dreamed of a city full of excitement and discovery. The Paris of today has plenty to offer adventurers, but you may want to fill up on dreams and atmosphere beforehand with works like the following:

FICTION & AUTOBIOGRAPHY

The Autobiography of Alice B. Toklas, Paris France by **Gertrude Stein**; *A Moveable Feast* by **Ernest Hemingway**; *Père Goriot* by **Honoré de Balzac**; *The Belly of Paris, Nana* by **Emile Zola**; *Down and Out in Paris and London* by **George Orwell**; *The Vagabond* by Colette; *L'Invitée* by **Simone de Beauvoir**; *Les Miserables, Notre Dame de Paris* by **Victor Hugo**; *My Double Life* by **Sarah Berhardt**; *Treat it Gentle* by **Sydney Bechet**; *Memoirs of Montparnasse* by **John Glassco**; *The Big Sea* by **Langston Hughes**.

NON-FICTION & BIOGRAPHY

The Banquet Years by **Roger Shattuck**; *Jazz Cleopatra (Josephine Baker in Her Time)* by **Phyllis Rose**; *Paris Journals, Paris Was Yesterday* by **Janet Flanner (Gênet)**; *Yankees at the Court, the First Americans in Paris* by **Susan Mary Alsop**; *Decline or Renewal, France Since the 1930's* by **Stanley Hoffman**; *The French* by **Theodore Zeldin**; *The Food Lover's Guide to Paris* by **Patricia Wells**.

USEFUL ADDRESSES

TOURIST INFORMATION

The main tourist information office is the ***Bureau d'Accueil Central*** (open every day from 9 a.m. to 8 p.m.) at 127 ave. des Champs-Elysées, 75008 (M° Charles-de-Gaulle-Etoile), 47.23.61.72. This excellent center is run by a friendly English-speaking staff, and has every brochure or service a tourist could desire. They find and reserve hotel rooms anywhere in France (no more than eight days in advance, a deposit is required), reserve and provide airline, train, theater and sightseeing tour tickets (for a small fee), sell Michelin guides and maps in English, and can direct you to any monument, office, bank or drugstore in Paris. However, they are virtually overwhelmed in summer and busy all year round, so be prepared to wait.

Other offices are located at the Gare du Nord, Gare de l'Est, Gare de Lyon, Gare d'Austerlitz and the Eiffel Tower (open from May to September). There are also tourist offices at the airports with hotel reservation services (a deposit is necessary). The offices at Orly Sud (near gate H) and Orly Ouest (near gate F) are open daily from 6 a.m. to 11 p.m. and at Roissy (arrival level near gate 36) from 7 a.m. to 10:30 p.m.

The ***Agence Nationale pour l'Information Touristique*** (ANIT) at 8 avenue de l'Opéra, 75001 (M° Palais Royal), 42.96.10.23, is open Mon. through Fri., 9:30 a.m. to 6:30 p.m. This agency provides advice on vacations in France and free tourist information by mail, but does not reserve hotel rooms. Open Mon. through Fri., 9 a.m. to 5:30 p.m., the Automobile Club at 8 place de la Concorde, 75008 (M° Concorde), 42.66.43.00, has useful information, and for a taped message in English listing the main events in Paris call 47.20.88.98 (updated weekly so you get the latest information).

If you would like to know before you go, contact one of the **French Government Tourist Offices** at:

645 North Michigan Ave.
Chicago, IL 60611
Tel: 337-6301;

9401 Wilshire Blvd.
Beverly Hills, CA 90212
Tel: 271-6665;

360 Post St.
San Francisco, CA 94180
Tel: 272-2661;

610 Fifth Ave.
New York, NY 10020
Tel: 757-1125;

372 Bay St., Suite 610
Toronto, M5H 2W9
Tel: 36-16-05;

1840 Ouest, rue Sherbrooke
Montréal 109
Tel: 931-38-55.

EMBASSIES & CONSULATES

Australia
4, rue Jean-Rey, 75015
M° Bir-Hakeim, 40.59.33.00
Mon. to Fri., 9 a.m. to 5:30 p.m.

Canada
35, ave. Montaigne, 75008
M° Franklin D. Roosevelt or Alma Marceau, 47.23.01.01
Mon. to Fri., 9 a.m. to 4:30 p.m.

New Zealand
7, rue Léonard-de-Vinci, 75016
M° Victor Hugo, 45.00.24.11

United Kingdom
(Embassy) 35, rue du Faubourg St.-Honoré, 75008;
(Consulate) 2, rue d'Anjou, 75008
M° Concorde or Madeleine, 42.66.91.42
Mon. to Fri., 9:30 a.m. to 5:30 p.m.

United States
(Embassy) 2, ave. Gabriel, 75008;
(Consulate) 2, rue St.-Florentin, 75001
M° Concorde, 46.96.12.02
Mon. to Fri., 9 a.m. to 6 p.m.

For the addresses and numbers of other embassies and consulates, check with the tourist office or in the phone book under "Ambassades".

CREDITS

29, 30, 31	**Archiv Fûr Kunst und Geschichte, Berlin**
22	**Beck, Steve**
170/171, 173	**Caisse de Depot, Paris**
189	**Cardot/Joly**
163	**F.S.G.T., Bobigny**
192/193	**Heaton, Dallas & John/APA**
158, 204, 207	**Hetier, Michel**
32/33, 174	**IAURIF, Paris**
182, 185, 202/203, 208, 209	**Karnow, Catherine**
210	**Messent, David**
14/15, 20, 23, 26, 164/165	**Musées de la Ville de Paris**
143	**Nowitz, Richard**
188	**Reiser, Andrej/Bilderberg**
140/141, 142, 144, 145, 146/147	**Sohiez, Jean-Bernard**
186/187, 206	**Tony Stone Worldwide**
102/103, 160/161	**Van Beek, Steve**
180, 181	**Van Riel, Paul**

All photographs are by Ping Amranand except for the abovementioned.

INDEX

A

B

C

D

E

F

G

H

N

O

P

Q

R

S

T

U, V

W

Y, Z